A Concise History of the Haitian Revolution

Viewpoints/Puntos de Vista: Themes and Interpretations in Latin American History

Series editor: Jürgen Buchenau

The books in this series will introduce students to the most significant themes and topics in Latin American history. They represent a novel approach to designing supplementary texts for this growing market. Intended as supplementary textbooks, the books will also discuss the ways in which historians have interpreted these themes and topics, thus demonstrating to students that our understanding of our past is constantly changing, through the emergence of new sources, methodologies, and historical theories. Unlike monographs, the books in this series will be broad in scope and written in a style accessible to undergraduates.

Published

Beyond Borders: A History of Mexican Migration to the United States
Timothy J. Henderson

Bartolomé de las Casas and the Conquest of the Americas
Lawrence A. Clayton

The Last Caudillo: Alvaro Obregón and the Mexican Revolution
Jürgen Buchenau

Spaniards in the Colonial Empire: Creoles vs. Peninsulars?
Mark A. Burkholder

Dictatorship in South America
Jerry Dávila

Mothers Making Latin America
Erin E. O'Connor

A History of the Cuban Revolution, Second Edition
Aviva Chomsky

A Short History of US Interventions in Latin America and the Caribbean
Alan McPherson

Latin American Cultural Objects and Episodes
William H. Beezley

Forthcoming

Emancipations: Latin American Independence in a Global Context
Karen Racine

Mexico Since 1960
Stephen E. Lewis

A Concise History of the Haitian Revolution

Second Edition

Jeremy D. Popkin
University of Kentucky
Lexington, KY

This second edition first published 2022
© 2022 John Wiley & Sons Ltd.

Edition History
John Wiley & Sons Ltd. (1e, 2011)

Registered Offices
John Wiley & Sons, Inc., 111 River Street, Hoboken, NJ 07030, USA
John Wiley & Sons Ltd, The Atrium, Southern Gate, Chichester, West Sussex, PO19 8SQ, UK

Editorial Office
111 River Street, Hoboken, NJ 07030, USA

For details of our global editorial offices, customer services, and more information about Wiley prod-ucts visit us at www.wiley.com.

Wiley also publishes its books in a variety of electronic formats and by print-on-demand. Some content that appears in standard print versions of this book may not be available in other formats.

Library of Congress Cataloging-in-Publication Data
Names: Popkin, Jeremy D., 1948- author. | John Wiley & Sons, publisher.
Title: A concise history of the Haitian Revolution / Jeremy D. Popkin,
    University of Kentucky, Lexington, KY.
Description: Second edition. | Hoboken, NJ : John Wiley & Sons, 2022. |
    Includes bibliographical references and index. | Contents: Introduction
    -- A Colonial Society in a Revolutionary Era -- The Uprisings, 1791-1793
    -- Republican Emancipation in Saint-Domingue, 1793-1798 -- Toussaint
    Louverture in Power, 1798-1801 -- The Struggle for Independence,
    1802-1806 -- Consolidating Independence in a Hostile World -- Afterword:
    The Earthquake Crisis of 2010 and the Haitian Revolution -- Recent
    Scholarship on the Haitian Revolution.
Identifiers: LCCN 2021020319 (print) | LCCN 2021020320 (ebook) | ISBN
    9781119746331 (paperback) | ISBN 9781119746348 (pdf) | ISBN
    9781119746263 (epub) | ISBN 9781119746362 (ebook)
Subjects: LCSH: Haiti--History--Revolution, 1791-1804.
Classification: LCC F1923 .P66 2022 (print) | LCC F1923 (ebook) | DDC
    972.94/03--dc23
LC record available at https://lccn.loc.gov/2021020319
LC ebook record available at https://lccn.loc.gov/2021020320

Cover image: © Lesueur, Jean-Baptiste (en 1749 - en 1826), dessinateur,
Musée Carnavalet, Histoire de Paris, CC0 licence
Cover design by Wiley

Set in 10/12.5 MinionPro by Integra Software Services Pvt. Ltd, Pondicherry, India

SKYB3871048-B1BA-4CF4-AE4C-E588F9C19A17_102021

Contents

List of Illustrations

Series Editor's Preface

Each book in the "Viewpoints/Puntos de Vista" series introduces students to a significant theme or topic in Latin American history. In an age in which student and faculty interest in the global South increasingly challenges the old focus on the history of Europe and North America, Latin American history has assumed an increasingly prominent position in undergraduate curricula.

Some of these books discuss the ways in which historians have interpreted these themes and topics, thus demonstrating that our understanding of our past is constantly changing, through the emergence of new sources, methodologies, and historical theories. Others offer an introduction to a particular theme by means of a case study or biography in a manner easily understood by the contemporary, non-specialist reader. Yet others give an overview of a major theme that might serve as the foundation of an upper-level course.

What is common to all of these books is their goal of historical synthesis. They draw on the insights of generations of scholarship on the most enduring and fascinating issues in Latin American history, and through the use of primary sources as appropriate. Each book is written by a specialist in Latin American history who is concerned with undergraduate teaching, yet has also made his or her mark as a first-rate scholar.

The books in this series can be used in a variety of ways, recognizing the differences in teaching conditions at small liberal arts colleges, large public universities, and research-oriented institutions with doctoral programs. Faculty have particular needs depending on whether they teach large lectures with discussion sections, small lecture or discussion-oriented classes, or large lectures with no discussion sections, and whether they teach on a semester or trimester system. The format adopted for this series fits all of these different parameters.

In this fifth volume in the series, Professor Jeremy Popkin provides an interpretation of the Haitian Revolution of 1791, at once a massive slave revolt and the second successful independence movement in the New World. The volume provides a clear and concise introduction to a historical process that, by raising the twin specters of freedom and violence, reverberated through the Atlantic world. Popkin discusses the legacy of the Haitian Revolution in global terms: the movement profoundly shaped other independence movements in Latin America and the Caribbean, and affected the political discourse in early nineteenth-century Europe. A singular strength of this book is its chronological scope, encompassing the nineteenth century and beyond. The author makes the case that the Haitian Revolution was a process of global historical significance, and that it deserves equal billing with the much more widely studied revolutions in France and British North America.

Jürgen Buchenau
University of North Carolina, Charlotte

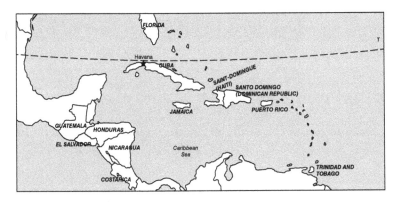

Map 1   Saint-Domingue/Haiti and the Caribbean.

Source: Adapted from Chomsky, *A History of the Cuban Revolution* (Oxford: Wiley-Blackwell, 2010).

Introduction

On 16 August 1791, a building on one of the hundreds of sugar plan-tations in France's wealthy Caribbean colony of Saint-Domingue, today's independent Republic of Haiti, was set on fire. The local white colonists immediately suspected one of the plantation's enslaved blacks. Under interrogation, he made a startling confession. "The most trusted slaves on the neighboring plantations and those in the adjacent districts had formed a plot to set fire to the plantations and to murder all the whites,"[1] he claimed. The authorities in the nearby port of Cap Français, the largest city in the colony, dismissed the idea that uneducated black captives could have conceived such a scheme. For years, a small minor-ity of whites had successfully exploited the labor of a far larger enslaved population; the whites could not imagine that the blacks they had treated with such contempt for so long were capable of organizing themselves to overthrow their oppressors. Less than a week later, on the night of 22–23 August 1791, the white colonists learned how wrong they were. Just as the suspect arrested for arson had said, bands of blacks attacked planta-tions in Saint-Domingue's richest sugar-growing area, setting fire to the crops and killing or driving out their white owners and overseers. It was the start of a movement that would culminate almost 13 years later, on 1 January 1804, when a leader who had once been enslaved, Jean-Jacques Dessalines, proclaimed the independence of the nation of Haiti.

A Concise History of the Haitian Revolution, Second Edition. Jeremy D. Popkin.
© 2022 John Wiley & Sons Ltd. Published 2022 by John Wiley & Sons Ltd.

The Haitian Struggle for Freedom

The success of the 13-year-long insurrection in the French half of the Caribbean island of Hispaniola, where Christopher Columbus had landed in 1492 and begun the era of European colonialism in the Americas, showed that the movement for freedom in America, begun by the white population of the British colonies in North America in 1776, had leaped across the boundary of race. For the first time, a population of African origin overthrew its white rulers. The main leader of the Haitian movement, Toussaint Louverture, proved that a black man born into slavery could command armies and govern as effectively as any white man. Most importantly for the future of the Americas and the entire Atlantic world, the Haitian Revolution struck a blow against the institutions of slavery and racial hierarchy. The constitution of the United States, drawn up in 1787, spoke of freedom, but left hundreds of thousands of blacks in servitude; even free black people were denied the full rights of citizens. In contrast, the Haitian constitution of 1805 proclaimed that "slavery is abolished forever" and that "all distinctions of color among members of the same family must necessarily stop." The Haitian Revolution's stand against slavery and racial discrimination made it the most radical of the American revolutionary insurrections against European rule. No study of the revolutionary era that laid the basis for the modern world can afford to ignore this movement.

Present-day Haiti is a small spot on the map of the Americas: it occupies less than half of the island of Hispaniola that it shares with the Spanish-speaking Dominican Republic. Particularly since the devastating earthquake of 12 January 2010 that killed more than 200,000 people and reduced its capital city of Port-au-Prince to rubble, media images of Haiti emphasize the country's poverty, environmental problems, and endemic political turmoil. Two hundred years ago, however, the territory that is now Haiti played a central role in world affairs. Ceded to France by Spain in 1697, Saint-Domingue had grown in less than a century to become the most profitable of all New World colonial settlements. In 1789, when the enslaved population in the 13 United States was only 650,000, Saint-Domingue had nearly 500,000 enslaved laborers and produced almost half of the entire world's supply of sugar and coffee, as well as valuable crops of cotton and indigo. At the moment when the Haitian Revolution began, Saint-Domingue was the biggest market for African captives, some 30,000 of whom were imported every year to keep its economy going, and the wealth of the colony's plantation-owners eclipsed that of even the richest Virginia and South Carolina planters. Vital to the prosperity of France, western Europe's largest country, Saint-Domingue was also a crucial trading partner for the United States: Yankee ships brought flour, salt meat and fish to feed the island's population, and took home molasses to supply New England's rum distilleries. The progress of the Haitian uprising was followed with passion and anxiety throughout the Atlantic world.

At the moment when the Haitian Revolution began in August 1791, the world's attention was focused on the revolutionary upheaval in France itself. Two years earlier, after the storming of the Bastille in Paris on 14 July 1789, the legislators of France's revolutionary National Assembly had issued their famous Declaration of the Rights of Man and Citizen, proclaiming that "men are born and remain free and equal in rights." The uprising in Saint-Domingue forced them to consider whether their principles applied to the 800,000 enslaved blacks in France's overseas colonies. Torn between their assertion that freedom was a universal human right and their equally strong belief that France needed overseas possessions to maintain its own power and prosperity, the French revolutionaries wrestled painfully with the problem of reconciling their principles with their country's national interest. In 1799 a successful general, Napoleon Bonaparte, seized power in France. In his mind, the liberty the French revolutionaries had proclaimed had proved to be incompatible with political stability and social order. He had even less sympathy for the attempt to build a free multi-racial society in France's Caribbean colonies. His attempt to reimpose white rule in Saint-Domingue in 1802–3 provoked the most violent phase of the Haitian Revolution. The defeat the island's population inflicted on his forces foreshadowed the disasters in Spain and Russia that would lead to his downfall in 1814.

Like revolutionary France, many other parts of the Atlantic world were powerfully affected by the events of the Haitian Revolution. In addition to its importance for American commerce, the fate of slavery in Saint-Domingue was a major concern for slaveowners in the southern states. The flight of white colonists from the island produced the first refugee crisis in the history of the United States, and the support the United States gave to the black leader Toussaint Louverture in the late 1790s was the first example of American intervention beyond its own borders. Napoleon's defeat in 1803 led France to offer to sell its territorial claims in North America to the young American republic. This "Louisiana Purchase" opened the way for the westward expansion of the United States and its growth into a continental power. Former residents of Saint-Domingue made up much of the early population of New Orleans and profoundly influenced that region's distinctive "creole" culture. Blacks in the United States saw in the success of the Haitian movement proof that members of their race could achieve freedom; the Haitian example inspired some of the slave conspiracies of the early nineteenth century and gave courage to those who campaigned for the rights of their people through legal means.

The Haitian Revolution affected the entire western hemisphere, not just the United States. Whether it was an inspiration for the uprisings that led to the independence of other Latin American countries in the early nineteenth century remains a matter of debate, however. Throughout the region, ruling elites feared the spread of ideas about freedom among their enslaved populations and dreaded the kind of violence that had characterized the Haitian movement. In South and Central America, independence movements in the 1810s and 1820s more closely resembled the movement of the free men of color that developed alongside the slave uprising during the Haitian Revolution, rather than the uprising of the enslaved population, and independence did not immediately bring the end of slavery in many of those countries when they first gained their freedom. The Caribbean islands closest to Haiti proved the most resistant to the Haitian example; slavery was finally abolished in them by their colonial rulers, not through insurrection, and independence came even later. Even today, not all of them are independent: the United States governs Puerto Rico and the Virgin Islands, and the islands of Martinique and Guadeloupe are overseas territories of France. In some Latin American countries the Haitian Revolution clearly promoted the growth of slavery rather than hastening its disappearance. White Saint-Domingue refugees brought their highly efficient sugar-growing methods to Cuba and Brazil, creating new centers of production that would make those two countries the last places in the Americas to abolish slavery.

In Europe, intellectuals such as the German philosopher Georg Wilhelm Friedrich Hegel pondered the implications of resistance to slavery, and British abolitionists, many of them motivated by religious principles, cited the Haitian movement as proof of the need to abolish slavery; in 1807 their efforts led the British Parliament to officially prohibit the slave trade. In Africa, the sudden disappearance of what had been the largest single market for black captives profoundly affected the destinies of thousands of men and women who would otherwise have been shipped to the Caribbean. Taught a harsh lesson by the success of the

Haitian Revolution, British and French governments and economic interest groups began to think that it might be more profitable to establish colonies in Africa itself, where black labor could be regimented to produce for the European market without the moral stigma associated with the Atlantic slave trade. The Haitian Revolution was thus linked to the beginnings of a new age of European imperialism that would, by the end of the nineteenth century, affect almost the entire continent of Africa and many other parts of the world.

Defining the Haitian Revolution

The term "Haitian Revolution" is a relatively recent way of labeling the dramatic events of the years from 1791 to 1804. Historians who use this phrase argue that these events should be put on the same level as the American and French revolutions in discussions of the origins of modern ideas of freedom and equality. The phrase "Haitian Revolution" also suggests, however, that there was a unity to the events from 1791 to 1804 and that their final outcome reflected the accomplishment of a program consciously laid out from the beginning. As we will see, these propositions are not necessarily accurate. The uprising that began in August 1791 affected only one of the colony's three provinces, for example, and it developed alongside another revolutionary movement, the uprising of Saint-Domingue's free people of color, that had very different goals. These two revolutionary movements were often in conflict with one another, a conflict that continued even after the declaration of Haitian independence in 1804. Initially, both of them fought against the French colonial government. From 1794 to 1801, however, both movements claimed to be supporting the French, until Napoleon's intervention in 1802 drove most of the population to turn against them. Waged by a largely illiterate population, the Haitian revolt against slavery never issued a manifesto defining its goals, and its history has to be written almost entirely on the basis of evidence provided by outsiders, most of whom were thoroughly hostile to it. Those events certainly had revolutionary consequences, but trying to force them into a mold derived from American and French models is misleading. Including the Haitian Revolution as one of the modern world's major revolutions requires us to rethink the very nature of such phenomena, and to recognize, for instance, that a revolution can develop without the leadership of a revolutionary party or movement.

Just as it is misleading to describe the Haitian Revolution as a unified movement with clearly defined and consistent goals, it is difficult to describe its principal leader, Toussaint Louverture, as a revolutionary leader in the mold of Robespierre or Fidel Castro. To this day, it remains unclear whether Louverture actually played any role in starting the slave insurrection in August 1791. When he joined the movement, he did not initially call for the complete abolition of slavery, and he even rejected the first French decree of emancipation in 1793. After he switched from fighting against the French to fighting on their side in 1794, Louverture consistently insisted that he was loyal to the French government, even when his actions appeared to undermine its authority. The laws he imposed on the population of Saint-Domingue during these years, however, were quite conservative and drove many blacks to revolt against him. Toussaint Louverture's demonstration that a black man could govern a key territory in the Atlantic world had revolutionary implications, but he cannot be seen as a self-conscious, ideologically motivated revolutionary in the mold of Thomas Jefferson, Thomas Paine, or the revolutionary French Jacobins.

It has been customary to see the Haitian declaration of independence of 1804 and the promulgation of the first Haitian constitution of 1805 as marking the end of the Haitian Revolution. Slavery, the fundamental institution of colonial society, had been abolished and, with the defeat of the French army and the massacre of the remaining white colonists, the pre-revolutionary ruling class was completely replaced by a new group of rulers. Nevertheless, the outcome of the Haitian Revolution did not become clear until many years after 1804. By the end of 1806, Haiti had split into two rival states that continued to fight each other until 1820. France did not recognize Haiti's independence until 1825, and it took several decades before the lasting features of post-revolutionary Haitian society became evident. The final chapter of this book outlines the major developments of Haitian history until the crisis of 1843, which may be seen as the last direct confrontation between the democratic and elitist currents coming out of the revolutionary period.

Studying the Haitian Revolution

Although people at the time were intensely aware of the importance of the events we now call the Haitian Revolution, outside of Haiti itself that movement has never commanded the same attention as the American and French revolutions of the same period. Whereas the United States rapidly expanded into a continental power, and whereas France remained a major factor in European affairs and ruled over a world empire well into the twentieth century, the small nation of Haiti did not have the same assets. As the only black-dominated country in the Americas, the new nation was treated with hostility by an outside world increasingly under the sway of racial prejudices that have still not disappeared. Lacking natural and cultural resources such as the vast farming regions and the educational institutions the United States inherited from its colonial past, Haiti was unable to follow the same path to prosperity as its northern neighbor. The two American republics born in the revolutionary era were both racked by civil conflicts in the nineteenth century, but the United States emerged from its Civil War of 1861–5 with its democratic institutions and its economy largely intact, whereas Haiti suffered a succession of coups, dictatorships, and foreign interventions that obstructed the development of a strong civil society, stable political institutions, and a diversified economy.

The "Black Lives Matter" movement that spurred demonstrations throughout the world in 2020 and initiatives such as the "1619 Project" that have highlighted the central role of slavery in the history of the Americas have underlined the importance of the events described in this book. As people in the United States and Europe have tried to grapple with the ambiguous legacies of their own histories, so strongly bound up with imperialism, racism, and the memory of slavery, and as our civilization has become truly global, with non-western countries playing an ever more important role in world affairs, the attention paid to the only successful uprising against slavery in history and the first successful non-white movement for national independence is growing. The catastrophic earthquake of 12 January 2010 focused the world's attention on Haiti, raising painful questions about the world community's responsibility to help those in need and about Haiti's own ability to implement the promises of freedom and equality of the revolutionary era. In the United States and Canada, the development of an important community of Haitian immigrants is drawing new attention to the history of the country that has produced such figures as the novelist Edwidge Danticat and the popular musician Wyclef Jean. Even for those with no personal connection to Haiti, like the American novelist Madison Smartt Bell, whose trilogy of dramatic novels about the Haitian Revolution, *All Souls' Rising* (1995), *Master of the Crossroads* (2000), and *The Stone That the Builder Refused*

(2004), was one of my own introductions to this history, the importance of the events of 1791 to 1804 is easy to understand.

Reconstructing the history of the Haitian Revolution is a complicated challenge. Participants in the American and French revolutions belonged to civilizations familiar with the written word; they left behind voluminous records from which historians can reconstruct their ideas and actions. The vast majority of the blacks who participated in the Haitian uprising were illiterate; the documents from which we have to piece together what happened between 1791 and 1804 come almost exclusively from whites, almost all of whom were hostile to the movement. The documents that we do have – French official records, letters from white colonists, newspaper articles published in the United States, memoirs by survivors of the revolutionary period – tell us much about the events of the period, but there are many questions about the Haitian Revolution that historians will never be able to fully answer. What did the ordinary members of the black population think they were fighting for? How did they view Toussaint Louverture and the other leaders of the movement, who did, in some cases, leave letters and other documents behind? What was the role of the blacks' *vodou* religious beliefs in shaping the insurrection? What influence, if any, did the free population of color exert over the insurgents? Historians disagree on the responses to these and many other questions about the events leading up to Haitian independence; the best we can do is propose answers based on the fragmentary and often one-sided evidence we do possess, knowing that some essential aspects of the past will always escape us.

As an example of the challenges of writing the history of the Haitian Revolution from documents generated by its opponents, let us consider the case of an eyewitness narrative of the early stages of the 1791 uprising that is cited in almost every account of these events, including this one. Gabriel Gros's *Historick Recital*, first published in French in Saint-Domingue itself in 1792, then translated into English in Baltimore in 1793 and republished in French in Paris in that same year, is a vivid account by a white colonist who was taken prisoner by the black insurgents in October 1791 and wound up serving as a secretary to Jean-François Papillon, one of the movement's early leaders. This document is one of the main sources about the events of the first few months of the insurrection, and includes, among other things, the earliest description of Toussaint Louverture's political actions. In addition to historians, starting with the nineteenth-century Haitian chronicler Beaubrun Ardouin and continuing down to the present day, Gros's dramatic story has inspired fiction authors, from the early nineteenth-century French novelist Victor Hugo to the contemporary American writer Madison Smartt Bell, who bases many episodes in his *All Souls' Rising* on it.

Gros was certainly a partisan witness, who left no doubt about his desire to see the rebellious blacks forced back into submission. Does this mean that we can dismiss everything he says? Even some of the most surprising details he gives, such as his claim that one of the white colonial military leaders fighting the blacks wrote a letter saying that he was prepared to sacrifice the prisoners rather than make any concessions to the insurgents, are confirmed by other documents. He gives a nuanced portrait of Jean-François, saying that he showed "a degree of good sense, a fund of humanity, and a ray of genius, far superior to any sentiment that might have been expected from his kind," although we must bear in mind the fact that one of the reasons he praised the black leader was that Jean-François proved willing to listen to Gros's advice.[2] On the other hand, Gros unfairly accused the white officials of being counterrevolutionary conspirators who set out deliberately to destroy the colony. In short, there is much to be learned from Gros's account, both about the black insurrection and about white attitudes, but his story has to be read with his own very obvious prejudices in mind and the assertions it makes have to be carefully compared with those in other sources.

Another issue facing historians of the Haitian Revolution that has taken on increased importance in recent years is what constitutes appropriate language to use in describing these events and the actors in them. Many of us have come to realize that to describe a human being as a "slave" is to accept the status imposed on that person by those who had taken away his or her freedom. The word "mulatto," routinely used to describe people of mixed racial ancestry even in relatively recent times, is derived from "mule," a word for animals bred by mating horses with donkeys, and is now recognized as offensive. The historical sources for the reconstruction of the Haitian Revolution routinely use racialized language that is no longer acceptable today. When we quote directly from such documents, however, it is sometimes necessary to reproduce its wording in order to convey the thought of the people who used it. In some cases, it is also difficult to find effective phrasing to replace terms that have been ingrained in the language for generations. In this revised edition of the *Concise History of the Haitian Revolution*, I have tried to avoid the word "slave" for individuals, but I have continued to use the phrase "slave revolt," for example, as a clear and direct way of describing collective acts of resistance to the condition of slavery. Some of my fellow historians now replace the name of the French colony of Saint-Domingue with "Haiti," the name the victors in the Haitian Revolution gave to the territory when they declared its independence in 1804. I continue to refer to "Saint-Domingue" prior to that date, both because it was the name used for the territory by all the actors in these events, including Toussaint Louverture, up to the moment when the Haitian Declaration of Independence was issued, and also because referring to Saint-Domingue as "Haiti" prior to 1804 obscures the fact that history might have gone in other directions. If Napoleon had not ordered his disastrous invasion of the island in 1802, for example, the territory, like the other French Caribbean islands of Martinique and Guadeloupe, might be still be part of France.

For Haitians themselves, the story of their ancestors' struggle for freedom has great symbolic importance, and its heroes remain sources of inspiration to a population facing what often seem like insurmountable challenges. This account, constrained by the guidelines of modern historical research, may strike some readers as less vivid than the colorful scenes of revolutionary events painted by many of Haiti's talented contemporary artists. Reconciling the living historical memory of the Haitian Revolution with the results of modern historical research is not a simple task. Nevertheless, historians' attempts to understand the events of the revolutionary period as the outcome of the actions of the men and women who participated in them have their own value, even if the historical record is not complete enough to answer all our questions. The aim of this book is, then, to provide students and general readers with a concise overview of the generally accepted historical facts about the Haitian Revolution, drawing on the scholarship of historians from Haiti itself as well as the research of those in the United States, Europe, and other countries who have contributed to the subject.

For much of the period from the declaration of Haitian independence in 1804 until the last decades of the twentieth century, serious historical scholarship on this subject by scholars outside Haiti remained quite limited. Haitian historians have produced many important works on the subject, despite the fact that most of the surviving documents about the revolution are in archives in France and not in Haiti itself, but their books, usually published in French, are often hard to find except in major research libraries. Outside of Haiti, few historians were attracted to a subject that inevitably raised troubling questions about the policies of the French Revolution and the national hero Napoleon, and that reminded Americans that the United States had refused to recognize Haiti's freedom for six decades. In recent decades, what the Haitian American scholar Michel-Rolph Trouillot eloquently denounced in a famous essay as the "silencing" of the Haitian Revolution for so long has begun to end.[3] In writing this short history, I have been able to draw on a rapidly growing body of modern scholarship from both sides of the Atlantic; the recommendations for further reading at the end of this book will point readers to many of the sources I have used. If this book encourages readers to explore the subject further on their own, it will have achieved its purpose.

1

A Colonial Society in a Revolutionary Era

The beginning of the Haitian Revolution in August 1791 shocked the entire Atlantic world because it occurred, not in some remote backwater of the Americas, but in the fastest-growing and most prosperous of all the New World colonies. By 1791 Europeans had been staking out territory across the Atlantic and importing African captives to work for them for 300 years, but nowhere else had this colonial system been made to function as successfully as in Saint-Domingue. In the 28 years since the end of the eighteenth century's largest conflict, the Seven Years War, in 1763, the population of the French colony had nearly doubled as plantation-owners cashed in on Europe's seemingly unquenchable appetite for sugar and coffee. Imports of enslaved Africans to the island averaged over 15,000 a year in the late 1760s; after an interruption caused by the American War of Independence, they soared to nearly 30,000 in the late 1780s. No other slaveowners had learned to exploit their workforce with such harsh efficiency: by 1789, there were nearly 12 enslaved blacks for every white inhabitant, and the wealthiest Saint-Domingue plantation-owners were far richer than Virginians like George Washington and Thomas Jefferson. Cap Français, the colony's largest city, was one of the New World's busiest ports; on an average day, more than 100 merchant ships lay at anchor in its broad harbor. The city itself, with its geometrically laid-out streets and its modern public buildings, was a symbol of European civilization in the tropics.

A Concise History of the Haitian Revolution, Second Edition. Jeremy D. Popkin.
© 2022 John Wiley & Sons Ltd. Published 2022 by John Wiley & Sons Ltd.

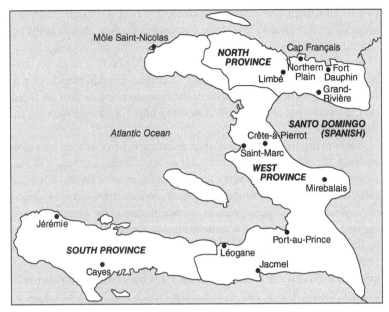

Map 2   The French Colony of Saint-Domingue in 1789.
Source: Adapted from Jeremy Popkin, *Facing Racial Revolution: Eyewitness Accounts of the Haitian Uprising* (Chicago: University of Chicago Press, 2007).

The Origins of Saint-Domingue

The island of Hispaniola, where Saint-Domingue was located, had been the site of one of the first contacts between Europeans and the peoples of the Americas: Columbus landed on its northern coast during his first voyage in 1492. The Spanish made it the first hub of their empire in the New World; the diseases they brought with them and their harsh exploitation of the population soon killed off the native Taino Indians. By the end of the 1500s, however, the Spanish had found richer opportunities for settlement in Mexico, Peru, and other parts of the Americas. Lacking gold and other easily exploitable resources, Hispaniola was virtually abandoned. During the early decades of the 1600s, the English, French, and Dutch, initially shut out of the scramble for territories on the American continents by the first arrivals, the Spanish and the Portuguese, began staking claims to some of the islands in the Caribbean. France established its first permanent colonial settlement on the small island of Saint-Christophe in 1626; in 1635, the French planted their flag on two larger islands in the eastern Caribbean, Martinique and

Guadeloupe. Together with a small colony on the coast of South America – today's French Guyana – and their outposts in Canada, these islands became the base of France's overseas empire. In the same period, small groups of seagoing adventurers, acting on their own, landed on the northern coast of Hispaniola. These early settlers, not all of them French, were known as *boucaniers* or buccaneers because of the *boucans* or open fires on which they smoked meat from the wild cattle and hogs they found roaming the deserted island.

Eager to expand their colonial domains at the expense of their long-time enemies, the Spanish, the French made a move to claim territory in Hispaniola by appointing a governor for the *boucaniers*' settlements in 1665. In 1697, at the end of the European conflict known as the War of the League of Augsburg, Spain officially ceded the western third of the island to France; the remainder of the island became the Spanish colony of Santo Domingo. By this time, Europeans all across the Caribbean had realized the enormous profits to be made by establishing plantations to grow sugar. The sugar boom first took hold in some of the smaller islands of the eastern Caribbean, such as the British colony of Barbados and the French island of Martinique. By 1700, however, much of the suitable land on those islands had already been used up. Saint-Domingue, a larger colony, offered new horizons for sugar production, and an ever-increasing stream of immigrants, dreaming of wealth, arrived on its shores. In 1687, there were just 4,411 whites and 3,358 enslaved blacks in Saint-Domingue; by 1715, the figures were 6,668 whites and 35,451 blacks, and in 1730 the enslaved population had risen to 79,545. Forty years later, in 1779, there were 32,650 whites and 249,098 enslaved blacks, a figure that would nearly double by the end of the 1780s.[1]

The geography of Saint-Domingue dictated its pattern of settlement. Sugar plantations needed flat, well-watered land; colonists rapidly staked out claims in the plain in the northern part of the island and later in the drier valleys between the steep mountain ranges in the west, where irrigation systems had to be built to make sugar-growing possible. The long southern peninsula of the island was the last part of the territory to be settled; harder to reach from France than the other parts of the colony, it was a center for contraband trade with the British, Dutch, and Spanish colonies to its south and west. The French administration divided Saint-Domingue into separate North, West and South provinces. Cap Français in the north and Port-au-Prince in the west were the main administrative centers; smaller cities such as Cayes, the capital of the South Province, were scattered along the coast, at points where ships could anchor and collect the products of the plantations for transport to Europe. By the mid-1700s, Saint-Domingue plantation-owners had discovered a new cash crop, almost as lucrative as sugar: coffee. Coffee trees could be grown on the slopes of the island's steep mountains, land that was unsuitable for sugar cane. Whereas sugar plantations required large investments of money to pay for the machinery needed to crush the canes, boil their juice, and refine the raw sugar, coffee plantations were cheaper to set up and attracted many of the new colonists who arrived after 1763. Indigo, grown to make a blue dye widely used in European textile manufacturing, was another resource for small-scale plantations, and, by the end of the century, cotton-growing was also becoming an important part of the colony's economy. In 1789 there were some 730 sugar plantations in the colony, along with over 3,000 plantations growing coffee and an equal number devoted to indigo.

In the early days of colonization, the labor force in the French islands included both white indentured servants and enslaved blacks. As the sugar boom created a growing demand for workers, however, plantation-owners throughout the Caribbean became more and more dependent on Africans to work their fields. After the end of Louis XIV's long series of wars in 1713, the French slave trade expanded rapidly. Throughout the eighteenth century, slave ships left the ports on France's Atlantic coast, carrying trade goods to the coast of Africa. There, they exchanged textiles, muskets, and jewelry for black men and women, often captives taken in wars between rival African states. Packed into the holds of overcrowded vessels, the terrified blacks knew only that they would never see their families and homelands again. Close to a sixth of the captives on a typical voyage died from disease or mistreatment before reaching the Americas. Those who arrived in Saint-Domingue were promptly put up for sale and found themselves taken off to plantations where, if they were lucky, they might encounter a few fellow blacks who spoke their native language. In this strange new world, they had to struggle to make some kind of life for themselves, under the control of masters whose only interest was in extracting the maximum amount of useful labor from them.

A Slave Society

Eighteenth-century Saint-Domingue was a classic example of what historians call a "slave society," one in which the institution of slavery was central to every aspect of life, in contrast to "societies with slaves," in which slaves were a relatively small part of the population and most economic activity was carried on by free people. Organized in work gangs or *ateliers*, enslaved blacks in Saint-Domingue performed almost all of the exhausting physical labor on which the growing and processing of sugar and coffee depended. Much of the field work – hoeing fields to clear away weeds, planting, and harvesting – was done by women; men were often trained to do more skilled jobs, such as sugar-processing, carpentry, or, like the future Toussaint Louverture, serving as coachmen. Children were assigned to a special *petit atelier* as early as possible, to accustom them to work, and those too old or sick to toil in the fields were used to guard the plantation's animals or its storeroom. At the top of the hierarchy among the enslaved workers were the *commandeurs* or drivers, who directed the work in the fields. The smooth functioning of a plantation depended on the *commandeurs*: even though the *commandeurs* were enslaved themselves, plantation-owners and managers treated them with respect to maintain their authority over the rest of the workforce. While most enslaved workers on the plantations worked in the fields or processed sugar and coffee, some were used as domestic servants for the masters and their families. The one skilled job usually reserved for women was the direction of the infirmary; supervising the care of the sick and ferreting out malingerers who were trying to escape work was an important task in the overall management of a plantation.

Caribbean sugar plantations were notorious for the demands they placed on their captive work force and the cruelty with which they were treated (see Figure 1.1). A French observer in the 1780s described the scene he witnessed in Saint-Domingue's sugar fields: "The sun blazed down on [the enslaved blacks'] heads; sweat poured from all parts of their bodies. Their limbs, heavy from the heat, tired by the weight of their hoes and the resistance of heavy soil, which was hardened to the point where it broke the tools, nonetheless struggled to overcome all obstacles. They worked in glum silence; all their faces showed their misery."[2] Sugar cane had to be processed as soon as it was cut, before the precious juice began to turn to starch and lose its sweetness. During the long harvesting season, from January to July every year, cane was cut in the fields and immediately fed through the heavy rollers of the crushing machine. The extracted juice then had to be boiled for hours in large cauldrons, while enslaved laborers stirred the syrup in the sweltering heat; it was then poured into molds so that the sugar could crystallize. The same workers who had toiled in the fields during the day were forced to work making sugar long into the night, and accidents caused by exhaustion were frequent; women who had to feed the cane stalks into crushing machines often lost arms that got caught in the machinery. Work on coffee plantations was not driven by the same need for haste as that involved in sugar production, but the endless routine of planting and caring for the trees, harvesting the beans, spreading them out to dry in the sun, and processing them kept enslaved workers equally busy. In addition to working for their masters, black captives were responsible for producing most of their own food: masters usually gave them small private plots to raise yams, beans, and other vegetables for themselves. In theory, they were supposed to be guaranteed one day a week to cultivate these gardens, but masters never hesitated to commandeer them for other tasks; the enslaved blacks had to make do with whatever free time they could find to tend their crops.

Vue Perspective de la Purgerie et d'une partie des Batimens.

Figure 1.1   Plantations and enslaved labor. An image commissioned by a French plantation-owner around 1780 shows the "purgerie," where enslaved blacks worked to refine sugarcane juice into sugar for export. In the foreground, a black woman on the right carries cane stalks to be processed, while on the left, a man with a raised whip chases another woman. Even at the height of the Enlightenment period, European whites were not embarrassed by the cruelty and the exploitative nature of the slavery system.

Source: © RMN-Blérancourt, Musée franco-américain du château de Blérancourt.

Living conditions for enslaved blacks on the plantations were harsh. Although Europeans considered blacks uniquely suited to work in the hot Caribbean climate because it resembled the weather in Africa, newly arrived captives fell victim to unfamiliar diseases in their new environment or succumbed to depression resulting from the traumatic ordeal they had been through; as many as a third of them died in their first year in the colonies. The average life expectancy of a enslaved black after arriving in Saint-Domingue was no more than seven to ten years. Most of them suffered from chronic malnutrition: the system of private plots rarely sufficed to provide enough food, and above all they were deprived of meat, a basic element of their diet in Africa. Slaveowners were theoretically obliged to supply their captives with adequate clothing, but few of them paid attention to this rule, and blacks often had only rags to wear or were forced to go around half-naked. Left to themselves, they tried to build huts similar to those familiar to them from Africa, but masters often preferred to force them to live in larger buildings where they could be supervised more easily. Masters discouraged marriages among their captives, for fear that having their own families would give them a sense of independence. Newly arrived blacks, called *bossales*, were sometimes put under the supervision of veterans who spoke their native language, but they still had to learn Kreyol, a combination of elements of French and various African languages that served as the general medium of communication in the colony. At the time of the revolution, African-born *bossales* made up at least half of the Saint-Domingue population. Many of the newly arrived captives at the time of the revolution had military experience, having been taken prisoner in wars in the Congo region of Africa; they would make an important contribution to the uprising that began in 1791.[3] Masters considered enslaved blacks born in the colony, known as *creoles*, easier to manage than the *bossales*; the *creoles* s grew up speaking the local language and had never known any life outside of the slave system.

Hanging over the enslaved workers at all times was the threat of brutal physical punishment if they angered their masters. Slaveowners and their hired managers routinely whipped them to force them to work and to punish them for any sign of insubordination. To make it easier to identify them if they tried to run away, enslaved blacks were branded with their owners' initials or other marks. Those who were caught after escaping were often forced to wear chains or iron collars, and might be shackled to a post at night. Masters were also legally permitted to cut off disobedient blacks' ears or to cut their hamstrings as punishment. Slaveowners often built private prisons or *cachots*, where enslaved blacks were locked up in the dark for various offenses. In theory, masters were not supposed to execute their captives, but in practice the authorities rarely intervened to protect them. In 1788, charges were brought against a Saint-Domingue master named Lejeune, who had tortured two enslaved women to death because he suspected them of poisoning other blacks on his plantation. Although Lejeune was initially convicted, other slaveowners protested so strongly against the verdict that it was overturned.

In theory, the treatment of slaves was regulated by the Code Noir or "Black Code" issued in 1685 by the French king Louis XIV. The Code Noir provided a legal basis for slavery in the French colonies, even though the institution was officially barred from the metropole where French judges had laid down the principle that "there are no slaves in France" in 1571. Although the Code Noir was meant to uphold the authority of slaveowners over their human property, it did include some provisions meant to prevent the worst abuses of slavery. Masters were made responsible for providing their captives with adequate rations, they were supposed to furnish them with two new sets of clothing every year, and they were encouraged to provide for their instruction in the Christian religion. In extreme circumstances, the code permitted enslaved blacks to appeal to the royal authorities for protection from their masters. In practice, however, both colonial plantation-owners and French administrators ignored these clauses of the code: enslaved workers were left to furnish most of their own food, clothing was distributed erratically, and little effort was made to Christianize the blacks, for fear that this would require recognizing that they had at least some minimal rights. Few among the enslaved population even knew that they were supposed to be able to protest about extreme mistreatment, and colonial officials rarely paid any attention to their complaints. Nevertheless, blacks who did become aware of the protections they were supposed to enjoy under the Code Noir began to think of themselves as having at least a minimum of rights. In this way, historian Malick Ghachem has suggested, the legal code that defined slavery served, paradoxically, to spread ideas that could ultimately undermine it.[4]

The Culture of the Black Population

Forced to live under the harsh discipline of their masters, the enslaved blacks in Saint-Domingue nevertheless managed to develop some communal life and to find ways to oppose the worst forms of oppression.

Although captives from different plantations were not supposed to mix, masters, knowing that a few concessions made them less likely to revolt against their situation, looked the other way when they gathered for meetings and dances on their weekly days off. When black captives came together they would often hold religious ceremonies that combined African rituals and elements of the Christian practices with which some of them had come into contact. Out of this fusion of elements there emerged in the course of the eighteenth century a distinctive religion, *vodou*, in which worshipers went into trances in which they were seized by the spirits of various African spirits or *lwa*, whom the blacks often identified with particular Catholic saints. *Vodou* ceremonies helped unify an enslaved population drawn from many different African ethnic groups. Individual enslaved blacks were sometimes able to build up a small *pécule* of personal savings by selling part of the crops they raised in their private food plots or by persuading their masters to let them hire themselves out; in certain cases, individuals were able to purchase their own freedom with these earnings.

The prerevolutionary life of the future Toussaint Louverture, then known as Toussaint Bréda because he lived on the Bréda plantation, is an example of the way in which one exceptional individual born into slavery in Saint-Domingue was able to gain free status during the colonial era. Claims that Louverture was descended from a West African king are probably unfounded, but stories passed down in his family that his intelligence, his determination, and his ability to work with animals distinguished him even as a youth are more plausible. He managed to learn to speak and read French; analysis of his largely phonetic spelling suggests that he acquired the accent of the colonists from southwestern France who were numerous in the colony. He became a devout Catholic and remained loyal to that religion throughout his life, although, like many blacks, he may also have practiced vodou. Even before he gained his own freedom, he formed a first marriage with a free woman of color, an unusual opportunity for an enslaved man. He became the coachman for the manager of the Bréda plantation on which he lived, and it was probably through this connection that he obtained his legal freedom in the 1770s. After his emancipation, he briefly owned a small plantation with several enslaved laborers, but this venture does not seem to have succeeded and he returned to work on the Bréda population, where his second wife Suzanne and several other relatives were among the enslaved population. Unlike enslaved blacks, Louverture was able to move around freely, which gave him the opportunity to build up a network of friends and contacts, many of whom would be useful to him when he emerged as a leader of the Haitian Revolution.[5]

Very few enslaved blacks were able to escape the limits imposed on them in colonial Saint-Domingue, but whenever they could, they expressed their opposition to their treatment through various forms of individual and collective resistance. What masters saw as the blacks' inherent laziness was undoubtedly a deliberate response to a system in which they were denied any benefits from their labor. Rather than bear children who would grow up under slavery, women used plants and herbs to induce abortions; like most enslaved populations in the Americas, the captive workforce in Saint-Domingue required constant importations from Africa to maintain its numbers. *Marronnage* or escape from the plantations was another common form of resistance. In some cases, it was a way for blacks to protest against a particularly cruel overseer or *commandeur*, and runaways might negotiate their return to the plantation in exchange for a promise of better treatment. Some groups of *marrons* succeeded in fleeing into the mountains and established independent bands; one group in a remote area along the border with Spanish Santo Domingo maintained itself for nearly a century, although its numbers were relatively small. Runaways could also take refuge in the colony's cities, where they might be able to pass themselves off as freedmen and make a living as day laborers.

Although they normally claimed that they could easily manage their enslaved workforces, masters lived in fear that the blacks might turn against them. Plantation-owners blamed any unexplained illnesses or deaths among their captives or their livestock on poisoning, which the colony's whites claimed was the blacks' main weapon. In 1757–8, the entire colony was swept by fear of a conspiracy, supposedly organized by an enslaved black man named Makandal, to poison all the whites and take over the island. The deaths attributed to Makandal were all among enslaved blacks, and it is not clear that they were due to poison rather than to disease, but he was tortured and burned alive in Cap Français in 1758. According to legend, he turned himself into a fly and escaped from his executioners. Even today, Makandal's name is remembered in Haiti as a symbol of resistance to oppression. Despite the whites' fears, overt collective resistance to the slavery system was rare: unlike the neighboring British island of Jamaica or the Dutch mainland colony of Surinam, for example, Saint-Domingue experienced no major slave revolts in the decades prior to 1791. This was certainly not because the blacks found their situation acceptable, but until 1791 they did not see any realistic prospect of changing it through collective violence.

The White Colonial Order

Although they were heavily outnumbered by the enslaved population, until 1791, Saint-Domingue's minority of white colonists seemed solidly in control of the island. Although the French government kept only a small garrison in the island, the 30,000 white inhabitants in 1789 used the constant threat of force and the resources of European technology to dominate the far more numerous blacks. Trained troops armed with European weapons, supplemented by local police forces, helped deter black resistance. European ships capable of crossing the oceans made the import of enslaved captives and supplies and the export of plantation products possible. Loans from France financed the slave trade and the expansion of colonial plantations. Whereas most enslaved blacks were illiterate, whites used written letters and printed documents to maintain communication between the colony and the metropole. After 1764, the Saint-Domingue newspaper, the *Affiches américaines*, printed notices describing escaped blacks, helping their masters to track them down. Few of the enslaved blacks in Saint-Domingue in 1791 had ever seen Europe, but all of them understood that the white colonists' connection with France made them formidable adversaries.

By 1791 a few of the whites in Saint-Domingue could claim several generations of ancestry in the island, but most of them, like the *bossales* on their plantations, had in fact been born on the other side of the Atlantic. Throughout the eighteenth century, Saint-Domingue was France's land of opportunity, a new frontier where enterprising individuals could hope to escape the restrictions of aristocratic society and make their fortunes. Even the high rate of mortality for new arrivals – whites were as vulnerable to tropical diseases as the blacks – did not discourage ambitious immigrants. The memoirs of one settler who arrived in the colony in 1785 are typical of those who crossed the ocean, looking for possibilities they could not find in Europe. Eager to escape from his domineering parents, this anonymous author enlisted in one of the French army's colonial regiments. Army discipline in Saint-Domingue was lax, and he was able to spend much of his time doing odd jobs to earn extra money. After a few years, he deserted his regiment and went to work as an *économe* or assistant overseer on a coffee plantation. He was soon making a salary of 3,000 *livres* a year, along with room and board, at a time when an ordinary worker's wages in France were about a sixth as much. He succeeded in winning the trust of the elderly plantation-owner he worked for; when that man died, he left his former employee 6,000 *livres* and "a young

American-born black woman, eighteen years old, for whom he knew I had affection." Using this money, the young man acquired more enslaved blacks of his own and established a coffee plantation in the southern part of the colony.[6]

Whereas newcomers from France had to struggle to establish themselves and were often referred to, even by the blacks, as *petits blancs*, "little whites" whose only asset was their skin color, the most successful *grands blancs* achieved fortunes that few Frenchmen at home could dream of. Itemizing his losses in the Haitian Revolution, one man listed a sugar plantation with 342 captive laborers, a coffee plantation with 46 others, a stud farm with 48 mares and 148 mules, and a lime-making establishment employing 25 enslaved blacks; he was by no means the wealthiest of Saint-Domingue planters.[7] Prosperous planters built large houses on their plantations and filled them with expensive furnishings imported from Europe. Freed from having to do any physical labor themselves, the colonists were known for their hospitality and their lavish spending, which often left them heavily in debt. Merchants in the colony's cities and in France's ports enriched themselves by supplying these free-spending customers, many of whom spent most of their time in town or left to live in France, appointing hired managers or *gérants* to run their properties. Critics of the slavery system claimed that these managers treated the blacks harshly and skimmed off money that should have been spent on their care, in order to accumulate as much money as possible for themselves, in hope of either buying their own plantations or of returning to France with their profits.

Separated from France by the Atlantic Ocean, the white colonists in Saint-Domingue resented the metropolitan government's attempt to regulate their lives. From the point of view of the distant authorities in Versailles, Saint-Domingue existed in order to enrich the mother country and help France compete with the other European imperial powers. France's navigation act, the *exclusif*, required the colonists to buy their supplies only from French merchants and to sell their products only in the mother country. Colonists complained that the merchant houses of Bordeaux, Nantes, and Le Havre overcharged them for products shipped from Europe and underpaid them for their sugar and coffee; especially in the South Province, colonists reacted by carrying on a lively smuggling trade with other Caribbean islands and Britain's prosperous North American colonies. The white colonists also resented the authority of the military governors and civil intendants sent from France to govern them.

Wealthy and self-confident, the island's plantation-owners wanted to run their own affairs, as colonists in the nearby British colonies usually did. After the end of the Seven Years War in 1763, the French administration tried to tighten its control over its most valuable colony, just as the British were doing in North America. While Britain's colonists demonstrated against measures like a new stamp tax, the Saint-Domingue colonists went further: in December 1768 they staged an outright rebellion which was not brought under control until the following summer. It was a warning of the independent spirit that the colonists would show when revolution broke out in France in 1789.

In the colony's main city, Cap Français, the white population recreated the features of modern European life. Le Cap, as it was commonly called, had a rectangular grid of streets, much easier to navigate than the crooked alleyways of Paris. A large and imposing building housed the colonial administration. The city, with a population of around 18,000 in 1789, was built largely of stone. In addition to its 1,500-seat theater, it boasted separate hospitals for men and women, elegant public squares, and a large barracks complex for the military garrison that protected the colonists from foreign invasion and the threat of a slave uprising. Le Cap's whites considered themselves full participants in the Enlightenment culture of France. The city had bookstores, Masonic lodges, and in 1784 it became the third community in the western hemisphere, after Philadelphia and Boston, to have a learned society, the Cercle des Philadelphes. Saint-Domingue's other cities were less impressive. Port-au-Prince, in the west, was the official capital, even though its population was smaller than Le Cap's. Most of its buildings were made out of wood and its streets were still unpaved at the time of the revolution. The smaller ports scattered along the colony's coastline served primarily as places where ships could anchor to take on the produce from local plantations.

The Free People of Color

Whites shared the cities with enslaved blacks and with members of the colony's third racial group, the free people of color. As in the countryside, enslaved laborers did most of the physical tasks in the cities, loading and unloading ships, working in the building trades, and caring for their masters' households. Enslaved urban workers enjoyed greater freedom than the more numerous laborers on the plantations. Masters often taught them artisanal skills and then let them hire themselves out, in exchange for a share of their earnings. Rather than being organized into work gangs, they could often circulate on their own, and the fact that it was difficult to distinguish enslaved blacks from free persons allowed runaway *marrons* to blend into the city population. The urban black population would show itself less eager to participate in the insurrection that began in 1791 than the enslaved blacks on the plantations.

Enslaved urban blacks tolerated their situation because they hoped to join the population of free people of color. This third racial category among the colony's population had begun to develop soon after enslaved blacks were imported to the island. Many, but not all, of the free people of color were the offspring of sexual relationships between white masters and enslaved black women: throughout the colony's history, there had always been many more white men than white women willing to leave Europe for the rigors of colonial life. White men routinely exploited enslaved black women for their sexual pleasure. Although the relationships between white men and women of African descent were profoundly unequal, white men often granted freedom to women who bore themchildren; the Code Noir explicitly authorized this practice. White women often resented their husbands' involvement with women of color; in 1791, a French official had to intervene when a jealous white wife physically attacked an enslaved woman in whom she decided her husband was taking too much interest.[8]

Populations of free people of color developed in all the American colonies, but in the course of the eighteenth century the group in Saint-Domingue came to be larger and more influential than in any of the other Caribbean colonies. Those free people of color who were descended from white fathers often inherited property, including enslaved blacks. Less averse to hard work than the whites, and less tempted by the prospect of leaving the colony for France, they were often more economically successful than the Europeans. Free people of color were essential to the running of the colony. Companies of free men of color were recruited to form the *maréchaussée* or rural police, used to hunt down runaway slaves, and entrepreneurs from this group ran many of the colony's small businesses. White men sought out free women of mixed race, who legend claimed were more skilled at the arts of sex than whites; white women often complained that European men preferred their mixed-race rivals. Sex was not the only reason why white males linked themselves to these women, however. It was not uncommon for white men to leave the management of their property to energetic free women of color, known as *menagères*, who might or might not also be their mistresses; many of these women became the founders of prosperous families and sought to guide their children into advantageous marriages with other members of the free colored group or even with white men willing to cross the color line in order to improve their economic situation. Like the children of white couples, some children from mixed-race families were sent to France for their education.

As their numbers and wealth increased – by 1789 official statistics showed 28,000 free people of color in Saint-Domingue, almost as many as the 30,000 whites – members of this group increasingly resented laws that condemned them to second-class status. In 1685, the Code Noir had specified that freed blacks had "the same rights, privileges, and liberties enjoyed by persons born free," and throughout the early part of the eighteenth century, there was little discrimination against them and their descendants in the colonies. From the 1760s onward, however, official policy and white colonists' attitudes became increasingly prejudicial toward the free people of color. The French government calculated that maintaining a clear separation between whites and non-whites would prevent the colony's free population from uniting to resist metropolitan authority. A series of laws attempted to limit new manumissions and banned free people of color from entering a long list of professions, including medicine and law, or from wearing fancy clothing and jewelry. Notaries drawing up legal documents had to use specific terms to identify them, and they were forbidden to use the family names of their white ancestors. In practice, many of these laws were often ignored, but free men of color were excluded from all government posts and from commanding military units. When the French Revolution broke out, they would be quick to seize on its promises of liberty and equality to demand the abolition of these restrictions.

Critics and Defenders of Slavery

In addition to the tensions generated by the slavery system and the conflicts between whites and the free people of color, Saint-Domingue in the years before 1789 was increasingly affected by new ideas coming from Europe and the newly independent United States. By the middle of the 1700s, some European thinkers were beginning to criticize slavery as an inherent violation of natural human rights. The idea of colonialism also came under fire. In 1770 the abbé Raynal's *Philosophical History of the Two Indies* made a scathing denunciation of the effects of European settlement in the Americas. Subsequent editions of this best-selling work added vehement denunciations of slavery. One passage, written by the French *philosophe* Diderot, mentioned slave revolts in several colonies, warning that "these bolts of lightning announce the thunder," and predicted that if slavery was not abolished, a black leader would soon "raise the sacred banner of liberty" and lead a movement to destroy the institution.[9] Raynal's book circulated freely in Saint-Domingue; it is often claimed that Toussaint Louverture had read it. Raynal himself had connections with royal administrators in charge of the colonies, and colonists feared that his ideas might influence official policy. Other critics challenged colonial policy on economic grounds, arguing that the cost of defending and administering overseas territories outweighed the profits they produced.

The French government's actions during the decades before the revolution were confused and often contradictory. While some officials hoped to reduce the cruelty of slavery, others were more concerned about the possibility of blacks entering France itself. A 1777 edict, the *police des noirs*, expressed fears about racial mixing and set up a registration system meant to exclude blacks from the metropole.[10] In Saint-Domingue itself, royal officials imposed new restrictions on the free population of color. The American Revolution added to the ferment under way in the New World. The conflict interrupted Saint-Domingue's trade with Europe and its supply of new captives from Africa, reminding the colonists of their vulnerability to disruptions resulting from France's foreign policy. White planters were alarmed when the French administration recruited free men of color to join a military expedition sent to besiege British forces in Savannah, Georgia, in 1779. Among the participants in this unsuccessful campaign were André Rigaud, who would later become Toussaint Louverture's most important political rival, and a number of other figures who would play important roles in the events of the Haitian Revolution.

With the end of the American war in 1783, Saint-Domingue's seemingly irresistible economic rise resumed. To make up for the cutoff of imported captives during the war, planters purchased record numbers of new African laborers, and a new wave of whites arrived from France. A decree in August 1784 opened Saint-Domingue's major ports to trade with the newly independent United States. Eagerly welcomed by the colonists, this breach of the *exclusif* was bitterly opposed by French merchant interests. Although they appreciated the new trade law, the colonists were jolted when the French government issued ordinances on 3 December 1784 and 23 December 1785 intended to mitigate some of the worst abuses of the slave system. Masters and plantation managers were required to keep accurate records of the food and clothing provided to their slaves, and the provisions of the Code Noir allowing enslaved blacks to complain about mistreatment were restated. The colonists reacted violently to what they denounced as an example of metropolitan "despotism." "This edict violates the sacred rights of property, and puts a dagger in the hands of the slaves, by giving control over their discipline and their regime to someone other than their masters," one of them wrote.[11] To silence this opposition, in January 1787 the French government shut down the Conseil supérieur, the main law court in Cap Français, and merged it with the court in Port-au-Prince. This measure further angered the white colonists, some of whom were ready to call for a revolt like the movement in 1768–9.

By the beginning of 1787, the French government's attempt to deal with its growing financial problems had started the chain of events that would lead to a full-fledged revolution two years later. Saint-Domingue's white colonists followed the stages of the pre-revolutionary crisis of 1787 and 1788 closely, and tried to calculate how to turn it to their own advantage. At the same time, they realized that they faced a new danger. In Paris in February 1788, a group of French reformers led by a well-known pamphleteer, Jacques-Pierre Brissot, founded the Society of the Friends of the Blacks. Inspired by the British campaign to abolish the slave trade, the Friends of the Blacks denounced slavery as a violation of natural rights. Its members, who included a number of wealthy aristocrats with properties in the colonies, shared the general European prejudice that blacks were the products of a primitive civilization. The society's manifestoes called for a gradual phasing out of slavery that, its members claimed, would do no damage to the interests of slaveowners. Despite the moderation of its program, the Society of the Friends of the Blacks clearly underlined the contradiction between the ideals of liberty and equality that the self-proclaimed "patriot" movement in France was demanding and the realities of colonial life. The fact that the French government tolerated the society's public meetings made the white colonists even more determined to defend their own interests.

Saint-Domingue and the French Revolution

When Louis XVI's ministers announced, in the summer of 1788, that they were going to summon an elected assembly, the Estates General, to deal with the monarchy's financial crisis, white landowners in Saint-Domingue immediately began a campaign to obtain seats for themselves. Their spokesmen cast the colonists as victims of an arbitrary government that imposed rules on them without consultation and favored metropolitan merchants over plantation-owners. Recognizing that the enthusiasm for liberty that was sweeping France made an overt defense of slavery risky, they emphasized the economic importance of the colonies and accused the Society of the Friends of the Blacks of promoting impractical utopian ideas. The Friends of the Blacks tried to persuade local electoral assemblies in France to include calls for the reform or abolition of slavery in the *cahiers*, or lists of grievances that they drew up in the first months of 1789. Few of the *cahiers* actually mentioned slavery, but those that did clearly identified the institution as a violation of natural rights and Christian values. On 17 June 1789, when the deputies of the Third Estate, the representatives of France's commoners, took the radical step of challenging the king and the country's privileged groups, the clergy and the nobility, by proclaiming themselves the National Assembly, the would-be representatives of the white colonists supported them. Some colonists threw themselves into the metropolitan revolutionary movement. Moreau de Saint-Méry, one of the main leaders of protests against the royal administration's actions in Saint-Domingue, presided over the Paris city council on the afternoon of 14 July 1789, the day the Bastille was stormed.[12]

Although many members of the new National Assembly voiced objections to slavery, on 4 July 1789 the deputies voted to give Saint-Domingue six seats, thereby acknowledging the colonies as an integral part of the new national community. By this time, some Saint-Domingue colonists had begun to realize the danger that the new national legislature, in which they were only a small minority, might pass laws that would endanger the institution of slavery, but their protests were ignored by other colonial property-owners who were eager to become deputies. Given that as many as 150 of the 1,200 National Assembly deputies had a direct economic interest in the colonies, it seemed unlikely that that body would do anything to jeopardize the islands' prosperity. The situation changed after the storming of the Bastille on 14 July 1789, which pushed the French revolutionary movement in a radical direction. Three weeks later, on 4 August 1789, the National Assembly voted to abolish all the special privileges that defined social hierarchy in France. One deputy called for the assembly to consider abolishing slavery as well, although his motion was ignored. On 26 August 1789, however, the assembly passed its famous Declaration of the Rights of Man and Citizen, whose first article proclaimed that "men are born and remain free and equal in rights." Honoré Mirabeau, one of the most prominent revolutionary spokesmen and a member of the Society of Friends of the Blacks, insisted in his newspaper that the clear meaning of the Declaration was that "there are not, and cannot be, either in France or in any country under French laws, any other men than free men, men equal to one another."[13] The assembly did not listen to Mirabeau, instead deciding that the question of whether the Declaration of Rights applied to the colonies would be settled at a later date. Slaveowners in the colonies understood the danger, however. In Saint-Domingue, the local authorities prohibited the circulation of any newspapers from France because of the subversive ideas they might spread. A short-lived slave uprising in Martinique in August 1789 stoked the white colonists' fears about the impact of news from France.

While Saint-Domingue's white colonists tried to exploit the French revolutionary crisis to gain autonomy for themselves without endangering slavery, members of the colony's free population of color saw the new principles of 1789 as an opportunity to claim political rights for themselves. Already in 1784 a wealthy free man of color, Julien Raimond, had gone to France to lobby on behalf of his group; he had received some encouragement from royal officials who saw his group as more loyal to France than the whites. When whites excluded free men of color from their movement for representation in the Estates General, Raimond and other members of the group in France objected. Initially, the Parisian spokesmen for the free people of color thought they might be able to make an agreement with the whites, who had organized themselves in the Club Massiac to defend their interests. Representatives of the free men of color addressed the group in August 1789, arguing that all of them shared a common interest in protecting slavery. The Club Massiac members rejected these overtures, however, insisting that only the white colonists in Saint-Domingue could make any changes in the colony's racial system. Raimond and his supporters then turned to the Friends of the Blacks, persuading Brissot and his colleagues that the granting of rights to the free men of color would be a blow against racial prejudice and a first step toward the eventual abolition of slavery. Until 1793, debates about the colonies in France focused on the issue of the rights of the free men of color, rather than on slavery itself. In March 1790, the

National Assembly passed two decrees promising that the colonies would be allowed to regulate their own internal affairs and authorizing "citizens" in the colonies to elect assemblies for this purpose. The language of these decrees did not specify whether free men of color were included in the category of citizens, as many French reformers demanded. The white colonists, however, interpreted the laws of March 1790 as giving them the right to decide on the matter, and they excluded the free men of color from the new political assemblies created in Saint-Domingue.

A Colonial Revolution

In Saint-Domingue itself, the collapse of royal authority after the storming of the Bastille allowed the white population to realize its dream of governing itself. The royal intendant François Barbé-Marbois, who had closed down the court in Cap Français in 1787, was forced to flee the island in October 1789. Colonists chose new local governments and imitated the revolutionaries in France by creating a National Guard made up of armed white citizens. Uncensored newspapers appeared in the colony's major cities, and local "patriots" established political clubs like those that had sprung up in France in 1789. In April 1790, an all-white Colonial Assembly convened in the western port city of Saint-Marc, at a safe distance from the royal army garrisons in Port-au-Prince and Le Cap. Although some of its members warned against taking steps that the metropolitan government might interpret as a claim of independence, the majority decided on a confrontational course. On 28 May 1790, they passed a colonial constitution asserting their right to decide on all laws concerning the internal affairs of the colony. When news of the Colonial Assembly's actions reached France, it provoked an uproar: supporters of the revolution denounced a plot to make Saint-Domingue independent of France, and possibly even to turn it over to France's main rival, Britain. In the colony, the royal governor, backed by those whites who had opposed the Colonial Assembly's actions, used force to disperse the deputies. Sailors on the French warship *Leopard*, stationed in Saint-Marc's harbor, however, mutinied in support of the assembly; they seized control of the ship and took 85 of the white colonists back to France, where they denounced the governor's actions. Although the National Assembly sternly rebuked these "Leopardins" for undermining metropolitan authority, they were allowed to stay in France, where they joined the Club Massiac in denouncing the danger of allowing revolutionary principles to spread to the colonies.

While the whites in Saint-Domingue disputed among themselves in 1789 and 1790, other parts of the colony's population were also recognizing that the revolution in France might change their lives. How much the enslaved black population heard about the revolution and how they interpreted the news is hard to measure. Despite the ban on French newspapers, reports about events there circulated widely in the colony, and some blacks undoubtedly heard their masters using the new language of freedom and natural rights. In October 1789, Julien Raimond's brother told him that blacks had heard that the red, white, and blue cockade or ribbon being worn by many whites stood for "liberty and equality," and that they had threatened to rise up for their own freedom.[14] The number of new black captives imported to the colony reached its all-time peak in those years, with more than 30,000 being brought from Africa in 1790 alone; these new arrivals could hardly have mastered Kreyol, let alone French, before the start of the slave uprising in 1791. The free population of color had better access to information. Julien Raimond wrote regularly to an extensive network of correspondents in the island, telling them about his efforts on their behalf. Some members of this group took initiatives of their own to try to obtain the rights that the new French principles seemed to guarantee them. In November, 1789, a white local official in the town of Petit Goâve was lynched by other whites when he helped the local free men of color draw up a petition on their own behalf.

Matters took a more explosive turn in October 1790, when Vincent Ogé, a free man of color who had been in Paris in 1789, returned secretly to Saint-Domingue and organized an armed revolt among members of his group in the mountains south of the Northern Plain, the richest sugar-growing area of the North Province (see Figure 1.2). Prior to the revolution, Ogé had been one of the most prosperous free men of color in Le Cap: he owned extensive property in the city and was accustomed to dealing with whites on a basis of equality. Ogé was convinced that the National Assembly's decrees of March 1790 had been meant to grant rights to his group; when he learned that the colony's whites had continued to exclude them, he decided to act. In his call for insurrection, which attracted only a few hundred followers, Ogé was careful to make it clear that he was not seeking the abolition of slavery, but he warned some of the whites he encountered that he might do so if his demands were rejected. White forces soon dispersed Ogé's movement. He and a few associates fled across the border into the Spanish colony of Santo Domingo, but the Spanish authorities turned them over to the French. After a quick trial in Cap Français, Ogé was tortured to death in Le Cap in February 1791, and over 20 of his supporters were also executed.

Figure 1.2 Vincent Ogé calls on the free men of color to demand their rights. This nineteenth-century illustration shows Ogé, carrying the French flag and wearing the uniform of the French revolutionary National Guard, being welcomed by a group of free men of color on his return to Saint-Domingue in October 1790. Ogé and his supporters, many of them slaveowners themselves, did not call for the emancipation of the slaves, but they were the first group to resort to force to challenge racial hierarchy in the colony.

Source: Bibliothèque nationale, Paris, Cabinet des Estampes.

Although Ogé's insurrection was quickly put down, it had major effects throughout Saint-Domingue and in France. For the first time, the colony's whites' greatest fear – a violent insurrection against the system of racial hierarchy – had materialized. Ogé's threat to offer freedom to the blacks in order to gain enough support to defeat the whites raised the stakes in the island's racial conflict to a new level, and the whites' brutal response made the free people of color realize that they were not likely to obtain the rights they sought peacefully. In the South Province, more than 600 armed free men of color, including André Rigaud, who would eventually become the group's main leader, gathered on a plantation outside the capital city of Cayes and beat off an armed attack from local whites.[15] As agitation among the free people of color increased, some of the colony's enslaved blacks also began to organize against the whites. In January 1791, a conspiracy involving several hundred blacks was discovered in the Port-Salut district in the South Province.

The impression that only force would lead to any change in the colony's racial order was strengthened by the violence with which some white colonists denounced the members of the colony's other racial groups. In 1790 the chevalier de Beauvois, a member of Cap Français's science academy, published a pamphlet asserting that "nature has created several species of men, as she has created several species of animals." Blacks, he claimed, were little better than apes, and they could never be part of a civilized society. As for people of mixed race, Beauvois insisted they should be kept in a subordinate position, forced to work for the benefit of the whites, and forbidden from owning land or having whites working for them.[16] Beauvois's pamphlet was one of the first expressions in print of the pseudo-scientific racism that would become widespread in the western world in the nineteenth and twentieth centuries. White violence was not just rhetorical. On 4 March 1791, a mob made up of colonists and sailors and soldiers from France, who had brought revolutionary suspicions of government authority with them, murdered Colonel Mauduit, the commander of the military garrison. Mauduit had fought in the American revolutionary war, and reports of his death shocked newspaper readers throughout the Atlantic world.

In France, the news of Ogé's execution and Mauduit's murder galvanized both supporters of racial equality and defenders of slavery. Brissot and the Friends of the Blacks denounced the harsh punishment inflicted on Ogé, a man who, they claimed, had all the qualifications needed to be a French citizen. Members of the slaveowners' lobby responded by pushing to make sure that their racial privileges were protected by French law. In mid-May 1791, the National Assembly held its longest and most heated debate about these issues. The colonial deputy Moreau de Saint-Méry challenged his opponents head on by moving that the new French constitution explicitly guarantee that no changes would be made in the institution of slavery without the consent of the white colonists. An outraged Maximilien Robespierre, one of the leaders of Assembly's radical Jacobin faction, replied that it would be better "to let the colonies perish rather than violate a principle" by mentioning the word "slavery" in the constitution of a free country. The best Robespierre and his allies could obtain, however, was an agreement to replace the word "slaves" with the phrase "unfree persons."

Unhappy at having allowed themselves to be pressured into recognizing the legality of slavery, a majority of the deputies voted for an amendment to this law proposed by the deputy Jean-François Rewbell that granted full political rights to free men of color whose parents had also been free. This "Rewbell amendment" would have benefited only a minority of the free people of color, but it did for the first time directly challenge the notion that only racially pure whites could be full citizens in the colonies. The significance of the law was clear to observers in the United States, where newspapers closely followed the French debate because of its implications for race relations throughout the Americas. Moreau de Saint-Méry and his supporters were infuriated by the amendment's passage. For two years, they had fought to establish the principle that only the colonists themselves could decide questions about what they called "the status of persons" in the colonies. By voting for the Rewbell amendment, limited as it was, the National Assembly had asserted the metropolitan government's power to make such decisions; the white colonists feared that the next step would be a law limiting the powers of slaveowners. Their fears were heightened by the assembly's vote to send a three-member Civil Commission to Saint-Domingue to oversee the implementation of the law. Although the members of this First Civil Commission were supposed to rely on persuasion to get the whites to accept the new decree, their appointment represented an effort by the French legislature to rein in the white colonists' dangerous tendency to act as though they were entitled to govern themselves.

When news of the law of 15 May 1791 reached Saint-Domingue at the end of June, virtually the entire white population rose in revolt. General Philibert Blanchelande, the new governor who had arrived in the island in November 1790, had to tell the French government that he would not be able to enforce the law if it was officially transmitted to him. The colonists' lobby launched a determined campaign to overturn the decree; on 24 September 1791, shortly before it dissolved, the National Assembly reversed itself and voted to leave the fate of the rights of free colored persons entirely in the hands of the white colonists. Meanwhile, however, the members of the First Civil Commission had already sailed for Saint-Domingue; they would arrive only to learn that one of the main purposes of their mission had been cancelled, thereby adding to the confusion in the colony. Because it took two months for news to cross the Atlantic, the assembly handed the white colonists this victory before anyone in France knew of the event that was to totally transform the situation in Saint-Domingue: on 22 August 1791, a massive slave insurrection had begun in the North Province.

2

The Uprisings, 1791–1793

When Haitians today imagine the beginnings of the struggle that would lead to the end of slavery and their country's independence, they often picture a scene like that portrayed on a postage stamp issued in Haiti in 1991 to mark the 200th anniversary of the uprising (Figure 2.1). In the center of this image, the insurrection's leader Boukman Dutty, a tall black man dressed in the red and blue colors of Haiti's national flag, stands, surrounded by a group of blacks gathered in a forest clearing, and looks up to a lightning-streaked sky. He brandishes a *vodou* rattle or *ason* in one hand and gestures dramatically with the other. Next to him, a white-clad woman raises her arm as she leads the dozens of men and women around her in swearing an oath to fight to the death for their freedom. This depiction is not based on eyewitness accounts – no first-hand testimony about the Bois Caïman gathering has come down to us – but it captures some vital elements of the Haitian movement. The enslaved blacks who were about to rise up and take the risk of challenging the powerful system of white domination were indeed making a dramatic decision, one that they knew might cost them their lives. They needed to forge a sense of unity, and they needed inspirational leadership. No doubt they sought courage and determination in the religious beliefs that helped unite a population made up of descendants of many different African ethnic groups. They would need whatever weapons they could obtain, beginning with the knives they used in the sugar-cane fields. The total intransigence of Saint-Domingue's white slaveowners left them convinced that they had no choice but to resort to violence to claim their freedom.

A Concise History of the Haitian Revolution, Second Edition. Jeremy D. Popkin.
© 2022 John Wiley & Sons Ltd. Published 2022 by John Wiley & Sons Ltd.

Figure 2.1   A Haitian postage stamp issued to commemorate 200th anniversary of the ceremony supposedly held at Bois Caïman to launch the August 1791 slave uprising shows the insurrectionary leader Boukman Dutty holding a *vodou* rattle or *ason*, while a *vodou* priestess joins him in leading in an oath. To modern Haitians, dramatic images like this one evoke the courage of their ancestors and the connection between their struggle for freedom and the rituals blacks brought with them from Africa. *Courtesy of the Haiti Philatelic Society.*

The Slave Uprising in the North Province

While recreations of the start of the Haitian Revolution such as the one on this postage stamp help us imagine the drama of that event, historians work with the surviving documentary evidence to reconstruct as precise a picture as they can of how the insurrection of August 1791 began. In the absence of actual testimony from any of those who helped plan the uprising, many questions about its outbreak remain difficult to answer. At the time, the white colonists were convinced that the enslaved blacks had been incited to rebellion by abolitionist propaganda from France and echoes of the French Revolution's debates about liberty. In fact, French anti-slavery reformers had always insisted that the institution could only be done away with over time, with compensation for the slaveowners, and there is no evidence that any of their printed propaganda had actually reached the enslaved population. On the other hand, Saint-Domingue's blacks had certainly been able to observe the growing disunity among the whites in the colony and between the whites and the free men of color, which the Ogé rebellion had highlighted. With their enemies divided, enslaved blacks could see that they had an opportunity to seize their own freedom through collective action, quite different from the individual forms of resistance like *marronnage* that some of them had engaged in before. The persistent rumor that Louis XVI had actually granted them new rights, but that the white colonists were refusing to implement his decree, may have provided further encouragement. The whites' very visible resistance to the National Assembly's decree of 15 May 1791 certainly made this idea plausible.

We do know, from evidence gathered at the time, that blacks from a number of plantations in the Northern Plain met together on Sunday, 14 August 1791, eight days before the start of the rebellion, not in a forest clearing like the one depicted on the stamp, but at a gathering on the Lenormand de Mézy estate, a large plantation about five miles outside of Cap Français. Those who organized the plot were often blacks who occupied the most responsible positions on the plantations, including a number of *commandeurs* or slave drivers, who were accustomed to giving orders, and coachmen, whose positions gave them opportunities to make connections on other plantations. At their meeting, the conspirators presumably set a date on which they would simultaneously attack their masters' plantations. They may have tried to coordinate this with an uprising in the nearby city of Cap Français, where, among other things, they might have hoped to kill the members of the new Colonial Assembly that was about to convene there. On 16 August 1791, however, blacks on one plantation jumped the gun and set fire to a building. Under interrogation, one of them revealed the details of the conspiracy. Fortunately for the plotters, the white authorities did not take his confession seriously. The secret meeting in the woods at a site known as Bois Caïman, which probably took place on the night of 21 August, may have included a *vodou* ceremony, and perhaps an inspirational speech like the one attributed to Boukman in a romanticized account first published 30 years later, in which the insurrectionary leader supposedly told his fellow-conspirators, "Couté la libeté li palé nan coeur nous tous" ("Listen to the liberty which speaks in the hearts of all of us"). Probably the main purpose of the meeting, however, was to decide how to react to the danger that the whites might have discovered the plan for the uprising. Since the first assaults on the plantations occurred the next night, the conspirators must have decided to act as quickly as possible.[1]

Even though they had warned for two years that the dangerous ideas of the French Revolution might lead to a slave revolt, the plantation-owners were caught off guard. Smugly certain of their superiority, they could not believe that the blacks who normally seemed so docile could have organized themselves so effectively. The manager of the Clément plantation, one of the first to be overrun, was awakened by his dog's barking in the middle of the night. He quieted the animal and went back to sleep, only to be jolted awake again a few minutes later by the sound of the black insurgents who had surrounded his house. "Hearing the noise they were making," he wrote, "I jumped out of my bed and shouted, 'Who goes there?' A voice like thunder answered me: 'It is death!'" His life was saved by the intervention of the insurrection's leader, Boukman Dutty, who had been enslaved on that plantation and knew him personally. Other whites were not so lucky. A number of them were killed, although in many cases blacks helped them escape even as they set fire to their plantations. The sugar-cane fields burned fiercely: the smoke from the fires could be seen miles away in Cap Français (Figure 2.2).

Moving rapidly from plantation to plantation in the densely populated flatlands of the Northern Plain, the first bands of insurgents gathered increasing numbers of supporters. Within a few days, almost the whole of the plain, the richest sugar-growing area in the colony, had been devastated, as had hundreds of the smaller coffee plantations in the mountains bordering it. The black insurgents guarding the manager of the Clément plantation told him that their plan was "nothing less than the destruction of all the whites except some who didn't own property, some priests, some surgeons, and some women, and of setting fire to all the plantations and making themselves masters of the country."[2] Although the leaders of the insurrection were men who had occupied relatively high-status positions on the plantations, the movement had support from the rest of the enslaved population as well. A white man taken prisoner by the insurgents reported that as he and other white captives were marched through the countryside, "old Negro men and women assembled before their doors were abasing us by their jargon," insulting the former masters in their Kreyol language. Women, often the victims of sexual exploitation by their white overseers, sometimes took the opportunity for revenge. On one plantation, a group of them, finding a white man who had been

Figure 2.2 *Esclavage: La Révolte des esclaves Noirs à Saint-Dominique.* This highly unrealistic engraving, part of a series depicting scenes from the French Revolution, emphasizes the violence that was a major theme of pro-slavery propaganda during this period. Blacks are shown butchering helpless whites and setting fire to plantation buildings. The original caption blames the revolt on the "contradictory decrees of the National Assembly" rather than on the oppressive nature of slavery.
Source: Paris, Musée Carnavalet, White Images/Scala WH09964D.

left for dead by the insurgents, taunted him by pulling up their skirts in front of his face. When they realized he was still alive, they beat him until he lost consciousness. In a number of cases, however, black women protected white women. A white woman prisoner testified that her life had been saved at the beginning of the insurrection by her own enslaved blacks, who hid her in their huts, and later by other formerly enslaved women who intervened with the black leaders on her behalf and cared for her on the plantations they had occupied.[3]

Overwhelmed by the initial shock of the uprising, many of the North Province's whites succumbed to panic. Suddenly, every non-white seemed like a potential enemy. Blacks suspected of sympathy for the uprising were massacred in Cap Français and on the plantations. Convinced that the blacks could not have conceived such an elaborate plan by themselves, many whites blamed the free men of color, who they accused of seeking revenge for the execution of Vincent Ogé. In Cap Français, a white mob killed a number of members of that group before the authorities intervened, pointing out that the whites would need their assistance to fight the uprising. The rapid spread of the insurrection during its first several months led white civilians to accuse the officers of the Régiment du Cap, the North Province's military garrison, of deliberately sabotaging efforts to repress it. The royal governor, General Blanchelande, was besieged from all sides by whites demanding protection for their rural properties, while the whites in Cap Français protested that he was leaving them vulnerable when he sent troops into the countryside. He and the Colonial Assembly that had just begun to meet in Cap Français when the uprising broke out sent urgent appeals for help to the neighboring colonies of Santo Domingo and Jamaica and to the United States, but they delayed informing the French government of the crisis. In the wake of the National Assembly's decree of 15 May 1791 granting rights to some free men of color, the white colonists had come to regard the metropolitan government as their enemy; they also feared that news of the uprising would deter French merchants from sending ships and supplies to the colony. While the whites quarreled among themselves, the insurrection continued to spread. A second wave of attacks on plantations in October 1791 gave the rebels control of the eastern part of the province, along the border with Spanish Santo Domingo.

The Revolt of the Free Men of Color

The shock of the uprising in the North Province was heightened by the almost simultaneous outbreak of a different kind of insurrection among the free men of color in Saint-Domingue's West Province, near the capital of Port-au-Prince. The two movements were not coordinated, and their goals were quite different. The free men of color, many of them slaveowners in their own right, were not seeking the immediate end of slavery or the destruction of the plantation system. Free men of color did recruit some enslaved blacks to fight for them, but they kept control over the movement and did not let it turn into a general assault on the plantation system. Like Vincent Ogé, the leader of the short-lived movement in October 1790, the free men of color demanded the political equality with the whites that the French Revolution's principles seemed to imply. Ogé had staged his insurrection in the North Province, where whites heavily outnumbered the free men of color; the movement that began in the west in August 1791 took root in rural districts in which free men of color often outnumbered the whites.

Angered by the whites' refusal to accept the National Assembly's law of 15 May 1791, delegates from a number of districts in the West and South Provinces gathered in the mountain town of Mirebalais on 7 August 1791. Whereas the blacks in the North Province had supposedly organized their movement at a *vodou* ceremony in the woods, the free men of color met openly in the local Catholic church to make their plans. Among those who participated in the movement were André Rigaud, who would later become the most important rival to Toussaint Louverture, and Alexandre Pétion and Jean-Paul Boyer, who between them would govern Haiti for much of the first half of the nineteenth century. The black insurgents in the north were joined by only a handful of individual whites and free men of color, but the movement of the free men of color in the west was supported by some of the conservative white plantation-owners, who decided that, in spite of the racial divide, they had more in common with these fellow property-owners than with the reckless *petits blancs* of the cities in the West and South Provinces. On 5 September 1791, the free men of color in the parish of Mirebalais, the center of the movement, made a treaty or concordat with the local white landowners that was soon copied in several other districts. In these concordats, the whites were forced to publicly confess that they had "sacrificed to the idol of prejudice" and oppressed the free men of color "by an incredible abuse of the laws and the power of government."[4] They had to agree to the replacement of the all-white local governments in their districts with new institutions in which members of both racial groups would be represented.

The Colonists' Response

Formidable as the two insurrectionary movements in the north and west looked, and incoherent as the initial white response to them was, the colonial order did not completely crumble. Although we may imagine the black insurrection like an avalanche, gathering strength steadily, in fact, like most rebellions throughout history, it struggled to achieve mass support. Oppressive as slavery was, not all of its victims were ready to risk their lives attempting to overthrow it. In the parish of Borgne, west of the Northern Plain, one slaveowner persuaded the blacks that they would lose their own huts and their private food plots if they joined the insurrection. He formed them into a private militia that defended that region for the next two years. Many of the recently arrived *bossales* were experienced in the methods of African warfare, such as ambushes of small units in remote areas, and their mass attacks, signaled by piercing blasts blown on *lambi* or conch shells that became a symbol of the insurrection, terrified the whites, but these tactics did not allow them to storm the coastal cities where the whites had taken refuge. When the heavily armed white troops did force the blacks to face them in regular battles, the insurgents' lack of firearms left them at a serious disadvantage. Whites who took part in these battles recognized the blacks' courage, but, as would be true throughout the Haitian Revolution, the black fighters suffered far heavier casualties than the whites. One white colonist estimated that 4,000 black insurgents were killed in the first few months of the insurrection, and an additional 4,000 captured; the blacks, he claimed, only had muskets and rifles for a fifth of their men.[5] In contrast, the members of the First Civil Commission estimated in January 1792 that 400 whites had been killed in the first four months of the fighting.[6] This was a substantial number, but it was not the wholesale massacre depicted in the propaganda the white colonists sent back to France.

By mid-November, the military situation in the North Province had begun to stabilize. Governor Blanchelande established a line of forts, the "Cordon of the West," to block the mountain passes connecting the North and West Provinces, thereby isolating the uprising in the north from the rest of the colony. Meanwhile, divisions developed among the black leaders who had led the first wave of attacks and proclaimed themselves as "generals." Jeannot Bullet, a particularly violent man who had tortured several white prisoners to death, was executed by a rival,

Jean-François Papillon. In mid-November, Boukman Dutty, the insur-rection's main leader, was killed in battle with the white forces. According to the white chronicler Gros, the news demoralized the black fighters: "They ran this way and that across the plain, making the air resound with this cry: 'Boukman tué, que ça nous va!'" ("Boukman is dead, what will become of us!")[7] The movement of the free men of color also suf-fered a setback when news of the French National Assembly's decision, on 24 September 1791, to repeal its decree of 15 May 1791 reached Saint-Domingue. The members of that group had justified their uprising by claiming that they were merely demanding rights that the metropolitan government had granted them; now the French assembly had publicly disavowed them, undermining their claim that it was the whites who were violating the law.

It was at this moment that the man who would eventually take over the leadership of the black movement and lead it to the brink of success first began to take a visible role in affairs. Whether the future Toussaint Lou-verture had participated in the planning of the insurrection in the north is unclear. In contrast to the other leaders of the movement, Louverture was no longer enslaved in 1791; he had gained his own freedom many years earlier. Unlike most of the leaders of the movement of free men of color in the colony, however, he had no white ancestry, and he had not become an independent property-owner. In 1791 he was working for Bayon de Lib-ertat, the manager of the Bréda plantation, and the other members of his family were still enslaved there. His connections with Bayon de Libertat and other whites were close enough that a story circulated as early as 1793 that he had actually organized the slave uprising on their behalf. Accord-ing to this conspiracy theory, mentioned in many biographies of Tous-saint Louverture, wealthy whites in the island had decided to provoke a limited slave uprising in order to demonstrate to the French government that the propaganda of the Society of the Friends of the Blacks was under-mining France's precious colony. They hoped to cause a backlash against the abolitionists in France that would discredit revolutionary ideas and strengthen not only their own position but that of King Louis XVI. Tous-saint supposedly overheard whites discussing the idea and volunteered to act as their agent. No firm evidence has ever been found to confirm this story, but the notion that he might have recognized that he could exploit the whites' idea and use it as an opportunity to launch a movement that would lead to freedom for the blacks fits well with the image of him as an unusually gifted politician who always saw further than his rivals.

Whether or not they had white encouragement to start their uprising, however, it is clear that once the blacks failed to destroy the white government, and once their leader Boukman had been killed, the surviving black generals decided to try to reach an agreement with the colonial government to end the uprising. Toussaint Louverture played a key role in this effort, which was encouraged by the arrival of the First Civil Commission in Saint-Domingue at the end of November 1791. The three civil commissioners, Philippe Roume, Edmond de Saint-Léger, and Frédéric Ignace de Mirbeck, had been sent to try to restore order in the colony; they also announced that the French king, when he accepted the new constitution drawn up by the French National Assembly in September 1791, had issued an amnesty for any political crimes committed during the first two years of the revolution. The two self-proclaimed black generals who had now emerged as the movement's principal leaders, Jean-François Papillon and his colleague Georges Biassou, were encouraged by some of their white prisoners, such as Gros, to hope that this measure might open the door to a peaceful end of the conflict. In early December, Jean-François and Biassou offered to end the fighting and persuade their followers to return to their plantations in exchange for freedom for themselves and few other leaders and a promise that the other blacks would not be punished for what they had done during the insurrection. Behind the scenes, Toussaint Louverture played an important role in these negotiations, consistently urging Jean-François and Biassou to moderate their demands. The first political document from the revolutionary period on which his signature appears is a letter dated 12 December 1791, urging the whites to accept the black leaders' offer.[8] He also intervened to protect the white prisoners captured by the insurgents and to urge the black leaders to follow legal procedures in dealing with them. From the start, Toussaint Louverture clearly sought to limit the violence of the uprising and guide the movement toward the creation of a new social and political order that would be acceptable to all the groups that made up the colony's population.

In hindsight, the negotiations between the black leaders and the whites at the end of 1791 mark the first instance of a phenomenon that would recur often in Haitian history: a small group of leaders trying to benefit themselves at the expense of the mass of the black population. Even as they bargained with the whites, however, Jean-François, Biassou, and Toussaint were aware that their followers might not accept such a settlement. When the white colonists rejected the black leaders' proposals, the black generals responded by warning them that "A hundred thousand men are in arms … and you will realize from that that we are entirely dependent on the general will, and what a will! That of a multitude of Negroes from the Coast [of Africa] who barely know two words of French but who, however, in their country were accustomed to making war."[9] The black leaders' ability to control their followers was never put to the test: the white colonists, confident that the French government would soon send troops to put down the insurrection, refused to accept their offer. The situation in the North Province hardened into a stalemate: the insurgents controlled most of the devastated Northern Plain and the mountains south and east of it, but they were unable to break through the defenses the whites had established in other parts of the region. The whites, for their part, despite the arrival of some 6,000 soldiers in early 1792, were unable to organize themselves to defeat the insurrection.

While these events were taking place in the North Province, the situation in the West and the South Provinces was also changing. Although some of the white planters in the countryside were willing to accept the concordats demanded by the free men of color, the majority of the urban white population of the area's largest city, Port-au-Prince, violently opposed any concessions to their foes. In the face of this intransigence, the leaders of the free men of color recruited an armed troop of blacks, nicknamed "les Suisses" ("the Swiss") because, like the Swiss soldiers hired to fight in the French royal army, they were willing to fight for pay. With these allies, the free men of color put Port-au-Prince under siege. By late October the whites in the city were forced to capitulate and accept the terms of the concordats. In return, however, they demanded that the "Swiss" be expelled from the colony. In their view, enslaved blacks who had borne arms against whites could never be trusted again. In exchange for achieving their political goals, the leaders of the free men of color agreed to disarm the "Swiss" and let them be shipped out of the colony. The white ship's captains entrusted with the mission tried unsuccessfully to put them ashore on a deserted part of the coast of Central America or to sell them as slaves in the British colony of Jamaica. When these efforts failed, most of the "Swiss" were returned to Saint-Domingue, where a number of them were murdered by hostile whites. The abandonment of the "Swiss" by the leaders of the free men of color created a lasting distrust between them and the rest of the black population and was remembered with bitterness even after Haiti gained its independence.

The negotiations that led to the betrayal of the "Swiss" failed to create a lasting peace between the free men of color and the whites. In the wake of the October agreement, the armed free men of color were allowed to enter the city, and elaborate festivities were held to mark the end of the fighting, but tension between the two groups remained high. On 19 November 1791, an incident between a white man and a free man of color set off violent fighting in the city in which 27 square blocks of houses and stores were burned down. News of the events in Port-au-Prince set off similar clashes in Cayes, the capital of the South Province, and in the cities of the Grande Anse, the western tip of the long peninsula, which would become a stronghold of the most intransigent whites throughout the revolutionary period. In the south, unlike the west, there were few wealthy whites willing to make alliances with the free men of color, and the hatred between the whites and the free men of color was as bitter as that between the whites and the black insurgents in the north. In Jérémie, in the Grande Anse, whites imprisoned local free men of color on a ship in the harbor and deliberately infected them with smallpox; only a third of them survived. The West and South Provinces became divided into a jigsaw puzzle of regions, some of them controlled by whites and others by free men of color. The breakdown of authority in these regions allowed enslaved blacks in some areas to stage their own insurrections. In contrast to the situation in the north, however, these revolts did not coalesce into a movement with recognized leaders capable of controlling a large area.

News of the Insurrection Spreads

News of the violence in Saint-Domingue spread rapidly across the Atlantic world. The government of the British island of Jamaica sent a delegation to Cap Français in September 1791 to promise aid against the rebels, although its leader, Bryan Edwards, concluded that "the case appeared altogether desperate from the beginning" because of the extent of the uprising.[10] The Spanish in the eastern half of Hispaniola had long envied the prosperity of their French neighbors. Some of them were quite happy to sell arms, gunpowder, and other supplies to the insurgent blacks. By late September 1791, news of the uprising had reached the United States, where newspapers published dramatic reports of the attacks on the whites and the burning of their properties. Southern plantation-owners shuddered at the possibility that their enslaved blacks might imitate the example of those in Saint-Domingue. New England merchants worried that supplies of sugar, coffee, and molasses would be cut off, disrupting their business, but shrewd Yankee traders also recognized that the crisis provided opportunities for them. A shipper in Boston urged a friend to rush a cargo of flour to Le Cap, since "in all probability government will take all they can lay their hands on for the use of their troops."[11] Throughout the period, American traders continued to do business with Saint-Domingue, bringing back a steady stream of news about developments there. In South America, reports of the Saint-Domingue uprising alarmed slaveowners, but, like North American merchants, they also saw opportunities for profit. Unable to sell black captives in Saint-Domingue, slave traders took them to other markets, such as Brazil, setting off an economic boom fueled by enslaved labor that lasted through the 1790s.

When the first reports of the uprising reached France at the end of October 1791, two months after its outbreak, they provoked stormy debates. The National Assembly, in which the white colonists had had strong support, had been replaced at the beginning of October with a new Legislative Assembly in which Jacques-Pierre Brissot and other members of the Society of the Friends of the Blacks, the French abolitionist movement, played leading roles. Under the new constitution of 1791, Louis XVI's powers were considerably reduced. His position was further weakened because, in June 1791, he had made an unsuccessful attempt to flee the kingdom; although the National Assembly's leaders had decided not to remove him from the throne, the supporters of the pro-revolutionary Jacobin movement had lost all trust in him. The news of the slave uprising struck many of the Jacobins as suspicious: was it a trick to give the king a chance to send troops across the ocean and perhaps even establish a refuge for himself on the other side of the Atlantic? From his refuge in Germany, the king's brother, the comte d'Artois, actually tried to appoint a counterrevolutionary governor for the colony, a usurpation of his authority that Louis XVI quashed.[12] Although only a few extremists openly supported the blacks' bid for freedom, Brissot and his supporters insisted that the white colonists be required to grant equal rights to the free men of color as a condition for receiving military assistance. Brissot, who was closely linked to the free men of color's representative Julien Raimond, argued that only a complete union between the two groups of free people in Saint-Domingue could defeat the slave uprising. A first contingent of 6,000 troops was sent to the colony in early 1792, but then Brissot and his party succeeded in holding up any further assistance until the question of rights for the free men of color was resolved.

After months of deadlock, Brissot's group finally got its way in March 1792, when they made a surprising alliance with the king. For very different reasons, Louis XVI and Brissot's party both wanted to declare war against France's European rival, Austria. The king thought that if the French army, badly disorganized by the effects of the revolution, was defeated, his absolute powers would be restored. Brissot, on the other hand, thought that the war would set off a wave of patriotic fervor in the country that would overwhelm the Revolution's enemies at home. Louis XVI agreed to appoint a new cabinet of ministers favored by Brissot to launch the war. As part of the deal, Brissot also insisted on approval of a new law granting full civil and political rights to all the free people of color in the French colonies. Signed by the king on 4 April 1792, this law also provided for the dispatch of an additional 6,000 troops to Saint-Domingue, under the supervision of a new Civil Commission whose powers were to be much greater than those of the first set of commissioners appointed in 1791. The two dominant members of this Second Civil Commission, Étienne Polverel and Léger-Félicité Sonthonax, were Jacobin activists who had both written newspaper articles denouncing slavery. Although their official instructions ordered them to defeat the black insurrection in Saint-Domingue, they had little sympathy for the white plantation-owners in the colony.

The Goals of the Black Insurgents

While the new civil commissioners and the military expedition accompanying them were slowly making their way across the Atlantic – they would not reach Saint-Domingue until September 1792 – the black insurgents in the North Province and the free men of color in the West and South Provinces were pursuing their own goals. The failure of the peace negotiations with the whites at the end of 1791 left the forces commanded by Jean-François and Biassou in control of the devastated sugar-growing region of the Northern Plain and the mountains south and east of it, along the Spanish border. The insurgents also held positions in the hills west of Cap Français. In these areas they began to organize a black-dominated society. They established a network of camps in the regions they held and appointed commanders for each of them, thus creating an elite of military officers who would eventually become the nucleus of a new governing class. Among these commanders was the future Toussaint Louverture, who thus acquired a power base of his own. Biassou built an imposing headquarters for himself at his base on the southern edge of the Northern Plain; one white colonist described it as a "royal palace." Although Biassou and Jean-François could not write, they dictated letters to secretaries. They issued legal documents, such as passes for travel in the territories they controlled, set up military tribunals to sentence prisoners, and held periodic councils to discuss policy.

While their leaders laid the basis of a society dominated by military commanders, ordinary blacks claimed land from the destroyed plantations to grow their own food, beginning the process of creating the rural peasantry that makes up the majority of the Haitian population to this day. From the outset, the goals of the black leadership and the mass of the population were in conflict. The formerly enslaved blacks had no interest in continuing to perform the disciplined labor necessary for growing sugar or coffee, nor did they care about the survival of the plantation system. The new ruling class, however, would have liked to substitute itself for the former plantation-owners and continue the production of cash crops. This would have enabled them to enrich themselves, but they also needed resources to pay for weapons and ammunition to supply their troops, which they had to purchase from Spanish Santo Domingo. In order to pay for these supplies, Jean-François and Biassou resorted to selling black prisoners of war, and women and children who could not participate in the army, to the Spanish. Their willingness to engage in this kind of slave trading, similar to the arrangements by which black rulers in Africa sold captives to the whites, indicates that these leaders had not yet come to see their movement as a revolt against the principle of slavery, as opposed to a movement for the benefit of those who were participating directly in it. Toussaint Louverture, while he continued to serve under Biassou's command, was notable for not engaging in this kind of exchange, however. Having been a free man before the revolution, and having had more exposure to white debates about slavery, he may have had a stronger commitment to the elimination of the institution than the other black leaders.

Unlike revolutionary movements in Britain's North American colonies and in France, the uprising in Saint-Domingue was carried out by a largely illiterate population. The movement did not define its goals in written manifestoes or other public statements. It is therefore difficult to know whether they had been influenced by the abstract principles of the

French Declaration of the Rights of Man. A letter from Jean-François, Biassou, and a third black leader named Belair, written in July 1792, probably in response to a letter from Philippe Roume, the one member of the First Civil Commission who remained in the colony after the spring of that year, refers explicitly to the Declaration, but also draws on language from the Bible and on Enlightenment notions of natural right to make a powerful argument for the equality of all people: "Being all children of one father created in the same image we are therefore your equals according to natural right and if it has pleased nature to diversify the colors of the human species it is no crime to be black or any advantage to be white." Despite the radical language it contains, the letter ends with fairly moderate proposals: if the whites would recognize the blacks' freedom, grant amnesty to those who had participated in the insurrection, and have the Spanish government guarantee the terms of the agreement, the insurgents, for their part, would return to their plantations and resume their work, in exchange for a fixed salary.[13]

Even as they proposed negotiations with Roume, the black leaders continued to look to the French king, rather than to the French revolutionary movement, as their most likely source of support. The counter-revolutionary white military commander Joseph Cambefort, who seized the black generals' letter and published it in Paris in January 1793, pointed out that the blacks had no reason to think that the French revolutionaries, who had taken no measures to abolish slavery, were on their side. As Cambefort remarked, in Saint-Domingue, "the civil and military authorities who were fighting [the insurrection] wore the patriotic colors" of the revolution.[14] The blacks were also offended by the French revolutionaries' hostility to religion. Even if their real faith was in *vodou* rather than Catholicism, the black population could not imagine a society without some kind of religious belief. In August 1792, Jean-François wrote that "I have always stood up for our God and the king."[15] On 10 August 1792, the Jacobin leaders in Paris mobilized the city's *sans-culottes*, the poorer members of the population, and overthrew the constitutional monarchy established the year before. When he learned that Louis XVI had been imprisoned in France, Biassou held a ceremony to proclaim himself viceroy, promising to "maintain order while awaiting instructions from the king our master, whose rights I hope to support, with the help of the Lord, until it pleases him to send us his own established laws."[16]

While the insurgents in the North Province were establishing their own society, with an elite of black leaders and a distinctive political

ideology, the men of color in the West and South Provinces were gain-
ing power as well. With the support of Saint-Léger, one of the members
of the First Civil Commission, a shaky truce was re-established in Port-
au-Prince at the beginning of 1792, and the free men of color helped
put down a violent uprising led by a charismatic figure who called
himself "Romaine the prophetess" in the area around Léogane, another
port city in the area. French officials considered Romaine's claim to
be possessed by a female spirit "ridiculous," but the story may reflect
vodou beliefs, according to which individuals can be seized by divini-
ties of the opposite sex.[17] North of Port-au-Prince, in the rich Croix-
des-Bouquets plain, the free men of color allied with another black
leader, Hyacinthe, who was able to instigate slave insurrections to in-
timidate the whites in the area without letting these movements get out
of hand. In April 1792 the free men of color, led by Pierre Pinchinat,
renewed their alliance with the conservative white plantation-owners
in the west by forming the Council of Peace and Union in the port city
of Saint-Marc. Pinchinat, whose political skills were recognized even
by the whites who most violently opposed him, turned the mixed-race
council into a powerful rival to the all-white Colonial Assembly, which
continued to meet in Cap Français and to resist any concessions either
to the free men of color or to the insurgent blacks.

When news of the French Legislative Assembly's decree of 4 April
1792 reached Saint-Domingue at the end of May 1792, however, the Colonial Assembly, recognizing the need for metropolitan troops to fight
the slave insurrection, had to abandon its diehard opposition to equality
with the free men of color. Although many whites privately continued to
nurse their hatred for the free men of color, as a violent clash in Cap Français in mid-August that nearly unleashed a civil war in the city showed,
the white leadership proclaimed its readiness to accept equality with
them. Secretly, many whites hoped that the revolutionary government
in France would soon collapse and that the rights granted to their rivals
would be repealed. In the meantime, however, Governor Blanchelande
was determined to enforce the new law. He gave his endorsement to the
Council of Peace and Union, even though it had been formed without
his permission, and arrested the Port-au-Prince agitators who had continued to fight for white supremacy. Saint-Domingue appeared to be on
the verge of becoming the first New World society in which distinctions
between free people of different racial backgrounds would be abolished.
Even if this reform was meant to strengthen the system of slavery rather

than to abolish it, the acceptance of racial equality was a momentous step with implications that affected all parts of the Americas.

Even as he moved to implement the decree of 4 April 1792, Governor Blanchelande continued to try to end the slave uprising. Blanchelande had decided not to challenge the powerful black insurgent movement in the north until more troops arrived from France, but at the beginning of August 1792 he launched an attack on a smaller group of insurgents who had freed themselves and established a "republic" at Platons, in the mountains near the South Province's capital of Cayes. The French troops had to separate into several columns to penetrate into the rugged terrain, and the insurgents were able to ambush and destroy them. It was the worst military defeat white forces had suffered since the start of the fighting in the colony. Crushed and humiliated, Blanchelande had to sail back to Cap Français to wait for the arrival of the new civil commissioners and the fresh forces accompanying them. Sent back to France and accused of having exceeded his authority by endorsing the Council of Peace and Union and of mismanaging the military effort against the slave insurrection, Blanchelande became the first prominent victim condemned to death by the new Revolutionary Tribunal the radical French revolutionaries set up in April 1793.

The Second Civil Commission Arrives

When the members of the Second Civil Commission landed in Cap Français on 20 September 1792 they thus found a colony in disarray. Their official instructions were to enforce the decree of 4 April 1792 by replacing the all-white political institutions in Saint-Domingue with new bodies in which whites and free men of color were both represented, and to put an end to any agitation for colonial autonomy. In addition, they were explicitly told to defeat the slave uprising. At the ceremony held to welcome them in Le Cap, the civil commissioners publicly swore not to do anything to undermine the institution of slavery. Soon after they arrived, the commissioners learned that the shaky French constitutional monarchy that had appointed them had been overthrown and replaced by a radical revolutionary regime whose leaders announced that France would henceforth be a republic governed by the principles of "liberty and equality." Determined to avoid a split with the white populations of the French colonies, however, the victorious Jacobin revolutionaries quickly gave assurances that this proclamation did not apply to France's overseas territories. In Saint-Domingue, the civil commissioners followed their instructions and dissolved the all-white Colonial Assembly, replacing it with an Interim Commission composed of equal numbers of whites and free men of color. While France itself was being transformed into a democratic republic in which all men – but not women – would have full political rights, the struggle to defend slavery in the colonies continued. The fact that the black insurgents in Saint-Domingue continued to proclaim their loyalty to the king allowed the slaveowners to portray them as dangerous counterrevolutionaries.

Initially, the newly arrived civil commissioners were more preoccupied with what they saw as the peril of white counterrervolution in Saint-Domingue than with the black insurrection. On 19 October 1792, self-proclaimed white "patriots," supported by many of the revolutionary soldiers who had been sent from France and by the free men of color, staged a local version of the Paris republican uprising of 10 August 1792 in Cap Français, forcing the civil commissioners to arrest and deport the royalist officers of the local military garrison and the remaining civil officials who had been appointed by the king. Having achieved this victory, the white "patriots" began to resist the implementation of the law of 4 April 1792. The most determined of the civil commissioners, Sonthonax, decided to confront them by appointing several free men of color as officers in the Régiment du Cap, the permanent army unit stationed in the city. In response, the city's whites staged another violent uprising, attacking Sonthonax and the armed free men of color who supported him. When the whites overwhelmed them, the free men of color seized one of the forts defending the city, threatening to allow the armed black insurgents from the countryside to breach its defenses. The leader of the free men of color, Pierre Pinchinat, negotiated a settlement with his followers; in return, Sonthonax ordered the arrest and deportation to France of the most prominent white agitators in the city. In the wake of this uprising of 2 December 1792, Sonthonax made a firm alliance with the movement of the free men of color, allowing them to form so-called "free companies" of militiamen with their own officers, outside the regular army chain of command. Meanwhile, Sonthonax's colleague Polverel, sent to the West Province, also encountered vehement opposition from the white population. Like Sonthonax, he turned to the free men of color for support. The French Republic now seemed committed to allowing that group to dominate the colony.

The alliance between the civil commissioners and the free people of color went along with a renewed military campaign against the black insurrection. Since their arrival in September, thousands of the troops from France had fallen sick from the tropical diseases that always claimed a heavy toll on new arrivals from Europe; Sonthonax and Polverel were eager to deploy those who remained healthy before their forces became too weak to be of any use. In January 1793 they launched major campaigns against the rebels at both ends of the colony. In the South Province, the black "republic of Platons" whose fighters had destroyed Blanchelande's army was overrun and its defenders forced to abandon their stronghold. In the north, Étienne Laveaux, a patriotic officer who would eventually become the colony's governor, drove Biassou out of his impressive headquarters and compelled him and Jean-François to flee into the mountains along the Spanish border. Thousands of blacks who had been living in freedom for a year and a half fell back under white control, and plantation-owners who had been cooped up in Cap Français since the start of the insurrection began making plans to return to their properties. Months later, after Sonthonax and Polverel had found themselves unexpectedly compelled to offer freedom to the blacks, Toussaint Louverture had still not forgiven them for chasing him and his soldiers out of his camp in the January offensive. "You had us pursued like ferocious beasts," he wrote to Sonthonax in August 1793.[18]

The offensives launched by the commissioners in January 1793 were a blow to the black insurrection, but the commissioners' resources were not sufficient to defeat the movement. After a few weeks of fighting in the mountains, General Laveaux's troops were too exhausted to continue their efforts, and even as they were celebrating their victories, Sonthonax and Polverel learned that they were about to face a new threat. At the beginning of February 1793, Britain and Spain joined the war against revolutionary France, and Saint-Domingue was now menaced with attacks from the neighboring colonies of Jamaica and Santo Domingo. In London, representatives of the Saint-Domingue colonists signed a secret treaty with the British, promising to help the latter occupy the colony in exchange for assurances that slavery would be maintained there. In response to the threat of invasion, the commissioners dropped their military campaign against the blacks and focused instead on crushing the last centers of white resistance to their decrees before the slaveowners could make common cause with France's foreign enemies. In April 1793, they drove white extremists out of the cities of Port-au-Prince and Jacmel, leaving the white stronghold in the Grande Anse as the last bastion of opposition to their authority.

Anxious to end the slave insurrection before they had to face the threatened attacks from the Spanish and the British, Sonthonax and Polverel were still unwilling to go beyond the instructions they had received from France by proclaiming emancipation. Instead, the commissioners tried to win the slave population over with more modest concessions. On 5 May 1793, they issued a decree reinstating all the provisions of the century-old Code Noir originally issued by Louis XIV in 1685. The clauses in the Code Noir that gave slaves some protections from their masters had always been ignored, but Sonthonax and Polverel insisted that they would now be enforced. To communicate their message to the blacks, they had the Code Noir translated into Kreyol and ordered that it be read aloud on all plantations, so that the enslaved blacks would know their rights. Although the reissuing of the Code Noir was hardly a step toward the abolition of slavery, the colony's slaveholders rightly saw the commissioners' action as a threat to their power: enslaved blacks would now know that they were not totally under the control of their owners. Sonthonax and Polverel were optimistic that their gesture would end the slave rebellion. They did succeed in putting down a slave uprising near Port-au-Prince. According to their report to the new French assembly, the National Convention, when the blacks heard about the 5 May 1793 decree, "they cried 'Long live the Republic, long live the civil commissioners. Our fathers won't allow anyone to cut off our ears or to bury us alive or to throw us in ovens for having displeased our masters.'"[19]

While the French civil commissioners were trying to reach out to the enslaved population, the leaders of the insurrection in the North Province were taking advantage of the declaration of war between France and Spain to strengthen their position. The Spanish authorities in Santo Domingo had been giving covert support to the insurgents since the start of the revolt. Now they were ready to make an open alliance with Jean-François and Biassou and promise freedom to their men if they agreed to fight under the Spanish flag. Additional Spanish troops were brought from the nearby colony of Cuba. While Spanish soldiers fought to conquer Saint-Domingue, Cuban plantation-owners took advantage of the disorder in the French colony to buy up sugar-making machinery and, sometimes, the enslaved workers who operated it, in order to build up the plantation economy in their own island.[20] Whereas Sonthonax and Polverel still hesitated to free enslaved blacks who were, legally speaking, the property of white French citizens and of the commissioners' allies among the free people of color, the Spanish had no such qualms. Furthermore, the Spaniards were royalists whose king was part of the same Bourbon family as the French monarch, and they were devout Catholics whose respect for religion was shared by the insurgent leaders. A Spanish priest, Father Vasquez, was one of the main intermediaries in the negotiations with the blacks, writing regularly to assure them that God was on their side.

The Crisis of 20 June 1793

As they were concluding their campaign against the recalcitrant whites in the West and South Provinces in May 1793, Sonthonax and Polverel suddenly received surprising news from Cap Français, in the north of the colony. On 7 May 1793, a new governor, General François-Thomas Galbaud, arrived in the colony's main city. Galbaud, one of the heroes of the patriotic French defense against the Austro–Prussian invasion in 1792, had been sent to replace the elderly commander who had accompanied the commissioners when they arrived in September 1792 and whom they had sent back to France soon afterward. Despite his revolutionary credentials, Galbaud owned plantations in Saint-Domingue and the commissioners assumed that he would oppose any concessions they made to the insurgents. They promptly ordered him not to take any action before they could return to Cap Français to meet with him, but Galbaud, eagerly welcomed by the local white population, immediately began implementing his own policies. Sonthonax's allies among the free people of color wrote him urgent letters, telling him that their position was in jeopardy if the commissioners did not return at once and confront the general; among other things, they resented the fact that Galbaud's wife refused to receive free women of color in her home.

Among the groups in the city that welcomed Galbaud most enthusiastically were the hundreds of French sailors on the ships in Cap Français harbor. Ever since the declaration of war with Britain, they had been forbidden to sail for France, for fear of being intercepted by the British navy. The commissioners had ordered the ships to assemble into a large convoy, to be protected by a squadron of warships, but months had passed while the convoy waited for the order to set sail, and the sailors, eager to go home, had become increasingly restless and resentful. Imbued with racial prejudices, the sailors frequently got into fights with free men of color when they came ashore to drink and look for women.

On 10 June 1793, the civil commissioners Sonthonax and Polverel returned to Cap Français and confronted Galbaud, accusing him of undermining their authority. Despite his military reputation, Galbaud was a weak and timid man; rather than arguing with the commissioners, he agreed to let himself be sent back to France. The commissioners put him on board one of the warships in the harbor. Their supporters among the free population of color, who had had to hold their tongues while Galbaud had been in charge of the city, celebrated the commissioners' triumph, further irritating the sailors. On the morning of 20 June 1793, following several incidents in which naval officers claimed to have been insulted by men of color in the city's streets, the fleet's anger boiled over. The sailors persuaded Galbaud to lead them in an assault on the commissioners. Their plan was to seize Sonthonax and Polverel and take them back to France, where Galbaud and the sailors would accuse them of abusing their authority. On the afternoon of 20 June 1793, the general and the sailors came ashore and nearly succeeded in storming the commissioners' headquarters. Sonthonax and Polverel were defended by armed free men of color, who drove the disorganized sailors back. Nevertheless, Galbaud's forces took over the city's arsenal and prepared to make a renewed attack on the following morning.

The First Emancipation Proclamation

The commissioners and their free colored supporters realized that they risked being overwhelmed once Galbaud and the sailors could deploy the cannon they had captured at the arsenal. On the night of 20 June 1793, Sonthonax and Polverel took a momentous step: they called on the thousands of enslaved blacks in the city, who had so far remained neutral in the conflict, to join their side, promising them their freedom if they did so. This offer fell well short of an emancipation proclamation: it applied only to men of military age, and those who responded had to agree to remain in the army as long as the war in the colony continued and even to fight against the black insurgency. Unlike previous occasions on which one faction or another in Saint-Domingue had armed enslaved blacks to fight for them, however, the commissioners' appeal was extended to any eligible man who wanted to take advantage of it. When Galbaud's forces renewed their assault on the morning of 21 June 1793, the commissioners had to flee the city and set up a camp in the nearby village of Haut-du-Cap. There they made contact with some of the organized insurgent bands in the hills surrounding the city. On 22 June 1793 two black commanders, Pierrot and Macaya, arrived with their forces, numbering around 2,000 men. The commissioners swore them into their army, telling them that they were now free men and citizens of republican France, and sent them into the city to drive back Galbaud's supporters.

When the commissioners fled the city on the morning of 21 June, Galbaud's victory had seemed assured. Just at that moment, however, a wave of panic seized the general and his followers. Even though they no longer faced any organized opposition inside the city, "everyone yelled that thousands of blacks were coming from Haut-du-Cap and that they were going to exterminate all of us," one eyewitness recalled.[21] The general himself ran to the waterfront and threw himself into the harbor to reach a passing boat. Seeing the general and the sailors seized by fear, the city's civilian population abandoned their homes and property and joined in the scramble for safety on the ships in the harbor. By the time the newly enrolled black soldiers entered Le Cap on the following day, the city had dissolved into chaos. White sailors and blacks competed to loot the empty houses and stores, and fire, always a danger in the crowded city, began to spread, increasing the disorder. By the evening of 23 June, the entire city was in flames, and the captains in the harbor, their ships overloaded with refugees, decided to ignore the commissioners' orders and set sail as fast as they could. To their own surprise, Sonthonax and Polverel found themselves back in power, at the head of an army in which newly freed "citizens of 20 June" outnumbered the free men of color who until then had been their main supporters. The events in Cap Français were a major turning point in the struggle in Saint-Domingue. The city had been a proud symbol of European civilization in the colony, and its destruction signaled the end of white colonial rule. The burning of Cap Français, which cost the lives of at least 3,000 people of all races, was the worst episode of urban violence in the entire history of the Americas. The decision by Sonthonax and Polverel to offer freedom to blacks who would join their forces marked the first time that representatives of France's revolutionary government had disavowed slavery.

Sonthonax and Polverel had thought that the limited offer of emancipation they made during the crisis of 20 June 1793 would bring the black insurgents who had been fighting for their freedom since August 1791 over to the French side. They quickly learned, however, that the insurgent blacks had ideas of their own. Macaya, one of the two leaders who had come to the commissioners' aid during the crisis in Le Cap, told them that he would not disobey his superiors, Jean-François and Bias-sou, and that, in his opinion, the French and Spanish should make an agreement to work together. Contacted by the local French commander, Toussaint Louverture replied that his men, "having fought up to now alongside their brothers to uphold the right of the king ... will all shed the last drop of their blood to defend the Bourbons to whom they have promised unswerving loyalty to the death."[22] Jean-François and Biassou briefly considered switching their allegiance to the French, but the Span-ish soon persuaded them that revolutionary France was on the brink of defeat by the coalition of European powers opposing it. The black gen-erals' soldiers followed their leaders in rejecting the French invitation. Meanwhile, in Le Cap, the commissioners had to give in to black pressure to broaden their emancipation offer. On 11 July 1793, they agreed to free the wives and children of black men who joined the army, although they used the occasion to insist that this offer would apply only to blacks who contracted marriages according to French law. The commissioners' ap-peals to the blacks to return to work on the plantations and to stop loot-ing the ruins of the city were clear indications that the black population was no longer willing to follow orders from whites. When an American merchant visited Cap Français in early August and commented that one of his surviving white friends was "working like a slave" to restore his property, the man warned him "not to use the word *slave* on any occa-sion, as it might cost me my life."[23]

By the end of August 1793, Sonthonax realized that nothing short of a general proclamation of emancipation would give him any chance of winning support from the blacks in the North Province. On 29 August 1793, he finally took the decisive step, announcing that the principles of the French Declaration of the Rights of Man would now be applied in Saint-Domingue and that all the enslaved blacks were now free. Sontho-nax's proclamation was a true historical turning point: for the first time, slavery was abolished in a part of the Americas where it had been the ba-sis of an entire society. Although he was opposed to slavery in principle, Sonthonax had not planned to take such a radical step so quickly. He was forced to act because of the need for black support in the unanticipated situation created by the crisis of June 1793 in Cap Français. Still hoping to preserve the plantation system on which France's prosperity depended, however, Sonthonax coupled his proclamation with an elaborate set of regulations that required the formerly enslaved blacks to remain on their plantations and continue to perform their regular duties. His colleague Polverel, who had returned to the West Province a few weeks before Sonthonax issued his proclamation, was unhappy that his colleague had acted so hastily. Finding himself in an area where the free men of color had considerable influence, Polverel had to take their concerns about maintaining a workforce on their properties into account. Nevertheless, he soon issued his own emancipation proclamation, which included an even more extensive set of restrictions on the plantation workers' freedom.

Sonthonax and Polverel had assumed that their emancipation proclamations would bring the mass of the black population over to their side, but they quickly discovered that even these radical measures had not convinced many of the blacks. The black generals were still not prepared to break their alliance with the Spanish, who persuaded them that promises made in the name of the revolutionary French government were of little value, since Spain and its allies were bound to win the war in Europe. On 29 August 1793, the day on which Sonthonax issued his general emancipation decree, Toussaint wrote a letter in which he used the name "Toussaint Louverture" for the first time, and in which he claimed that he, like the French, was fighting for "liberty and equality." Rather than joining the French, however, he told his correspondents that they were "deceivers who only want to bring you down," and he reasserted his loyalty to the Spanish.[24]

Ordinary blacks who were not part of the insurgent army often took advantage of Sonthonax's and Polverel's proclamation to desert plantations that had continued to function, but they were unwilling to submit themselves to the system of controlled labor the civil commissioners wanted to create. To make the new arrangements more palatable, the commissioners relabeled the black *commandeurs* as *conducteurs*, and official documents called the former slaves *cultivateurs*: the new terms were supposed to emphasize the consensual nature of labor arrangements on the plantations. Whipping was no longer permitted as a form of discipline, but the *cultivateurs* were still expected to perform the same tasks they had under slavery; in exchange, they were to receive a share of the profits from the plantations. Polverel attempted to establish a system under which the *cultivateurs* would be made part-owners of the plantations in exchange for continuing to work, but he found that they often opted instead for more free time for themselves, even at the price of a lower income.[25] Women were particularly opposed to the commissioners' regulations, which gave them only two-thirds of the wages for men, on the grounds, as Polverel put it, of "the natural inequality between women and men, their constant or periodic infirmities, or the time they take off when they are pregnant, give birth, and feed their children."[26] They resisted by refusing to work at night and demanding more time off to care for their children.

Any chance that Sonthonax and Polverel had of implementing their abolition plans depended on their ability to keep at least part of the colony under French control. Throughout the fall of 1793 they suffered one setback after another. In September 1793, white colonists allowed British forces to land in the southern port of Jérémie and the naval base of Môle Saint-Nicolas in the northwest of the colony. Soon afterward, the two commissioners learned that the French National Convention had expelled their patron Brissot and his supporters, and that on 16 July 1793 the deputies had voted to recall Sonthonax and Polverel themselves and put them on trial. This action made it uncertain whether the French government would recognize the abolition decrees the two men had issued. Just before the news of the French Convention's vote reached Saint-Domingue, Sonthonax had arranged the election of deputies to represent the North Province in the National Convention. A "tricolor" delegation, consisting of equal numbers of whites, blacks, and men of mixed race was sent to Paris to defend the radical measures Sonthonax had taken in the colony. Fearing that if they abandoned their posts Saint-Domingue would be overrun by France's enemies, Sonthonax and Polverel decided to continue their work until a government official arrived to deliver the recall decree, but in November 1793 the free men of color in Saint-Marc, a key city in the West Province, reacted to the news by going over to the British. By this time, Sonthonax had retreated from the North Province, leaving General Laveaux in control of the parts of it that had not been occupied by the Spanish and their black allies, and Polverel had taken refuge on a plantation in the South Province. In spite of all these setbacks, however, the two commissioners did not give up hope. Sooner or later, they were convinced, the blacks would realize that it was the French, not the Spanish and the British, who were truly committed to giving them freedom, and the tide would turn in their favor.

3

Republican Emancipation in Saint-Domingue, 1793–1798

The dramatic events of the two years from the beginning of the insurrections of black slaves and free people of color in August 1791 to the French civil commissioner Sonthonax's proclamation of general emancipation in August 1793 constituted a genuine revolution. In 1791 Saint-Domingue had been the wealthiest and most exploitative of the New World's slave societies; by the end of 1793 the slave system in the island was in ruins, and the black population were all legally free. In 1791 whites had monopolized political and military power in the colony; two years later, much of the white population had fled the island, while free men of color had risen to top positions in the French army and held a large share of political power. At the same time, Saint-Domingue had become a battlefield in the war between revolutionary France and its European enemies, a conflict whose outcome hung in the balance as the year 1793 drew to a close. No one knew whether the spectacular changes in the colony were laying the basis for a new, racially egalitarian society or whether Saint-Domingue was doomed to be consumed by chaos and violence.

A Republican Colony of Free Men

Between 1793 and 1798, the violence in Saint-Domingue gradually subsided and a new society, from which slavery had been officially banished and in which people of all colors enjoyed the same legal rights, started

A Concise History of the Haitian Revolution, Second Edition. Jeremy D. Popkin.
© 2022 John Wiley & Sons Ltd. Published 2022 by John Wiley & Sons Ltd.

to take shape. An army largely composed of soldiers of African descent, fighting under the French colors, defeated the foes – the forces of the black insurrection, the Spanish and the British – who had nearly over-run the colony in 1793. Out of the midst of the power struggles in the island, a powerful personality – Toussaint Louverture – emerged, using his military and political talents to make himself the ruler of most of the colony. France's government appeared to accept the idea that a black man who had once been enslaved would govern its most valuable overseas territory as part of a republican empire from which racial distinctions had been banished. Other governments, particularly the British and the Americans, initially fearful that the upheavals in Saint-Domingue would spread to their territories, began to adjust to the new situation and even envisage how they might turn it to their advantage in their struggles with republican France.

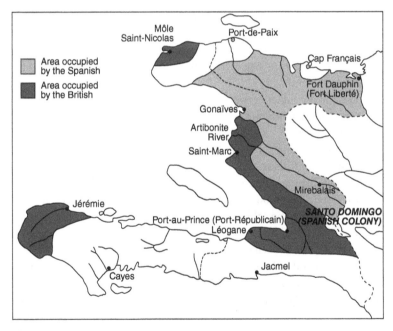

Map 3   Saint-Domingue, May 1794.
Source: Adapted from J. C. Dorsainvil (SP), *Manuel d'histoire d'Haiti* (Port-auPrince: H. Deschamps, 1958), p. 84.

While the period of "republican emancipation" from 1793 to 1798 suggested the possibility of a peaceful outcome to the struggles that had begun in 1791, the new order that took shape during those years proved to be a fragile one. Although the members of the new governing elite that developed in Saint-Domingue, drawn mostly from the military leaders of the movements against white rule that had developed since the start of the insurrections, all claimed to support the elimination of slavery, they remained convinced that the basic features of the plantation system that created the colony's wealth had to be maintained. The French government, too, remained determined to see Saint-Domingue restored to its function of providing the metropole with the valuable products it had exported before 1791. To most of the black population, however, the plantation system was synonymous with slavery. Neither Saint-Domingue's new governing elites nor the French government were able to find ways to make the mass of the formerly enslaved population feel that they had a stake in the success of the new social order. And as metropolitan France retreated from the radicalism of its own revolutionary experience, its acceptance of the drastic changes that had taken place in Saint-Domingue diminished as well. In reaction, the colony's dominant political figure, Toussaint Louverture, began to challenge France's authority over the territory. At the end of 1798 Saint-Domingue was still a part of the French empire, but a conflict between the colony and the metropole that would destroy the trans-Atlantic experiment undertaken in 1793 was becoming ever more likely.

Five years earlier, at the end of 1793, the chances that the civil commissioners Sonthonax and Polverel would be able to implement their decrees abolishing slavery and preserve the colony of Saint-Domingue for the French Republic had seemed slim. Separated from each other, with Polverel having taking refuge in the south while Sonthonax made his way to Port-au-Prince, now officially renamed Port-Républicain, in the west, the two French officials could do little but wait to see how events in the island and in France played themselves out. Where they could, the black population took advantage of the commissioners' proclamations of general liberty to desert the plantations, but in the areas controlled by the British and the Spanish the emancipation decrees had no effect. Black troops under commanders loyal to the Spanish surrounded Cap Français and pushed into the mountains between the North and West Provinces, while the British occupied most of the port cities on the west

coast. Even in the areas that remained under French authority, the abolition of slavery did not necessarily bring rapid change in the population's
life. Polverel in particular, strongly influenced by the free people of color
in the south and west, was determined to make sure that the plantation
system continued to operate, even without slavery.

Across the Atlantic, the embattled French Republic managed to turn
the military tide against its foes by the end of 1793, but its legislative
assembly, the National Convention, and in particular the Committee
of Public Safety, set up earlier in the year to direct the war effort, were
swayed by the lobbying efforts of white colonists who denounced Sonthonax and Polverel as traitors bent on destroying Saint-Domingue in
order to aid the country's enemies. On 16 July 1793, the Convention had
voted to recall the two national commissioners and put them on trial
for abusing their powers. Although no one was sent to Saint-Domingue
to implement this decree, news of it reached the Caribbean by September 1793, adding to Sonthonax and Polverel's difficulties: their enemies
could now claim that they had been disavowed by their own government.
If the two men had abandoned their mission, Saint-Domingue would
have been divided between foreign occupiers and local warlords, and the
chance of carrying out the abolition decrees Sonthonax and Polverel had
issued would have been lost.

The Turn of the Tide

Desperate as the situation in Saint-Domingue appeared in late 1793,
events gradually began to turn in favor of the French cause and the cause
of emancipation. The foreign invasions proved less threatening than they
initially looked. Like the white troops sent from France, the redcoated
British soldiers who had landed in the western part of the island suffered
heavy losses from disease. Even with the help of white French colonists
and blacks enrolled to fight on their side, they were unable to penetrate
inland from the coastal positions they had seized. Although many free
men of color had initially welcomed the British, they soon learned that
the occupiers did not intend to treat them equally with the white French
colonists, and increasing numbers of them switched their support to the
French. The black generals who had allied themselves with the Spanish,
Jean-François, Biassou, and Toussaint Louverture, remained hostile to

the French, but they spent as much energy squabbling with each other as they did in attempting to eliminate the remaining French positions. They failed to capture Cap Français or to destroy General Laveaux's small remaining force, based on the north coast at Port-de-Paix. The black population also became increasingly aware that the Spanish support for the insurgent armies did not mean support for the abolition of slavery. When the Spanish government in Santo Domingo tried to win over the remaining whites in the French colony by guaranteeing their properties, even its own officials wondered how they were going to fulfill the contradictory promises they had made to the whites and the blacks. In the summer of 1793, the Spanish had been able to convince the black leaders that the French Republic was near defeat, but by the end of the year news of French successes in Europe had reached the Caribbean, making some blacks consider that they might have chosen to back the wrong side.

The Abolition Decree of 16 pluviôse Year II

Meanwhile, in France, revolutionary policy on the issue of slavery was about to be dramatically transformed. Three of the deputies whom Sonthonax had had elected in September 1793 to seek the Convention's endorsement of his general emancipation decree of 29 August 1793 – the white colonist Louis Dufay, the free black army officer Jean-Baptiste Belley, and a free man of color named Jean-Baptiste Mills – reached Paris at the end of January 1794. En route, they had stopped in the United States, where they were assaulted by white French refugees in Philadelphia, and where their presence led to rumors that they meant to organize a slave rebellion in the American South. Despite frantic efforts by the pro-slavery colonists to have them arrested after they landed in France, the three men managed to present themselves to the National Convention on 3 February 1794 and they were seated as representatives of Saint-Domingue's North Province. On the following day, Dufay gave a long speech to the Convention, arguing that the abolition of slavery was the only way to keep Saint-Domingue French and promising the deputies that the grateful blacks would eagerly work and fight to restore the colony. Although Dufay was careful to emphasize the limits Sonthonax had placed on the freed blacks' rights, the Convention deputies seized the occasion to make a dramatic gesture on behalf of human freedom. In a decree dated 16 pluviôse Year

II according to the revolutionary calendar that France had adopted the previous October – 4 February 1794 according to the Gregorian calendar – the Convention decreed that "slavery of the blacks is abolished in all the colonies; consequently, it decrees that all men living in the colonies, without distinction of color, are French citizens and enjoy all the rights guaranteed by the constitution."[1]

The Convention's decree was unexpected. It had only limited support from the Committee of Public Safety, whose leaders, including Robespierre, were more concerned with the ongoing war against Britain and the opposition to their policies from rival political factions in Paris than with the question of slavery. Nevertheless, the Convention's decision was a momentous one. For the first time in history, the national government of a trans-Atlantic empire abolished the institution on which the social structure and the economy of its American colonies had been based since their establishment. In addition, the French legislators decreed legal equality for people of all races, and made the formerly enslaved blacks full citizens of France. This promise was given concrete form by the seating of Belley and Mills as members of the Convention. Belley would continue to serve in the French legislature until 1798; a full-length portrait of him by the leading French artist Anne-Louis Girodet-Trioson has now become one of the iconic images of the French revolutionary period (Figure 3.1). The decree of 16 pluviôse was celebrated with a great public ceremony in Notre Dame cathedral, which the revolutionaries had converted into a "Temple of Reason." Speakers at the ceremony proclaimed that the freeing of the blacks marked a new era of human history, restoring the natural liberty that all human beings deserved to enjoy.

Toussaint Louverture Joins the French

While the French Convention's decree of 16 pluviôse was a major turning point in the struggle against slavery, the chance of its being successfully applied in Saint-Domingue depended on the outcome of the military struggle in the colony. The decisive break came at the beginning of May 1794, when Toussaint Louverture, the most effective of the black military leaders, shifted his allegiance from the Spanish to the French after black fighters in his area attacked the Spanish garrison in Gonaïves, on

Figure 3.1 Anne-Louis Girodet-Trioson, *Portrait de Jean-Baptiste Belley.*
From 1794 to 1799, the republican colony of Saint-Domingue was represented
in the French legislature by deputies, most of whom were black or of mixed racial
ancestry. Jean-Baptiste Belley, born in Africa, had gained his freedom before the
revolution and fought on behalf of the republican commissioners Sonthonax and
Polverel in the crisis of June 1793 in Cap Français. In this portrait by the leading
French artist Girodet, he is shown wearing his deputy's uniform and standing next
to a statue of the French Enlightenment author Raynal, whose *Histoire des Deux
Indes* had criticized slavery and colonialism.
Source: Chicago Art Institute.

the west coast. The motives and the exact details of Louverture's "turna-round" are obscure. It is not clear whether the black commander had learned of the Convention's abolition decree and decided to join the French in order to promote the cause of emancipation, or whether he was motivated primarily by his ongoing rivalry with the other black leaders and his calculation that changing sides would help him advance his own interests. By mid-May, however, Louverture had put himself under the command of General Laveaux, explaining that he had only fought for the Spanish because he had been "misled by the enemies of the Republic and of the human race."[2] For the embattled French repub-licans, Louverture's conversion was an enormous relief. "Since the brave Toussaint Louverture ... has finally seen his mistake, we have the hope of seeing all the Africans in the north imitate his generous repentance, and coming to defend their freedom by fighting for France," Sonthonax and Polverel wrote to him.[3]

The two republican civil commissioners who had proclaimed the end of slavery in Saint-Domingue never met the black general who would ultimately guarantee the success of their efforts. On 8 June 1794, a French naval vessel brought the first official copy of the Convention's decree of 16 pluviôse to the colony, but its captain also carried out his orders to ar-rest Sonthonax and Polverel and take them back to France, in accordance with the earlier decree of 16 July 1793. General Laveaux was appointed as governor of the colony, but, even with Toussaint Louverture's support, his chances of holding off the British, who had captured Port-au-Prince on 4 June, and the Spanish and their black allies, still seemed dubious. Sonthonax wrote Laveaux a farewell letter telling him to "hold out until you have fired your last cartridge and then follow the course that pru-dence will dictate."[4] Because of the British naval blockade, there was no possibility of sending additional troops or supplies from France, and the overthrow of Robespierre on 9 thermidor Year II (27 July 1794) left the future of French colonial policy in doubt. In the political "thermidorian reaction" that followed Robespierre's fall, many of the radical measures the Convention had enacted during the "Reign of Terror" in 1793–4 were overturned, and white colonists lobbied furiously to have the abolition of slavery reversed. In response to their complaints, in November 1794 the Convention set up a commission of inquiry to examine the events in Saint-Domingue. Its sessions dragged on until the early fall of 1795, by which time Polverel, exhausted by his grueling experience in the colo-ny, had died.

Toussaint Louverture's decision to join the French did not immediately end the military threat to Saint-Domingue and to the prospects of carrying out emancipation, but it greatly altered the balance of power in the colony. Louverture's 4,000 soldiers – a force larger than that under Laveaux's own command – were added to those of the led by the free men of color André Rigaud and Louis-Jacques Bauvais in the south and the troops led by another free man of color, Jean-Louis Villatte, who had successfully defended the city of Cap Français. In military terms, the territories occupied by Louverture's forces were critical. During the fighting in 1793, Louverture had gained control of most of the former "Cordon of the West," the chain of posts that divided the North Province from the West. His territory separated the British positions on the west coast from those held by the other black generals and the Spanish in the interior of the island. From his stronghold in the western mountains, Louverture could threaten both these enemies. Although he had less military experience than the leaders of the free men of color, many of whom had served in the French expedition to Savannah, Georgia, during the American War of Independence, Louverture also proved to be the most capable of the group.

A Black Leader Emerges

Toussaint Louverture's background helps explain why he was able to make himself the dominant figure in Saint-Domingue after 1794. Born into slavery in the colony in the mid-1740s, he was the son of an African captive whose own father had been a military commander in the kingdom of Dahomey in West Africa. Through his family, Louverture no doubt heard stories about Africa and knew that blacks were not inherently condemned to inferior status; they could also be rulers and lead armies. Before the Revolution, as we have seen, Louverture had benefited from the openings that the slave system created for a few successful individuals to enter colonial society's "intermediate class" and had learned how to pursue his own interests in a white-dominated world. Unlike most of the other black insurgents, he was able to read and write. In contrast to the wealthy members of the mixed-race elite, however, who often received inheritances from a white ancestor, Louverture did not manage to accumulate much of a fortune before the revolution.

Whether or not Louverture played any role in the launching of the August 1791 slave uprising remains in dispute, but he was soon recognized as one of its leaders. Older and less imposing physically than the two principal generals, Jean-François and Biassou, Louverture nevertheless became by the summer of 1793 the third most important of the insurgent commanders. By this time he had recruited an outstanding cohort of officers from the ranks of the insurgents; some of them, like Jean-Jacques Dessalines and his nephew Moïse, were men he had known even before the start of the revolution. In June 1793, when he rejected the initial French offer of limited emancipation after the destruction of Cap Français, Louverture had had over 30 of his subordinates sign his reply to the French, indicating that he associated them with his decisions in a way that the other black leaders did not. Many of Louverture's officers, like Dessalines, Moïse, and Henry Christophe, would go on to play major roles in the military and political struggles of the years ahead. Whereas letters written in the name of the other black generals were in broken French, Louverture took pains to recruit white secretaries who could help him express his thoughts clearly and effectively. Conscious that the struggle in Saint-Domingue was part of a larger political picture, he kept himself informed about events in Europe and elsewhere.

The long series of letters Toussaint Louverture wrote to General Laveaux in the years from 1794 to 1796, one of the most important sources for our understanding of the black leader, reveal the qualities that made him such an effective commander. Attentive to every detail of the military situation confronting him, he never lost sight of the larger strategic picture. He regularly reminded Laveaux of the importance of providing food, uniforms, and ammunition for his troops. To improve his soldiers' skills, he employed captured white prisoners with military experience as trainers. No skirmish was too small to escape his attention, and he was skilled at deducing his enemies' intentions even from seemingly minor moves on their part; in addition, as he reported to Laveaux, he had recruited a network of informants among the blacks serving the British and Spanish. He pushed Laveaux to reward the officers serving under him with promotions and honors, and although he always addressed the French general respectfully, even calling him "Papa," Louverture never hesitated to criticize his superior for his lack of initiative and imagination.

From the time when he participated in the first negotiations with the French in December 1791, Louverture distinguished himself by his keen understanding of the realities of politics. He knew how to win the loyalty of subordinates, by praising and rewarding them, and he was quick to react to anything that seemed to undermine his authority, reining in those who tried to operate independently. Skilled at assessing the motives of others while keeping his own concealed, Louverture outmaneuvered a long succession of rivals and opponents. From the start, he assumed that a successful ending of the black insurrection would require the creation of an orderly society that integrated members of all three of Saint-Domingue's racial groups, the blacks, the free men of color, and the whites. He was careful to keep up good relations with members of all these groups, while avoiding being totally identified with any of them. His seriousness impressed both the Spanish and the French officials with whom he corresponded in 1793, and in the years after 1794 he proved equally adept at negotiating with the British military authorities in Saint-Domingue.

Exactly what Toussaint Louverture's political ideas were is difficult to determine. Like all good politicians, he knew how to frame arguments to appeal to the different audiences he wanted to win over and to change his language to suit new circumstances. Having decided to join the French side, he publicly embraced the republican principles he had denounced when he was fighting for the Spanish. "We are republicans," he wrote in a proclamation in June 1795, "and consequently free according to natural right. It can only be kings ... who dare to claim the right to reduce to slavery men like themselves, whom nature has made free." A free man himself even before the revolution, he could have stood aside from the insurgency, but after the failure of the negotiations with the whites in December 1791, he clearly committed himself to the fight against slavery. Although he consistently defended the freedom of the former slaves after 1793, he was equally firm in insisting that freedom did not mean the right for the freed blacks to do anything they wanted, and he was not trying to create an entirely black-dominated society. Like Sonthonax and Polverel in their 1793 emancipation proclamations, he wanted to keep the plantations functioning. After he occupied the parish of Mirebalais in the fall of 1795, he reported to Laveaux that he had been careful to implement the regulations for plantation labor in every detail. "All the cultivators are back home and working hard," he claimed, adding that he had named a white officer as the area's military commander and treated the white plantation-owners in the district humanely. Facing down a revolt among blacks in one region of the North Province in February 1796, he told them that they should be grateful for the "beneficent decree that gives them liberty" and that they should show France that they were worthy of its support "by their submission to the laws, by their work and by their obedience."[5] Louverture thus put himself in opposition to the rural black *cultivateurs'* desire to take over land for themselves and escape from the constraints of the plantation system.

Even as he emphasized his loyalty to France and to the ideal of a multi-racial society, however, Louverture also underlined his special relationship with the colony's black population. In a proclamation to "you Africans, my brothers" that he issued in early 1796, he called himself a "father who adores them" and urged them to remember "that it was I who first raised the standard of insurrection against tyranny." While exhorting the blacks to remain loyal to France, he also reminded them that "there are more blacks in the colony than there are men of color and whites combined ... and we are the strongest."[6] Another area in which Toussaint Louverture distinguished himself from orthodox French republicanism was the question of religion. Even as it abandoned many of the radical policies adopted during the Reign of Terror, the French government remained violently hostile to the Catholic Church. Louverture, on the other hand, continued to express his religious sentiments. In late 1794 he told Laveaux that "I have always held in horror those leaders who like to shed blood; my religion forbids it and I follow its principles," and when Laveaux complained about his own problems in 1796 Louverture counseled him, "Let us imitate Jesus Christ who died and suffered so much for us," words that no French republican of the period would have used.[7]

In addition to maintaining his own distinctive ideas, Toussaint Louverture clearly sought to increase his power and influence at the expense of the other principal military commanders fighting on the French side. He regularly complained to Laveaux about Villatte, the commander in Le Cap, and he emphasized the importance of the efforts he had made to support Rigaud and Bauvais in the south, implying that they were unable to hold off the British on their own. In addition to cultivating Laveaux's support, Louverture appealed directly to the French government to recognize his contributions to its cause. As early as June 1795, one Paris newspaper had mentioned "Toussaint Bréda ... who marches with his troops under the republican banner"; this may have been the first reference to him in the European press.[8] In December 1795, Louverture oversaw the election of deputies to represent the West Province in the French legislature. The men he selected were officially instructed to report "the great and memorable services he has rendered to the country and to all the citizens who have lived under his kind and humane command."⁹

Louverture's Rivals

Although Toussaint Louverture was destined to become the most important figure in Saint-Domingue, the revolutionary upheavals from 1791 to 1793 had also produced several other powerful leaders in the colony. Pierre Pinchinat, who had played a major role in negotiating the concordats with white royalists in 1791 and 1792, had switched to the republican camp in late 1792 and continued to exert a strong influence among the former free men of color. By 1794, however, he was overshadowed by André Rigaud, the military commander in the South Province. Operating independently of General Laveaux in the north, Rigaud successfully prevented the British forces in Port-au-Prince from linking up with those in the Grande Anse, at the western end of the southern peninsula. In June 1794, when the civil commissioners left the island, Polverel officially appointed Rigaud as governor of the South Province. Rigaud's position was especially important because the South Province had been less affected by slave uprisings and military operations than the other parts of the colony. American trading ships continued to reach the ports on the island's south coast, where they purchased sugar and coffee and sold supplies. Rigaud's territory was therefore the only part of Saint-Domingue that continued to function economically, and French officials hoped to use its resources to fund the defense of the rest of the colony.

Rigaud had committed himself to the French republican cause well before Toussaint Louverture. As early as May 1793, Rigaud had also offered freedom to enslaved blacks who joined his army, and the majority of the troops in the "Legion of the South" he had created were black. Nearly all the officers commanding them, however, were, like Rigaud himself, light-skinned men of mixed race. Even as he claimed to accept the abolition of slavery and the equality of the races, Rigaud rigorously enforced the regulations imposed by Polverel to keep the blacks working on their former plantations. Whereas Toussaint Louverture's black skin and his background as a former slave allowed him to put himself forward as a representative of the colony's black majority, Rigaud embodied the elitist pretentions of the wealthy free men of color. Although the free men of color were more imbued with French culture than the blacks, they were not necessarily favored by the French. From the French point of view, the free men of color seemed dangerously prone to think that they could run the colony by themselves; in addition, many of them had shown themselves willing to ally with the British in the West Province. As it had since the start of the revolution, the rivalry between the free men of color and the blacks greatly complicated events in the colony.

The British and the Spanish

While Toussaint Louverture and André Rigaud both proclaimed the end of slavery in the areas under their control, the blacks in the regions oc-cupied by the British were still subjected to legal servitude. Even in these areas, however, the system was becoming increasingly difficult to main-tain. The fighting in the area disrupted the routine on plantations that had not been affected by the uprisings between 1791 and 1793. Some 60,000 to 70,000 enslaved blacks – perhaps a sixth of the total black pop-ulation in the colony – lived in the regions under British occupation, although a disproportionate number of them were either too young, too old, or too feeble to have joined the insurgents or the French army. The free population of color in the occupied areas generally backed the Brit-ish, although they were disappointed when they realized that they were not being given the same privileges as the remaining whites. Some of the white colonists agreed to serve under British command, despite the tra-ditional hostility between the two nations. "To carry arms against the re-volting slaves of Saint-Domingue is not to be traitorous to one's country; it is to serve it," one of the French who enrolled under British command wrote.[10] Ironically, however, this French plantation-owner found himself commanding black soldiers who had been promised their freedom in return for military service: as British troops fell victim to disease, there was no other source of manpower to counter the republican forces. Jean Kina, a talented black military commander who had turned against the French in 1794, was allowed to lead his own unit, which came to include some free men of color and a number of enslaved blacks Kina had pur-chased from Jamaica. Even in trying to defend the system of slavery, the British and their French colonial allies thus found themselves forced to contribute to its destruction by allowing blacks to earn their freedom through military service.

While Toussaint Louverture and André Rigaud held off the British in the west, events in Europe drove the Spanish to abandon their attempt to take over parts of the French colony. In July 1795, after their attempt to invade southern France had been driven back, the Spanish signed the treaty of Basel and withdrew from the war. As part of the peace agreement, Spain agreed to cede its colony of Santo Domingo to France. Jean-François and Biassou, Toussaint Louverture's main rivals among the leaders of the black insurrection, departed from the island along with the Spanish forces, taking with them some of their troops; others joined Louverture's forces. The disappearance of his former rivals left Toussaint Louverture as the only major figure who could claim to have earned his position by his participation in the uprising that had begun in August 1791, and the only black man among the military leaders of the French forces. Elsewhere in the Caribbean, the French had already reconquered Guadeloupe, briefly occupied by the British in early 1794, and turned it into a base for privateering operations that disrupted British commerce. Under the dictatorial leadership of the French commissioner Victor Hugues, blacks in Guadeloupe were recruited for military positions and given civil rights, although Hugues, a former member of the white "patriot" movement in Saint-Domingue that had vehemently defended slavery, refused to implement the provisions of the decree of 16 pluviôse making them full citizens. Even though the British retained control of the third major French Caribbean colony, Martinique, which they had occupied in 1793, the French successes in Saint-Domingue and Guadeloupe, made possible largely by black troops, ensured the survival of a significant French presence in the region.

The Directory and the Villatte Affair

General Laveaux recognized the services Toussaint Louverture and the other leading commanders in Saint-Domingue had performed by recommending that they be promoted to the rank of generals in the French army. The Convention approved promotions for Louverture, Rigaud, Bauvais, and Villatte in July 1795, thus officially recognizing that the defense of the colony had become dependent not just on black troops but also on military commanders of African descent. A month later, the Convention approved a new republican constitution for France, creating a regime known as the Directory that would govern the country until

Napoleon Bonaparte's coup d'état in November 1799. Even though the new French Constitution of 1795 represented a conservative reaction against many of the radical innovations of the revolution and restricted the rights of the poor in France itself, the Directory maintained the abolition of slavery in the colonies and promised that they would be fully integrated into the French Republic, living under the same laws as the metropole. "The abolition of slavery was solemnly decreed, and you would not want to change it," the chairman of the constitutional drafting committee told the deputies. "It was a consequence of your principles, a result of your revolution, and you could not fail to proclaim it forcefully."[11] The outgoing Convention's commission of inquiry finally concluded its work in September 1795, fully vindicating the measures Sonthonax and Polverel had taken in 1793.

This vindication came too late for Polverel, who had died midway through the hearings, but it allowed Sonthonax the opportunity to resume his work in the colony. In January 1796, the French legislature approved the appointment of a new Civil Commission. Like the commissioners sent to the colony in 1791 and in 1792, the five members of this Third Civil Commission were given broad powers. Sonthonax, whose name alone symbolized the policy of emancipation, was the most prominent member of the group. His colleagues included Julien Raimond, a well-known representative of Saint-Domingue's free men of color who had been lobbying on their behalf since the start of the revolution, as well as Philippe Roume, a former member of the First Civil Commission who was sent to supervise the French takeover of Santo Domingo, and two other white officials, Pierre Leblanc and Marc Antoine Giraud, appointed for their supposed expertise in colonial matters. The five men sailed from France at the beginning of April 1796, accompanied by 1,200 troops under the command of General Donatien Marie Joseph Vimeur de Rochambeau, who would later command the last French forces fighting against the blacks under Napoleon. They brought with them some 20,000 muskets to arm the black troops who now constituted the bulk of the French army, and they expected additional reinforcements from France who would enable them to defeat the British invaders, although in fact the Directory soon decided that it could not keep this promise.

While the Third Civil Commission was preparing to depart from France in early 1796, the end of the threat from the Spanish and from the black forces fighting under their banner led to a sharpening of rivalries within the French camp in Saint-Domingue. Villatte, the mixed-race general who had commanded the region around Cap Français since 1793, became increasingly impatient at having to submit to the orders of General Laveaux, the white French military man who had become governor of the colony when Sonthonax and Polverel were arrested in June 1794. When Laveaux moved his headquarters back to Le Cap in late 1795, the conflict between the two men intensified. Laveaux's clear preference for Toussaint Louverture further widened the gap between him and Villatte. On 30 ventôse Year IV (20 March 1796), Villatte staged a military coup in Cap Français, putting Laveaux and other white officials under arrest and declaring himself governor of the island. His action was a direct challenge to the French government, and it raised for the first time the possibility that Saint-Domingue could come under the control of a ruler who was not white and who had not been appointed by the French government. On the surface, Villatte's coup seemed to represent a bid for power in the name of the free population of color, a group that had challenged the whites earlier in the revolution, and an effort to exclude the more numerous blacks from the leadership of the colony. Matters were complicated, since many of Villatte's own troops were black and not all men of color joined his movement; the other generals from that group, Rigaud and Bauvais, made no move to support him. Nevertheless, Villatte's move had the potential to reopen racial divisions between the *anciens libres*, or citizens of 4 April, and the black *nouveaux libres*, or citizens of 20 June, that had been papered over in the years since the 1793 emancipation proclamations.

The Villatte crisis allowed Toussaint Louverture the opportunity to present himself as the savior of French authority in Saint-Domingue. Louverture had been at odds with Villatte ever since he joined the French forces. After Villatte's coup, black military officers in Le Cap appealed to Louverture for aid, and the black general quickly marched toward the city from his base in the western mountains. Seeing his forces outnumbered, Villatte abandoned his plans and released Laveaux from prison. Villatte's supporters accused the French general of plotting to restore slavery in the island, and Louverture made an elaborate show of investigating and disproving this accusation, thus demonstrating his commitment to maintaining the freedom of the blacks. The outcome of Villatte's coup attempt was thus to underline Toussaint Louverture's dominant position in the northern part of Saint-Domingue. Laveaux, who owed the restoration of his freedom and perhaps his life to Louverture's intervention, rewarded the black general by naming him deputy governor of the colony, elevating him above the mixed-race generals. In the weeks that followed the coup attempt, troubles broke out in a number of rural areas in the north. Even though he emphasized that he had mixed-race supporters as well as black ones, Louverture blamed these disturbances on followers of Villatte, casting the men of color as fomenters of disorder in the colony.

The Third Civil Commission

The arrival of the Third Civil Commission in Cap Français on 11 May 1796 opened a new period of political struggle in the colony. Sonthonax and his colleagues immediately reaffirmed the French commitment to the abolition of slavery and the equality of people of all races, but they were equally determined to rein in the power of the successful generals whose power had grown steadily during the previous two years, when the metropole had been unable to intervene directly in the colony's affairs. The black population remembered Sonthonax's role in proclaiming general emancipation in August 1793 and welcomed him warmly; it was by no means certain that they would automatically prefer a black leader like Toussaint Louverture to this white Frenchman who had demonstrated his genuine concern for the colony's welfare by accepting a second mission to Saint-Domingue and who had shown his indifference to racial prejudices by marrying Marie Eugénie Bléigeat, a woman of color he had met on his first stay there and who had borne him a son during their stay in Paris in 1795. Recognizing the threat that Sonthonax's presence posed to his authority, Toussaint Louverture maneuvered carefully to preserve his own power, avoiding an open confrontation while waiting for an opportunity to rid himself of this powerful rival.

The Third Civil Commission landed in Saint-Domingue in the midst of the crisis caused by Villatte's coup attempt, and at first its members were more concerned with the challenge to French authority posed by the mixed-race generals than with that represented by Toussaint Louverture. Villatte himself was promptly deported to France, and Rochambeau wrote to France warning that "the men of color are loudly announcing projects for independence."[12] In June 1796, the Third Civil Commission sent three white delegates of its own, along with a white general, to re-establish French authority in the South Province, where

André Rigaud had made himself the virtual ruler of a considerable territory. The members of the delegation openly blamed the men of color in the region for exploiting the blacks, and urged the latter to demand their rights. General Edme Desfourneaux sought to break up Rigaud's army, the Legion of the South, and put its units under independent commanders. Desfourneaux also ordered Rigaud to undertake a poorly prepared attack on the British forces in the Grande Anse, at the western end of the South Province's long peninsula, and blamed Rigaud when the effort failed.

In the face of these provocative actions, the free men of color reacted strongly. On 11 August 1796, blacks roused to action by the local free men of color invaded the city of Cayes, the region's capital, and massacred a number of whites. The delegation's members, fortunate to escape with their lives, were forced to appeal to Rigaud, who had kept himself at a distance from the violence, to restore order. After bringing the killings in Cayes to an end, Rigaud expelled the delegates whose confrontational tactics had provoked them. Although Sonthonax issued a proclamation denouncing Rigaud, he had no way of ousting him from his southern stronghold and in fact needed the general's help in fending off a renewed British effort to conquer the colony. The South Province thus remained a virtually autonomous fiefdom under Rigaud's control, a situation that forced Sonthonax to rely even more heavily than before on the seemingly more loyal Toussaint Louverture for support.

The British, despite disappointing results in 1794 and 1795, had decided in July 1795 to make a more substantial effort to capture the French colonies in the Caribbean. By July 1796, 12,000 fresh British troops had landed in Saint-Domingue. The conflicts between Toussaint Louverture, the free men of color, and the French commissioners encouraged the British to think that they could finally achieve success. In mid-1796 the British did inflict some significant defeats on Louverture's forces, but they were unable to achieve a decisive victory. By the end of the year, even though the military situation in the island was still relatively favorable for them, the British government had concluded that the Saint-Domingue expedition had become too costly to be sustained. A new commander, General Simcoe, arrived in February 1797, with orders to make cutting costs his top priority; even before he departed in July 1797, it was clear that the British were preparing to abandon their effort to seize the colony.

Toussaint Louverture, Laveaux, and Sonthonax

Toussaint Louverture played a major role in defeating the British in 1796, but he was equally concerned with consolidating his own power and warding off the French attempt to re-establish control over the colony. From his point of view, the only way to guarantee that no future French government would go back on its commitment to the abolition of slavery was to have a black man like himself in charge of Saint-Domingue; at the same time, he was clearly pursuing his own ambitions. Rather than resorting to a coup d'état, as his rival Villatte had done, Louverture used more subtle means to rid himself of the French officials who stood in his way. In August 1796, the Civil Commission organized elections to choose deputies to represent Saint-Domingue in the Directory's legislative assemblies. It is unclear how much of the population actually participated in the election process: few blacks would have met the stiff qualifications for voting imposed by the French constitution of 1795 that supposedly governed them. Louverture exerted heavy pressure on those who did take part, urging them to include General Laveaux and Sonthonax among the deputies. He thus hoped to get the two most influential white figures in the colony, and the only two who had some personal popularity among the black population, to return to France.

Laveaux, who had been serving in Saint-Domingue since 1792, put up little resistance to Toussaint Louverture's pressure; he may have accepted the black general's argument that he could be more useful defending the freedom of the black population in France than in the colony. With his departure, Louverture became the commanding general of the French forces there. Sonthonax was more reluctant to leave. Many of the blacks in the North Province, where he had established himself, urged him to stay, and he therefore continued his mission through most of 1797. Although he treated the powerful black general with elaborate politeness, the two came into conflict on numerous issues. Both agreed on the need to restore the plantation system, despite the resistance of the former slaves who did not want to find themselves back under strict discipline, but Louverture ignored Sonthonax's suggestion that too many blacks were serving in the army and that some of them should be returned to farm work. Sonthonax recognized that Louverture was trying to fill all key positions in the army with officers personally loyal to him. Sonthonax imitated Victor Hugues in Guadeloupe by encouraging privateering attacks on British and especially on American merchant ships trading with the British-held ports on the west coast. This was in line with French policy: by 1796, the Directory had decided to punish its former ally's policy of neutrality in the war between the two European powers, thus starting what came to be known as the "Quasi-War" with the United States. Sonthonax insisted that the supplies of grain and meat seized from captured American vessels were vital to feed the troops and the civilian population, but Louverture objected that Sonthonax's policy would cut off normal trade with the Yankees and perhaps make them give up coming to the Caribbean altogether. While Sonthonax remained determined to enforce the French republicans' antireligious policy, Louverture wrote to Henri Grégoire, a French Catholic priest and politician who supported the abolition of slavery, to ask for help in recruiting priests to restore the church in the colony.

A change of political atmosphere in France undermined Sonthonax's position and encouraged Toussaint Louverture to take decisive steps to oust him. In April 1797, counterrevolutionary forces scored major gains in the first parliamentary elections held in France since the start of the Directory in 1795. Egged on by white colonists who had fled to France, the counterrevolutionary deputies made the dismissal of Sonthonax and the restoration of "order" in Saint-Domingue one of the first issues on their agenda; many of them openly expressed their hope that slavery could be restored. Louverture decided that it was urgent for him to ensure that there was no representative of the French government with even nominal authority over him left in the island. Two of the white commissioners had already left Saint-Domingue; the third, Roume, was in the former Spanish territory of Santo Domingo and unable to intervene in the conflict. Julien Raimond, the commissioner who had represented the free men of color in France, threw in his lot with Louverture, who helped him to enrich himself by acquiring a number of abandoned plantations. On 20 August 1797, Louverture and several of his generals sent Sonthonax a peremptory letter telling him that his duty was to "go tell France what you have seen, the prodigies which you have witnessed. Be always the defender of the cause we have embraced, for which we shall be eternal soldiers."[13] Faced with this ultimatum, Sonthonax abandoned his resistance and returned to Paris.

While Toussaint Louverture claimed that Sonthonax was needed to defend emancipation in France, he also wrote to the Directory, accusing the commissioner of having plotted to make the island independent of France. Even as he tried to destroy Sonthonax's influence, however, Louverture did not overlook the menace posed by the white colonial lobby in France. In a long letter addressed to the Directory, he explicitly refuted the arguments put forward by the pro-slavery spokesmen. He reminded the French government that "it was the blacks who, when France was threatened with losing the colony, used their arms and their weapons to conserve it," and he warned that if the French tried to use force to reassert their authority in Saint-Domingue, the black population, "with the Constitution in one hand ... will defend the liberty it guarantees." But, he claimed, there was no need for France to worry about the future of the colony. According to him, the formerly enslaved blacks were already returning to fieldwork and the property rights of the former white plantation-owners were fully respected. "We see the whites, the reds [people of mixed ancestry], and the blacks living in the most perfect equality," he claimed.[14] Louverture's letter offered the French government a choice between accepting the freedom of the black population and his own control over Saint-Domingue, or embarking on a policy of confrontation that would risk losing the colony altogether.

By the time Toussaint Louverture's letter and the exiled Sonthonax arrived in France in the fall of 1797, the political situation in the metropole had changed once again. On 4 September 1797, militant republican members of the Directory, backed by the man who had emerged as the most powerful of their army commanders, the young general Napoleon Bonaparte, had staged a coup against the counterrevolutionary deputies elected to the legislature the previous April. Arrest warrants were issued for the leading right-wing deputies, and others were ousted from their seats. One consequence of this coup of 18 fructidor Year V was a reaffirmation of the Directory's intention to maintain the abolition of slavery in the colonies and the ex-slaves' integration into the metropolitan political system. A new law passed on 12 nivôse Year VI (1 January 1798) outlined procedures for extending French civil institutions to the colonies, reasserted that "black or colored individuals ... enjoy the same rights as an individual born in French territory as long as they work as *cultivateurs*, serve in the army, or exercise a profession or trade," and promised, among other things, to "favor growth in population by encouraging marriage and rewarding the fertility of legitimate unions" and to organize public schools.[15] Sonthonax, although he accused Toussaint Louverture of plotting to make Saint-Domingue independent of France, echoed the black general in arguing that conditions there were improving. "A provisional police force, organized across the whole territory, has put down vagabondage, and the love of work is so strongly engraved in their hearts, that the blacks from plantations that had been burned are restoring the buildings themselves," he claimed.[16]

A New Black Society

While the French government at the beginning of 1798 seemed ready to accept the result of the emancipation proclamations and the rise of Toussaint Louverture, the colony's mostly black population continued to forge a new life for itself. Conditions in the colony were neither as chaotic as the counterrevolutionary faction in France pretended, nor as orderly as Toussaint Louverture and Sonthonax claimed. Thanks to the emancipation proclamations of 1793, blacks living in the French-controlled parts of the island were now legally free. French officials watched vigilantly to be sure that old distinctions based on race and legal status were not revived. In 1796, Sonthonax threatened to punish anyone who recalled the former slaves' condition by labeling them "freedmen." Although those blacks who were still on the plantations were obligated to continue performing field labor, they were now entitled to a salary for their efforts. Whipping and other physical punishments were prohibited. Blacks could marry and form their own families, and many of them took advantage of their new rights to obtain documents legalizing the informal unions they had formed during the era of slavery. The French administration strongly encouraged them to embrace European-style family arrangements, although it is not clear how much success this policy actually had. Blacks could acquire property and make contracts, and some of them took over businesses in the cities that had formerly been run by whites.

Although they were now legally free, the colony's blacks faced many difficulties during these years. The enslaved population had not benefited from the exploitative system that was destroyed in the uprisings of 1791, but the disruption of the colony's economy often left the freed blacks struggling to make a living. Saint-Domingue had never produced enough food to feed itself, relying on imports for most of its meat, fish, and grain. Freed blacks took over some of the fields previously used for sugar in order to grow food crops, but they could not replace the supplies that had formerly arrived from overseas. In the nineteenth century, Haiti would gradually be transformed into a peasant society, with small farmers producing food for themselves and a surplus to feed the rest of the population, but there were still many obstacles in the way of this process in the 1790s. One of the most important of these was the uncertain legal status of the land that had formerly belonged to white plantation-owners who had fled the colony. Sonthonax and Polverel had been willing to deprive the whites of their human property by freeing the enslaved blacks, but they refused to take such drastic steps with regard to real estate. They took over the management of abandoned plantations in the name of the French government, but the question of ownership remained uncertain.

According to French law, owners who had fled to enemy countries were classified as rebels, and their property was supposed to be confiscated outright, but those who had left because their lives were in danger, particularly if they had gone to neutral countries like the United States or to France itself, had the status of refugees and their estates were legally protected. In either case, however, French policy was to try to keep plantation properties intact, so that sugar production could eventually be revived, rather than dividing them into smaller farms for individual families. Where they could, the authorities appointed managers to run the abandoned plantations until the legal disputes over their ownership could finally be resolved. When this system proved vulnerable to corruption, French officials turned to leasing the properties to private owners who had the resources to run them, a policy that favored wealthy and well-connected figures, such as army officers who had enriched themselves during the war. Toussaint Louverture and many of his officers were among those who acquired extensive properties for themselves in this way, and Julien Raimond, supposedly responsible for helping to maintain French authority in the colony, became notorious for taking advantage of the system. Blacks who had less influence were not sure whether the former white owners were really gone for good. In May 1798, one ex-slave wrote to his former master in France, announcing that he had obtained the lease on the master's plantation and had put three of its four sugarcane fields back in production. "When you return, you will find your property in good shape," he concluded.[17] Poorer blacks found that the only way of establishing themselves as independent farmers was to take over marginal land in the island's mountain regions, where they could hope to eke out a living as subsistence farmers. The blacks who settled in the mountains would form the backbone of resistance to the French invasion of 1802, but this shift in settlement patterns also exacerbated the problems of deforestation and soil erosion that had been noticeable even before the start of the revolution, as black peasants cut down trees to clear land for their plantings.

The situation of the black population living on former plantation land at the end of the 1790s is illustrated by the memoirs of one white owner who was able to visit his family's property in 1799. Although he certainly wanted to emphasize the dilapidation of the property caused by the ouster of the slaveowners, his observations reflect the difficulties caused by the events of the intervening years. An illegitimate mixed-race son of the former owner had been leasing the property, but he did not have the resources to maintain the buildings. Most of the plantation's livestock had disappeared, and many of the fields were overgrown with weeds. Lacking draft animals to pull a plow, the remaining blacks were working the land with hoes and other hand tools, and most of the working-age men had disappeared, although the total number of people living on the property was about the same as it had been before the start of the revolution. "Any reasonable man must suffer to see nature herself saddened by not being able to show her generosity, made impotent by devastation," the former colonist wrote.[18] In view of the overall drop in agricultural production, there is little doubt that simply obtaining food was a struggle for much of the population during these years.

One reason younger men were scarce on the plantations was that many of them had joined the various armies that disputed control of the colony in the 1790s. In 1795, a letter published in a South Carolina newspaper claimed that "half the population are soldiers, a fourth are farmworkers and the other fourth are roaming brigands."[19] By late 1798, Toussaint Louverture had some 23,000 men under his command, not counting the sizable army created by André Rigaud in the South Province; in addition, according to Louverture, some 15,000 blacks had been serving in the British forces at the time of their withdrawal from Saint-Domingue in 1798.[20] In France itself, the revolutionary wars had also resulted in a great increase in the size of the army and an overall militarization of society, but the army of 700,000 men that the revolutionaries had raised in 1793–4 represented only about 2.5% of the total population, and the number of soldiers declined during the Directory. In Saint-Domingue, by 1798, between 10 and 15% of the population may have been under arms. The fact that so many men acquired some military experience during these years would eventually enable them to resist Napoleon's effort to reconquer Saint-Domingue, but the diversion of so much of the colony's younger male population to soldiering had a negative effect on the economy. Military service came to appear to be the best way of furthering one's own interests, and soldiers became accustomed to taking what they needed to feed themselves, without having to work for it. Women, of course, were excluded from the opportunities for advancement that military service provided for many men.

With so many of the colony's resources being diverted to military purposes, efforts to build the basis of a racially egalitarian civil society took second place. The task was a daunting one. Under slavery, blacks had been excluded from any possibility of education, and the French colonial administration had deliberately prevented the creation of secondary schools even for children of wealthy white and mixed-race families, preferring to make their parents send them to Europe for their education so that they would not develop a distinctive "American" identity. Sonthonax and the members of the Third Civil Commission set up a model school in Cap Français and claimed that the blacks in rural districts wanted them to send "young European children, who know how to read and write, to instruct them."[21] Faced with an almost complete lack of teachers, textbooks, and other resources, however, the commission was unable to make much progress in this area. Continuing the policy of the colonial era, the French government invited some of the black and mixed-race leaders to send their children to France, where they would be educated at government expense. Toussaint Louverture was one of those who accepted this offer. As he discovered, this made his sons Isaac and Placide virtual hostages of the French government, which would later try to use them to make him submit to its authority.

Unable to make much progress in establishing schools, the republican government had somewhat more success in re-establishing civil administration in the colony. New courts modeled after those set up in France were established in the towns, although it was difficult to find men with enough education to staff them. During the time of his mission in 1796 and 1797, Sonthonax wrote regularly to the local officials he had appointed, urging them to spread the republican gospel of "Liberty, Equality, Prosperity" and to administer the laws fairly. A locally printed newspaper was set up to guide the newly named officials in their work. In a society where the law had always been an instrument of oppression in the hands of a small privileged group, however, it was difficult to convince the population that the government was now going to defend their interests. Accusations of corruption and favoritism were common, and the large proportion of the population serving in the various armies in the island were in a position to ignore the law whenever they chose to.

In spite of all these obstacles, there were some signs of progress in those areas that were no longer directly affected by warfare. Cap Français, the colony's major city, began to recover from the devastating fire that had destroyed it in June 1793. By early 1797, more than half of the burned buildings had been rebuilt; in many cases, their stone walls had survived the flames, so that they only needed new roofs and interiors. The city's streets and public squares were given new names, such as Liberty and Equality, designed to inspire the population with republican ideals. A returning white colonist in 1796 wrote, "I saw citizens of all colors doing business as tinsmiths, smelters, ironworkers, barrel-makers, shoemakers, carpenters, wagonmakers, storekeepers, and so on. I saw thirty to a hundred mules loaded with coffee arriving every day during the harvest, and wagonloads of sugar." This man also reported that the former blacks who had once been enslaved on his plantation were keeping up production. "They showed me that their love of liberty went along with a love of work," he wrote. Other observers complained, however, that the black laborers now asserted their rights and contested the authority of the managers. "They are always in dispute with their employers about how much of the product belongs to them," a disgruntled observer wrote in 1795.[22]

Despite these difficulties, the withdrawal of the British forces from Saint-Domingue in 1798 appeared to open the way for the development of a society unlike any other in the Americas. Slavery, the central institution of colonial Saint-Domingue, had been abolished. A formerly enslaved black man, Toussaint Louverture, was now the official head of the French government in the island. Although he had succeeded in ridding himself of the supervision of white officials sent from France, he had by no means created an all-black government: with his encouragement, whites continued to play an important role in Saint-Domingue's economy, while former members of the free population of color occupied leading positions in the army. Saint-Domingue's economy was still suffering from the impact of years of civil war and foreign invasion, but its future prospects seemed promising. The Americans and the British were eager to revive trade with the island, and a population of independent peasants was laying the basis for a new agricultural economy. Compared to the United States after the end of its war of independence, Saint-Domingue was woefully poor in "social capital," but efforts were under way to create institutions such as schools and local courts. The active participation of deputies from Saint-Domingue, many of them black or of mixed race, in

France's legislative assemblies seemed to show that the mother country was genuinely committed to doing away with racial distinctions and to integrating its colonies into its political system. In an Atlantic world still dominated by monarchical empires with slave colonies and in which the only other free republic, the United States, denied political rights even to the free members of its black population, Saint-Domingue in 1798 formed a remarkable exception, and one capable of inspiring movements for change elsewhere. In August 1798, for example, spokesmen for a conspiracy formed by mixed-race artisans in the Brazilian city of Bahia referred to Saint-Domingue in calling for a democratic government based on "freedom, equality, and fraternity" and the end of slavery.[23] On both sides of the Atlantic, however, developments soon undermined the prospects for the stabilization of the multiracial republican colony that had emerged in Saint-Domingue.

4

Toussaint Louverture in Power, 1798–1801

The departure of the French emancipator Sonthonax for France in late 1797 left no doubt that Toussaint Louverture had become the most powerful figure in Saint-Domingue. In the four years since he had joined the French in 1794, the black general had defeated the foreign invaders who had threatened the colony and skillfully outmaneuvered both the French authorities and his rivals for power in the colony. He now had the chance to implement his ideas about how a society without slavery could be developed in what had been the most extreme example of a "slave society" in the Americas. In the years from 1798 to 1801, Louverture laid the basis for what the several modern Haitian scholars have called the "Louverturian state," a system of centralized authoritarian government that has had a lasting influence on Haiti's destiny.[1] Louverture's experiment in state-building came at a high price, however. As he tried to create a powerful government capable of protecting the freedom of the black population from slavery, he found himself caught up in a series of conflicts with opponents who resented his authority. These opponents included his rival André Rigaud and other "anciens libres," members of the mixed-race elite, who resented the rise of a black man to the colony's top position. They also came to include many ordinary members of the island's black population, whose vision of freedom was more concrete than his, centering on their right to claim land for themselves and establish self-sufficient farms. By 1801, for the first time, he had to defeat

A Concise History of the Haitian Revolution, Second Edition. Jeremy D. Popkin.
© 2022 John Wiley & Sons Ltd. Published 2022 by John Wiley & Sons Ltd.

a revolt led by one of his own officers, General Moïse, who took the side
of the black population and opposed Louverture's effort to create a society in which whites would still have a significant position.

The Dilemmas Facing Toussaint Louverture

Even as he used increasingly violent means to maintain his authority
against these challenges from within the colony, Toussaint Louverture
also became increasingly concerned about the danger of an assault from
outside: not from the British or the Spanish, whom he had defeated, but
from France, the country whose interests he had defended. In the same
years when Louverture was building his regime in Saint-Domingue,
another successful general with political skills and great ambitions, Napoleon Bonaparte, assumed power in France. From the start, Napoleon
made it clear that he did not intend to let France's most valuable colony
escape from the mother country's control. Louverture, who had played
the game of politics so skillfully under the divided and unstable republican government of the Directory, could not find a successful strategy
to avoid a clash with the new French ruler. Even though he denied such
a plan, Louverture's actions convinced Napoleon that the black leader
meant to make Saint-Domingue independent. By the end of 1801, a conflict between Louverture's nascent state in the Caribbean and Napoleonic
France had become inevitable.

If Toussaint Louverture frequently felt compelled to take strong measures to impose his authority and destroy his opponents, it was because
he was convinced that the freedom the formerly enslaved blacks had won
after 1793 remained vulnerable to threats from the outside world. As the
year 1798 began, Saint-Domingue remained a key theater of the trans-
Atlantic conflict between revolutionary France and Britain. To defend
the gains made during the revolution, Louverture realized that he had
to enter the international arena, dealing not only with the French, who
continued to regard Saint-Domingue as their possession, but with the
British and with the representatives of the United States, whose involvement in Saint-Domingue constituted the first of what would become
many American interventions in Caribbean affairs. The formerly enslaved Louverture now had to understand the interests of governments
in London and Washington and calculate how to take advantage of them
to protect his own power and the interests of the population he governed.

At the same time as he learned to play the game of international politics, Louverture also had to keep his eye on events in Paris. The war with Britain that Napoleon inherited from the Directory kept him from intervening directly in Saint-Domingue for several years, but Louverture understood that, when circumstances permitted, the new French ruler would surely do his utmost to reassert control over his country's most valuable overseas territory. Although Napoleon insisted publicly that he had no intention of restoring slavery, he clearly had little sympathy with abstract notions about human freedom: the new constitution he drew up for France dropped the declaration of basic rights that had been a major feature of France's three earlier revolutionary constitutions. Preparing to meet a possible threat from France, Saint-Domingue's supposed protector, became Louverture's constant preoccupation.

Hédouville and the British

At the beginning of 1798, Napoleon's ascent to power was still unforeseeable, and the main issues facing Toussaint Louverture were dealing with a new representative of the French government, General Gabriel de Hédouville, who arrived in Saint-Domingue in March 1798, and ending the British occupation of the west coast. The appointment of Hédouville, known for his success in pacifying the rebellious territory of the Vendée in France, was meant to signal the French government's determination to rein in Louverture's growing power. He had originally been named at the moment when the right-wing deputies elected to the French legislature in April 1797 were in the ascendant, but the Directory maintained his mission even after his political allies had been defeated in the coup d'état of fructidor in September of that year. Hédouville's instructions directed him to restore the property rights of white plantation-owners who had not been classified as émigrés and to restart production, a mandate that was bound to put him in conflict both with the new owners who had taken over the plantations and the formerly enslaved blacks whose labor was necessary to make them function.

Hédouville alarmed Toussaint Louverture by disembarking in the Spanish part of the island, rather than coming directly to Cap Français where Louverture was in control. Despite his authoritarian personality, Hédouville soon realized that he had no means to effectively oppose the black leader. François Kerverseau, another French officer who had been in the colony for several years, warned the newly arrived Hédouville to stay on good terms with Louverture. "With him, you can do anything; without him, you are powerless," Kerverseau wrote.[2] The largely black army was loyal to Louverture, and Hédouville's effort to reclaim state-owned plantations that Louverture had given to his officers further alienated the military. Louverture undercut Hédouville by dispatching an agent to France to accuse him of stirring up trouble in the colony. At the same time, however, Louverture allowed Hédouville to issue a set of regulations obligating the freed black cultivators to continue working for a minimum of three years on their former plantations, in exchange for a one-quarter share of the profits. These regulations were quite similar to the rules Louverture himself had imposed in the West Province, but Louverture was able to deflect complaints from the black fieldworkers by blaming the French general for the measure, and even encouraging rumors that Hédouville's rules were a first step aimed at restoring slavery.

Hédouville found the southern territory governed by the military strongman André Rigaud better administered than the parts of the island under Louverture's control, but the French were still wary of Rigaud, who was blamed for the massacre of whites in Cayes in 1796 and who seemed even less respectful of metropolitan authority than his black rival. Colonel Charles Vincent, a French military officer well acquainted with the colony who went to France at the end of 1797, had warned the Directory that Rigaud had established "a horrible and tyrannical government that responds to nothing but his own will."[3] Furthermore, throughout the summer of 1798 Rigaud and Louverture – who had met personally for the first time in July 1798 – were cooperating to drive the British out of their last strongholds. At the same time, Louverture was conducting negotiations with the new British commander, General Thomas Maitland, about a British withdrawal from the island. Having decided that the campaign in Saint-Domingue was costing them too many men and too much money, the British deliberately exploited these negotiations to create further friction between Louverture and the French government. By addressing himself to Louverture rather than to Hédouville, Maitland encouraged the black general to ignore his supposed superior and to promote his own interests.

The terms of the final agreement reached between Toussaint Louverture and Maitland in August 1798 were calculated to cause further damage to Louverture's relations with Hédouville. Stories circulated that the British had offered to support an independent government led by

Louverture, and even to help him proclaim himself king. Louverture recognized that the British were not reliable allies; among other things, they were determined to prevent him from creating his own navy, whose sailors might spread dangerous ideas to their own colonies. To avoid falling under their control he maintained a degree of loyalty to France, but he did not hesitate to defy the metropolitan government on the details of the treaty. Whereas official French republican policy banned white colonists who had fought alongside the British from French territory, Louverture agreed to let those who wished to remain to do so, and to continue managing their plantations. In conducting his own diplomacy without regard to the wishes of the Directory government in Paris, Louverture was following the example of Napoleon Bonaparte, who had shown a similar spirit of independence during his campaign in Italy in 1796–7. Separated from France by the Atlantic Ocean, Toussaint Louverture was even harder to control.

Strengthened by his agreement with the British and the Americans, Louverture decided to rid himself of Hédouville's inconvenient presence. The black governor was alarmed by an outbreak of violence in the city of Fort-Dauphin, east of Cap Français, in which white troops clashed with a unit commanded by General Moïse; he feared that it might be the prelude to a French attempt to land major forces in the island. The incident set off an insurrection in the countryside around Cap Français, which Louverture himself may have helped to instigate. Louverture insisted that this movement could not be pacified if the French representative remained in Saint-Domingue. On 23 October 1798, Hédouville left the colony, acknowledging that his effort to reimpose French government control had failed. Unable to do anything else to limit Louverture's power, he tried to prevent the him from claiming total control in Saint-Domingue by writing a letter officially freeing André Rigaud, the military strongman in the South Province, from any legal subordination to Louverture. Subsequent Haitian historians have often blamed this maneuver for the violent conflict that soon broke out between Louverture and Rigaud, but the struggle between Rigaud, a representative of the mixed-race class that had sought to establish its own dominance throughout the revolutionary decade, and Louverture, who claimed to represent the black majority of the population, had deeper roots, even if the two men had cooperated in the final campaign against the British. Nevertheless, Hédouville's action showed that the only chance the French had of undermining Louverture's supremacy was to encourage civil conflict in the colony. To avoid the appearance of a complete break with France, Louverture replaced Hédouville with Philippe Roume, the only member of the Third Civil Commission still in Saint-Domingue, recalling him from the city of Santo Domingo where he had been sent to prepare for the French takeover of the Spanish colony authorized by the 1795 treaty of Basel. Surrounded by a black population loyal to Louverture, Roume was in no position to oppose the black general.

Having defied French policy in his negotiations with the British, Louverture demonstrated his independence even further by establishing friendly relations with the United States. Since 1796, the American republic and France had been locked in an undeclared "Quasi-War" caused by the French decision to treat Yankee merchant vessels as fair game subject to seizure by privateers based in the Caribbean. Despite this risk, American traders continued to visit Saint-Domingue; the high prices commanded by colonial products made up for the losses they suffered if their ships were captured. In 1798, when the corrupt French foreign minister Talleyrand demanded bribes from American representatives sent to try to negotiate a settlement of the conflict – a scandal known as the "XYZ affair" because the report President Adams sent to Congress about the matter referred to the three French intermediaries involved as X, Y, and Z – President John Adams and his supporters decided to retaliate by imposing an embargo on all American trade with France and its colonies. Toussaint Louverture encouraged the Americans to treat Saint-Domingue as a special case, however. He sent a personal representative to the United States bearing a letter to Adams, promising that "You can be assured, Mr. President, that Americans will find protection and security in the ports of the Republic and St. Domingue."[4] Although many legislators from the southern states feared that any official dealings with the emancipated blacks in Saint-Domingue would inspire uprisings among their own enslaved blacks, in February 1799 Congress passed an amendment to the trade embargo policy authorizing trade with any parts of the French empire that were not directly involved in the war.

Everyone recognized that this measure, known as "Toussaint's Clause," amounted to an invitation to the black general to defy the French government. Louverture and the American representative sent to Saint-Domingue, Edward Stevens, promptly negotiated an agreement in which Louverture promised to end raids on American shipping by vessels based in the colony in return for an exemption from the trade embargo. The British also joined in this agreement, with Louverture assuring them that they could trade with Saint-Domingue and that he would not make any effort to stir up trouble among the slaves in Britain's neighboring colony of Jamaica, whereas the French government hoped to incite a slave uprising there. When the French representative Roume managed to send an agent to Jamaica to try to start a revolt, Louverture betrayed the man to the British, who arrested and hanged him. Secretly, the British and American governments agreed that it would be undesirable to let Louverture make himself ruler of an independent state, but they both hoped that the fear of his doing so would put pressure on the French to make peace with them.

The Conflict with Rigaud

Assured of supplies from the United States, Toussaint Louverture was now prepared to settle accounts with André Rigaud, his most serious rival for power in the colony. Ever since 1793, Rigaud and his army had dominated Saint-Domingue's South Province. Like Louverture, Rigaud had defied the French officials in the island and established relations with the British, who were happy to see Saint-Domingue remain divided after they decided to end their effort to conquer it. Rigaud's method of government was not very different from Louverture's: both men had built up military regimes that relied on force to compel the mass of the black population to work on the plantations. The crucial difference between them was one of race or caste: Rigaud's regime appeared to amount to the substitution of an elite drawn from the mixed-race population for the former white ruling class. In February 1799, Louverture gave a menacing speech in which he accused the former free men of color of plotting to force the blacks back into slavery. He denounced the mistreatment of the "Swiss," the armed black slaves who had been betrayed by the men of color in 1791, and accused Rigaud of refusing to accept his authority because of his black skin. As tension mounted between Rigaud and Louverture, Rigaud wrote to Roume, insisting that he was more loyal to France than his rival and protesting that "my crime is … that I won't bow my head before the idol."[5]

Open warfare broke out in June 1799, when some of Rigaud's men tried to retake the town of Petit-Goâve, which Toussaint Louverture's forces had occupied. Louverture's army had a significant advantage in numbers, but Rigaud's smaller force was initially better organized. The American agent

Edward Stevens commented that Rigaud's "infantry are well disciplined, and his cavalry the best in the colony," whereas Louverture's army, at the start of the war, was "in want of everything." Nevertheless, Stevens predicted, once Louverture had obtained supplies, "the contest will be but short" since he could count on the support of the black population and of most of the whites, who resented the pretensions of those they called "mulattoes."[6] As Stevens had foreseen, Rigaud proved no match for Louverture as a leader. With relentless determination, the black general drove his forces to conquer his rival's strongholds. He was careful not to convert the conflict into a straightforward race war; some mixed-race officers continued to serve in Louverture's forces, while others remained neutral. Louverture's relations with the United States paid off: armed American ships blockaded the ports in the South Province, depriving Rigaud's forces of supplies.

The conflict, known as the "war of the knives" or "the war of the South," was fought with great brutality on both sides; captives were often tortured and killed with bayonets, and as many as 4,000 people may have starved to death during the four-month siege of the southern port of Jacmel, where a future president of post-revolutionary Haiti, Alexandre Pétion, commanded the defense. In his public proclamations, Louverture insisted that he was only fighting Rigaud and his supporters, not the entire group of men of mixed race, and promised to protect all those who came over to his side. He professed to be shocked by the violence used by his main field commander, General Dessalines. When Dessalines reported what he had done, Louverture supposedly responded, "I told you to weed the field, but you tore everything out by the roots."[7] By July 1800, Rigaud was forced to abandon the struggle and flee to France. Although Louverture had prevailed, former supporters of Rigaud remained numerous, especially in the south. Their lingering resentment against Louverture and Dessalines would lead some of them to welcome the French when they reoccupied the colony in 1802.

Toussaint Louverture Builds His State

Toussaint Louverture's victory in the conflict with Rigaud eliminated the last resistance to his authority in Saint-Domingue. The period from mid-1800 to the end of 1801 was the height of his power, and his actions during this interval give us our clearest picture of the sort of society he imagined for the emancipated blacks of Saint-Domingue. The principles of the

"Louverturian state," to use the phrase adopted by many contemporary Haitian scholars, were laid out in the comprehensive labor code Louverture issued in October 1800, in the colonial constitution he had drawn up in 1801, and in his speeches and proclamations. The fundamental justification on which Louverture rested his assertion of authority was his defense of the abolition of slavery and racial hierarchy in Saint-Domingue. These had been the all-pervading characteristics of the pre-revolutionary colonial social order, but Louverture declared them entirely eliminated. The 1801 constitution explicitly announced that "there can be no slaves in this territory; servitude is abolished within it forever" and that "all men, whatever their color, are eligible for all positions." The constitution did foresee, however, the possibility that new captives from Africa might be introduced to Saint-Domingue to restore the population losses caused by the revolutionary wars. They were to enjoy legal freedom, but they would be assigned to work on the island's plantations.

In the context of the time, the abolition of slavery and of racial privileges were radically revolutionary propositions. The white American revolutionaries of 1776 had seen no contradiction between demanding freedom for themselves and maintaining slavery; even the northern states that did abolish slavery after 1780 usually imposed restrictions on the rights of black residents or tried to force them to emigrate. In metropolitan France, the granting of citizenship rights to black residents in 1791 affected only a tiny minority, whereas in Saint-Domingue the overwhelming majority of the population consisted of formerly enslaved black people. The black *nouveaux libres* were the main beneficiaries of this radical change, but Toussaint Louverture's intent was not to create a new black privileged class. From the start of his public career, he had consistently advocated a society in which blacks, whites, and people of mixed race would coexist on a basis of equality. The promise of racial equality meant that the *anciens libres*, the former free people of color, and the whites who remained in Saint-Domingue also retained rights, including the right to occupy official positions. Indeed, although the army officer corps was dominated by blacks, Louverture appointed whites and men of color to most key positions in his civil administration. From the point of view of the newly freed blacks, however, this meant that members of these minority groups continued to occupy a disproportionately large number of privileged positions in the new society.

Although Toussaint Louverture insisted that freedom and equality were the fundamental bases of the new society in Saint-Domingue, his definition of freedom was very different from that of the French revolutionaries who had declared in 1789 that "liberty consists in being able to do anything that does not harm another person." In Louverture's view, freedom did not give people the right to be idle, or even to decide for themselves what kind of occupation to pursue. In his field labor regulations of October 1800, he insisted that "agriculture ... is the foundation of commerce and wealth, the source of arts and industry." Everyone who could not "produce the proofs of their having an occupation or profession sufficient to gain their livelihood" was in principle to be employed in the fields. Louverture compared agricultural laborers to soldiers, insisting that they had to perform their duties or else be subject to punishment. They were "forbidden to quit their respective plantations without a lawful permission," either to seek easier jobs in the towns or to try to establish private farms in the mountains.[8] The French emancipators Sonthonax and Polverel had incorporated similar restrictions in their abolition decrees in 1793 and 1794, but they had had very few means for enforcing them. Thanks to his army, Louverture was in a better position to try to impose his will on the population.

In addition to ensuring that all inhabitants of Saint-Domingue were compelled to work, Toussaint Louverture was determined, officially at least, to impose a strict code of morality on them. In this respect he was more conservative than the French officials who had preceded him. His labor regulations ordered parents "to attend to their duty towards their children" by instructing them "in good morals, in the Christian religion, and the fear of God," and by making sure they learned a productive trade. Rather than being sent to school in the towns, he intended that children should be set to work in the fields from an early age. Recognizing that the war had caused more casualties among men than among women, he was concerned about the behavior of the colony's numerous unmarried women, especially those in the cities who "are entirely devoted to their appearance and want to do absolutely nothing useful," as he complained in a proclamation issued in November 1801. The constitution he issued in 1801 praised marriage, which "encourages the purity of morals," and promised special protection for faithful spouses and legal advantages for children born to properly married parents. Although the French government had officially legalized divorce in 1792, Louverture's constitution banned it in Saint-Domingue.[9]

The army was the dominant institution in the Louverturian state. Even after the end of the "war of the knives," Toussaint Louverture kept many more men under arms than the colonial regime ever had. In part, this was a reaction to the threat of a French military expedition, but it also reflected the fact that Louverture relied on the army to take the place of a civil administration. Army officers were appointed as district commanders and ordered to "promote agriculture by every means in your power"; in exchange, they were promised that they would share in the profits of the restored plantations. The constitution of 1801 called for an elected assembly to approve laws and outlined a system of local administration and law courts modeled after French institutions, but these clauses were never put into effect. Whether Louverture would have managed to create civil institutions that could balance the power of the army if he had stayed in power longer remains uncertain.

At the center of Toussaint Louverture's new society was the general himself (Figure 4.1). He clearly regarded his continued rule as the only guarantee that the revolutionary changes carried out since 1791 would last. The constitution of 1801 specified that, "in consideration of the important services he has rendered the colony, in the most critical circumstances of the revolution, and on the request of its thankful inhabitants, the reins [of government] are confided to him for the rest of his glorious life." He was also authorized to name his own successor. Unwilling to risk delegating any of his authority, Louverture was constantly on the move from one part of Saint-Domingue to another, trying to make it appear that he was personally supervising the entire territory. "One never knew what he was doing, if he was leaving or staying, where he had gone, from whence he had come," the French general Pamphile De La Croix wrote.[10] Wherever he went, he insisted on being received with the honors due to a ruler. Aware that he had accumulated many enemies – Rigaud had attempted to have him assassinated during the "war of the knives" – he ate only food prepared under his own supervision and avoided making himself visible from windows that might have made him a target for gunshots.

It is ironic that all of our descriptions of the black leader at the height of his power come from whites, many of whom were hostile to him. Some of the French army officers who remained in Saint-Domingue after Hédouville's departure did come to admire his talents. Colonel Vincent, an army engineer who worked closely with him, wrote to France that "Toussaint … is the most active and indefatigable man of whom we can form an idea; we may say, with truth, that he is found wherever instructions or danger render his presence necessary."[11] Another French officer, General Jean-Pierre Ramel, praised him for appointing only "honest, moral, and

Figure 4.1   *Toussaint Louverture: Chef des Noirs insurgés de Saint-Domingue.*
Like all of the existing pictures of Toussaint Louverture, this engraving of the black
general on horseback was done by an artist who had never seen his subject. Nevertheless, this dramatic depiction captures the strong impression that the black
leader made on all those who met or heard about him.

Source: Courtesy of the John Carter Brown Library at Brown University.

intelligent men" as administrators.[12] He was said to dictate more than a hundred letters a day to his secretaries, and those who observed him working were impressed with his ability to express himself. "I watched him condense the substance of his addresses into a few spoken words, rework awkward or misunderstood sentences, and deal with several secretaries who took turns presenting him with their versions," Michel-Etienne Descourtilz, a young white doctor who lived in Saint-Domingue for several years, recalled. "He showed that he was worthy of being considered the natural genius forecast by Raynal," the author of the best-selling pre-revolutionary *Histoire des Deux Indes*, which had predicted the emergence of a black liberator if slavery was not reformed.[13]

When he was residing in one of the major cities, Toussaint Louverture held official receptions and imposed a rigorous etiquette on their participants. "When he appeared in the grand hall where his guests had gathered in advance," General De La Croix wrote, "everyone, without distinction of sex, had to rise. He required that they maintain a highly respectful attitude and especially liked the whites to address him with decent manners.... . He wanted the women, especially the white ladies, to dress as if they were going to church, and their bosoms had to be completely covered."[14] Admitting whites, including former plantation owners and even his own former master, to these gatherings was a way of emphasizing Louverture's policy of promoting understanding among the races, but he left his guests in no doubt about who was now running things. Whites were dependent on him if they wanted to have any chance of recovering control of their properties. Doctor Descourtilz was one of many who suffered from Louverture's "nasty habit of sometimes making a plantation owner travel a long distance, on the promise of listening to him; then, after having had him brought to his lodging, of disappearing through a hidden doorway without saying a word ... and disappearing, leaving the suppliant in the most embarrassing situation. He treated such sorts of things as a game." Descourtilz and others also noted that Louverture made a great show of religious piety, attending Catholic mass whenever he could. "He often interjected himself into the functions of the clergy," Descourtilz recalled, "interrupting the curé's sermon, haranguing the congregation and his soldiers." Descourtilz was one of many observers who doubted that Louverture practiced the strict morality he preached, however; the doctor noted that "at the end of each service he gave private audiences to favored women, one on one and with the doors closed."[15]

The Life of the Black Population

It is much harder to assess Toussaint Louverture's relations with the island's black population. His military victories and his defense of the blacks' freedom certainly assured him a reservoir of support. "The soldiers revered him as an extraordinary being, and the field-Negroes prostrated themselves before him as if he were divine," General De La Croix wrote. Nevertheless, he added, the soldiers were subject to rigorous discipline, and "the junior officers and soldiers were kept in an obedience differing little from slavery." In compensation, Louverture allowed the soldiers to bully the fieldworkers. "A soldier was always right when he complained against a black civilian," De La Croix observed. The harsh regulations that Louverture sought to impose on the rural population undoubtedly alienated many blacks, as periodic revolts in the countryside demonstrated. Doctor Descourtilz was sure that the blacks working on the farms, "constantly harassed by any soldier who comes along … would throw off the yoke if they could."[16] Even those blacks who were admitted to Louverture's receptions were often treated demeaningly, according to De La Croix. "He enjoyed embarrassing the blacks who attended these audiences" by asking them questions designed to reveal their lack of education and "reproaching [them] for their ignorance and incapacity."[17] There is little doubt that Louverture was often more feared than loved.

When they were able to pursue their own lives, the blacks in the countryside organized themselves in family groups and villages on the former plantations and created the basis of a new society that had little in common with Toussaint Louverture's vision of a militarized machine for agricultural production. Descourtilz, a careful observer in spite of his overt racial prejudices, described family groups in a remote village gathering outside their huts in the evenings, "some talking, the older ones in an African language, others singing some kind of *calenda* song, while the little ones crawl around and keep the fire going with dried cow patties, whose smoke drives away the mosquitos." Young men would play the *banza*, the African instrument we know as the banjo, and the women would dance. From his European perspective, Descourtilz was critical of the way black men treated women. When they went to market, he noted, men rode the family mule, while their wives walked, carrying heavy loads on their heads. Although they often left agricultural work to the women, as was common in the West African societies from which many of them had come, Descourtilz noted that the men were often skilled in hunting and handling animals. Some were talented craftsmen, who decorated the pots and baskets in their houses with "designs made with taste and proportion, without the aid of a ruler or a compass." In the absence of whites, black folk healers and midwives cared for the population's health, and Descourtilz was allowed to witness a *vodou* religious ceremony, where he repaid his hosts by killing the sacred snake they were worshiping, in order, he claimed, to cure them of their superstition. Although it was Louverture's official policy to encourage white plantation-owners like Descourtilz to resume the management of their plantations, the blacks found ways to sabotage these efforts. Instead of dictating to their workforce, whites were now dependent on the blacks to share some of their crops with them. Even when an unskilled black coachman took him on a terrifying ride through the countryside and became thoroughly lost, Descourtilz did not dare complain.[18] Whatever he or Louverture intended, the black population of Saint-Domingue would not be forced back into a life of disciplined obedience, either to their former white masters or to the black leader who had risen from their ranks.

The Rupture with Napoleon

By early 1800, news of Napoleon Bonaparte's seizure of power in France the previous November had reached Saint-Domingue. It soon became clear that the new French ruler meant to change the country's policy toward its colonies. Although the Directory had reasserted that the emancipation of the slaves was an official principle in its law of 12 nivôse Year VI (1 January 1798), Toussaint Louverture's expulsion of Sonthonax and his increasingly authoritarian policies had turned many French republicans against him. After his return to France, Sonthonax himself denounced Louverture as an agent of the counterrevolutionaries, citing his agreement with the British, and even some of the black deputies from Saint-Domingue turned against him, urging the government to support Rigaud instead. The members of the Society of the Friends of the Blacks and the Colonies, a group of politicians and officials founded in 1798 to promote interest in colonial affairs that included many of the surviving members of the earlier Society of the Friends of the Blacks, including

Henri Grégoire, was dominated by critics of Louverture. This division among the republicans made it easier for Napoleon to adopt a new colonial policy.

Article 91 of the hastily approved Constitution of the Year VIII (1799) that Napoleon imposed on the country specified that the French colonies would henceforth be governed by "special laws": in other words, their populations could no longer assume that they would have the same rights as those of metropolitan France. That the "special laws" in the colonies might include slavery became clear when Napoleon officially abandoned any effort to apply the emancipation law of 1794 in France's distant Indian Ocean island colonies, whose white colonists had successfully resisted the Directory's attempt to carry out abolition in 1796. Napoleon may not have been so certain about what to do in the colonies where slavery had been abolished, however. In a proclamation issued to the "citizens of Saint-Domingue" in December 1799, he assured the population that "the sacred principles of the liberty and equality of the blacks will never be attacked or modified." Three representatives were sent to bring the news of the change in government to the colony, and, among other things, to see that the motto, "Courageous Blacks, remember that only the French people recognizes your liberty and the equality of your rights," was embroidered on the battle flags of all of its military units. Toussaint Louverture, however, angrily rejected this proposal, telling Colonel Vincent, "We are free today because we are the strongest. [Napoleon] maintains slavery in Martinique and the Ile Bourbon: we will also be enslaved when he becomes the strongest."[19]

Toussaint Louverture's suspicions about Napoleon's intentions were a reaction to several gestures that the new French ruler had made to placate the pro-slavery colonists in France. Former colonial officials from the pre-revolutionary days were appointed to key ministerial positions, and former slaveowners and slavetraders were allowed to publicly defend the institution. It is not clear, however, that Napoleon had decided from the outset that all French colonies had to have the same policy regarding slavery. In late 1799 and early 1800, he had his newly appointed minister of the navy, Alexandre Forfait, solicit the views of a wide range of people interested in the colonies about future policy there. Some of the responses argued strongly for the reimposition of slavery, in order to restore the colonies' economic value, but others, like the former plantation-owner Paul Alliot, thought that the step taken in 1794 was irreversible. "Since the Negroes are free, it is important that they enjoy their freedom, that they work, and that they be paid," he wrote. The participants in this debate also gave conflicting advice on the question of how to deal with Toussaint Louverture. A French official from the southern Saint-Domingue city of Cayes denounced the black general for having "openly raised the standard of revolt against the French republic," while Colonel Vincent, one of the three agents sent by Napoleon to report on the situation in the colony, claimed that Louverture, who was then preoccupied with the war against Rigaud, remained loyal to France, although he resented the fact that the French government did not support his effort to put down the mixed-race general's revolt. "Toussaint, I repeat, is the only one who can still save everything, it is absolutely necessary for the government to give him strong proof of its confidence in him. He will do the greatest good if he is properly handled; everything is lost if things are done otherwise," Vincent warned.[20]

Toussaint Louverture Prepares for War

In the short run, Napoleon could not take any decisive action about the colonies in the Caribbean: France was still at war with Britain, whose navy made the sending of any substantial military expedition impossible. In the meantime, Toussaint Louverture did not remain idle. The news of Napoleon's ascension reached him during the "war of the knives"; it could only have strengthened his determination to make sure that there was no rival leader in the island whom the French could recruit as an ally. The strongly militaristic tone of the labor regulations Louverture issued in October 1800 reflected his conviction that the population of Saint-Domingue might soon have to turn all its efforts to defending the colony. By this time, Louverture had also decided to occupy the Spanish territory of Santo Domingo in the east of the island of Hispaniola. Although Spain had agreed to cede its colony to France in 1795, the transfer of control had never taken place, and the Spanish authorities had continued to govern the region. Rather than rushing to take control of Santo Domingo, the French government had decided not to press the issue, perhaps realizing that it might be to its advantage to have a part of the island that was not under the control of Toussaint Louverture and where French troops could land unopposed, as the agent Hédouville had done in 1798. For the same reason, Louverture was determined to bring the Spanish territory under his rule. As a pretext for his action, he cited incidents in which black women and children had been kidnapped from the French part of the island and sold into slavery in the Spanish colony. When the French commissioner Roume refused to authorize Louverture's move, Louverture had him put under house arrest in the remote country town of Dondon.

At the beginning of January 1801, Toussaint Louverture dispatched an army of 20,000 men to take Santo Domingo. His forces, commanded by his trusted subordinate General Moïse, easily defeated the small Spanish army. Louverture extended the laws in effect in the rest of the island to the Spanish territory, proclaiming the freedom of the 25,000 enslaved blacks there – although it is not clear that this measure was fully implemented – and opening access to government appointments to the mixed-race population, which amounted to half of the total population. He promised to encourage the economic development of the region, which had been thinly settled and much less prosperous than the French colony, and his policies were welcomed by many of the inhabitants; in January 1802, when he visited the capital city of Santo Domingo, he received a tumultuous reception.[21] The news of Louverture's initiative was not well received in France; it underlined the black general's alarming tendency to make his own decisions, without regard for French policy. Louverture compounded his offense by notifying Napoleon of his action only after it had been carried out, in a letter in which he also announced that he had, on his own authority, given promotions to some of the officers who had participated in the operation. Napoleon did not even respond to Louverture's letter, but when he was preparing to send his own military expedition to Saint-Domingue later in the year, he issued a decree stating that "the takeover of the Spanish colony carried out by Toussaint is hereby nullified."[22]

Even more serious than Toussaint Louverture's occupation of Santo Domingo was his decision to have a constitution for the colony of Saint-Domingue drawn up, without any consultation with the French government (Figure 4.2). When the white colonists' assembly had taken a similar step in 1790, the metropolitan government had reacted with outrage, and Louverture must have known that Napoleon would be equally perturbed. Nevertheless, in early 1801 he appointed a committee, consisting of white property-owners and a few men of mixed race, to draft a constitutional document that would incorporate his own ideas about how the colony should be governed. The Louverturian constitution was not the result of a democratic process: the vast majority of the population had no voice in designing the document, and no formerly enslaved blacks were on

Figure 4.2 Toussaint Louverture proclaiming the Saint-Domingue Constitution of 1801. The constitution that Toussaint Louverture had drawn up for the colony in 1801 proclaimed the abolition of slavery and promised the black population that they would have the full rights of French citizens. It also proclaimed Louverture governor for life. Although the constitution reaffirmed Saint-Domingue's status as a French colony, Napoleon interpreted it as a challenge to metropolitan rule and decided to use force to reassert his authority there.

Source: Library of Congress LC-USZ62-7861.

the committee that drew it up. Napoleon's proclamation that the French colonies would be governed by "special laws" provided a legal opening for the project: if Saint-Domingue was not to be governed according to the French constitution, it logically needed laws of its own. The constitution's first article, while stipulating that Saint-Domingue – including the recently occupied Spanish territory – was part of the French empire, asserted that it was to be governed by the "special laws" that followed.

Much of Toussaint Louverture's constitution followed the pattern of the various constitutional documents produced in France after 1789, and some of its language was directly copied from them, but it had some unique features. A section of the constitution devoted to "the inhabitants" specified the irrevocable abolition of slavery in Saint-Domingue, a guarantee that applied not only to those born in the colony but to anyone who lived or died there; this provision was probably meant as a response to the argument that some white colonists in France had made during the Directory, claiming that the majority of the blacks in the colony were not entitled to the rights of Frenchmen since they had been born in Africa. Article 4, which said that official positions were open to all men, regardless of their skin color, was meant both to reassure members of the white and mixed-race minorities and to prevent the re-establishment of discrimination against the black population.

Unlike the French revolutionary constitutions, Louverture's document did not provide for freedom of religion: only the Catholic Church was to be allowed to organize public worship. Most subsequent Haitian rulers until late in the twentieth century would follow Louverture's lead in refusing to grant recognition to the practice of *vodou*, the religion of the majority of the population. While Louverture meant to favor Catholicism, he also claimed control over the Church, giving himself the power to assign priests to the various parishes and forbidding them to act as a collective body. As we saw earlier, Toussaint Louverture's constitution committed the government to favor European-style marriages, and went beyond French law by forbidding divorce altogether. Like the French constitutional documents of the 1790s, Louverture's document strongly defended the right of property, which was proclaimed "sacred and inviolable." Various provisions in the constitution were meant to deal with the complicated situation caused by the departure of so many of the plantation-owners during the revolution, but the general effect was to protect the rights of the former owners and the interests of the military officers and government officials who had acquired control of abandoned plantations. Louverture himself was one of these, along with Dessalines and other leading generals. Rather than being promised any possibility of obtaining their own land, the mass of black fieldworkers were reminded that "the colony … cannot afford the slightest interruption in work on its crops," and that they were subject to the authority of the landowners employing them, although they were to be paid for their labor.

Like Napoleon's own constitution of the Year VIII, the Louverturian constitution created a barely disguised dictatorship. A legislative assembly, chosen by members of the local governments who themselves were to be named by Toussaint Louverture, was to meet in secret and could only vote to approve or reject laws proposed by the governor; it could not introduce legislation on its own. Although Napoleon would modify his own constitution in 1802 to ensure that he could stay in office for life, Louverture had done the same thing a year earlier. Like his French rival, Louverture had complete power to appoint civil and military officials and was commander in chief of the armed forces. The constitution created a system of press censorship, prohibited the formation of political clubs or assemblies, and authorized the extrajudicial arrest of anyone suspected of conspiring against the government. Louverture's conception of freedom did not include any notion that the population should have a say in the choice of its rulers or the making of its laws. A proclamation issued to the island's people justifying the constitution promised them that the new institutions would protect them from "the political tempests that arise from the imposition of laws made far away from you" in France.[23]

It was not the authoritarian character of Toussaint Louverture's constitution that angered Napoleon, but rather the black general's presumption in ordering such a document to be drafted and printed without permission from Paris. Although Louverture had been careful not to declare the independence of the colony, he had acted as though he had no need to take the views of the metropolitan government into account. Colonel Vincent, who greatly admired Louverture but who understood the dangers of an open confrontation with Napoleon, tried to persuade the black general not to insist on putting the constitution into effect on his own, but Louverture ignored him. Vincent was ordered to deliver a copy of the document to France, along with a covering letter asserting the necessity of the colony deciding on its own laws. Louverture's letter informed Napoleon that the constitution had already been put into effect, and that it had been "welcomed with transports of joy by all classes of citizens."[24] By the time Vincent arrived in Paris, Napoleon had already made the decision to send a military expedition to Saint-Domingue, but the news of Louverture's action redoubled his determination to restore French authority in the colony and to remove the black leader.

Toussaint Louverture's Motives

There is little doubt that Toussaint Louverture had deliberately chosen to challenge French authority when he ordered the occupation of Santo Domingo and had a colonial constitution drawn up, but his motives for taking these risky actions are unclear. He may have been convinced that Napoleon intended to try to restore slavery in Saint-Domingue, despite the French ruler's denials, and that making emancipation a constitutional principle in Saint-Domingue would help prepare the population to resist. The provisions of the constitution imposing forced labor on the black farmworkers and protecting the rights of plantation-owners were hardly calculated to build popular support, however. Louverture seems also to have thought that Napoleon would recognize the many contributions the black general had made to the success of French arms in the Caribbean. His strongest argument was his progress in restoring the colony's economy: according to official figures, by 1801 coffee production had reached three-fifths of the level of 1789, and sugar production, although much lower and consisting almost entirely of less valuable raw sugar rather than the refined product that had been the colony's main cash crop, was steadily increasing as well.[25] Louverture thought he had grounds to say that he had "done more for France than any other general," and he repeatedly complained that Napoleon refused even to answer his letters, a slight that clearly angered him.[26]

Louverture may also have underestimated the possibility that the French would reach a peace agreement with the British that would allow them to mount a major trans-Atlantic expedition; his proclamation justifying the issuance of his constitution referred to the "inability of the metropole to aid and feed this great colony during the war with the naval powers" as one of the reasons for his action.[27] By this time, however, the United States and France had already ended the "Quasi-War" with a formal treaty, and Thomas Jefferson, the Virginia slaveholder elected president at the end of 1800, was far less willing to support Louverture than his New England Federalist predecessor John Adams had been. Negotiations between France and Britain were also nearing their conclusion, with Napoleon insisting on France's right to send military forces to its colonies without British interference. The British, for their part, helped to keep Saint-Domingue isolated by intercepting ships that tried to leave the island for other ports. By February 1800, more than 500 black sailors from Saint-Domingue were being held in prison in Jamaica.[28] The international situation was therefore much less favorable for Louverture than it had been in 1798 and 1799.

While the news of Toussaint Louverture's constitution was increasing Napoleon's determination to reassert French dominance in Saint-Domingue, the black general was also facing severe problems in the colony itself. In October 1801, blacks on the plantations in the North Province, in the region where the slave uprising had first begun in 1791, revolted against the strict discipline being imposed on them, killing several hundred whites; only swift action by Henry Christophe, the black commander of Cap Français, prevented violence in the city. Louverture ordered Dessalines, considered the harshest of his commanders, to crush the rebellion in the countryside. He blamed the military commander of the North Province, Moïse, one of his oldest comrades-in-arms, whom he had even adopted as his nephew, for allowing the movement to spread. Moïse had a reputation for being more sympathetic to the position of the black farmworkers than Louverture and the other leading military commanders. He had repeatedly criticized Louverture's protection of the remaining white colonists; in 1798, when Hédouville was expelled, Moïse had reportedly threatened that he would "make all the whites leave and abandon their properties." When Louverture criticized him for not enforcing the labor regulations with sufficient rigor, Moïse responded that he was unwilling to be the "executioner of my color." He supposedly told the American consul Stevens that "although he was Toussaint's nephew, he detested his ingratitude, his dishonesty, and his atrocious ambition," and that he was working to build a following among the field laborers in the region.[29]

In the wake of the uprising, Toussaint Louverture had Moïse arrested. After a hasty trial, he was executed in November 1801. The uprising and the punishment of Moïse underlined both the extent of discontent among the black population and the fact that Louverture had come to distrust even his closest followers. Perhaps the years of effort and tension he had endured since he first committed himself to the slave uprising in 1791 had begun to take their toll on the indefatigable black leader, who was by now in his late fifties. He seemed to have lost the keen political instincts that he had shown in the earlier years of the revolution. His was still a name to conjure with in Saint-Domingue, but at the same time his strict policies had made him a considerable number of enemies. All those who had reasons to complain about him – the black fieldworkers, the mixed-race population, the whites, and now his own generals, traumatized by the treatment of Moïse – would at least have grounds to think twice about continuing to support him if the French seemed prepared to favor their interests. As the French fleet neared the shores of Saint-Domingue in early 1802, the "Louverturian state" he had painstakingly labored to construct was a deeply troubled polity.

5

The Struggle for Independence, 1802–1806

By the end of 1801, the stage was set for a violent confrontation over the future of Saint-Domingue. For more than ten years, since the beginning of the slave insurrection in August 1791, France's prized colony had been largely out of the metropole's control. During that time, profound changes had taken place in Saint-Domingue. The formerly enslaved population had experienced freedom and now wanted to live their everyday lives as they saw fit. The black general Toussaint Louverture had become the representative of French power in the colony, and had then liberated himself from French control and established his own system of government. Many changes had also taken place in France during those years. After the fall of Robespierre in 1794, the French population and its leaders had turned away from radical ideas about human freedom. Napoleon's seizure of power in 1799 represented a triumph for pragmatists who had little concern for liberty and were more interested in expanding France's power by building up a strong government. Particularly after the provocative moves he had made in invading Spanish Santo Domingo and issuing his own colonial constitution, Louverture represented a major challenge to the French government's authority. In both Saint-Domingue and in France, however, the great question was whether bringing him to heel would also mean ending the freedom of the black population.

A Concise History of the Haitian Revolution, Second Edition. Jeremy D. Popkin.
© 2022 John Wiley & Sons Ltd. Published 2022 by John Wiley & Sons Ltd.

The War against Napoleon

The conflict that racked Saint-Domingue from February 1802, when the French army landed on the island, to November 1803, when the last French troops gave up the fight, was the most violent period of the Haitian revolution.[1] The armies on both sides massacred civilians, enemy prisoners, and those they regarded as potential traitors in their own ranks. As the fighting intensified, any prospect for the maintenance of a society in which members of the island's three racial groups lived together on a basis of equality, as Toussaint Louverture had hoped they could, disappeared. So, too, did the possibility of Saint-Domingue remaining a part of a trans-Atlantic French empire. Independence, which some white colonists had called for during the first years of the French Revolution in order to defend slavery, now became the program of the black and mixed-race populations fighting against Napoleon's army. The precarious balance that Louverture had tried to maintain by creating a black-dominated government in the island while continuing to acknowledge French sovereignty was no longer tenable. Like Britain's North American colonists after 1776, the population of Saint-Domingue found themselves fighting not only for their freedom as individuals, but for their right to found a new nation.

The man who provoked this radicalization of the conflict in Saint-Domingue, Napoleon Bonaparte, had been born in 1769 in the Mediterranean island of Corsica at a time when that territory, acquired by France only a year before his birth, was governed by the French ministry of the navy and regarded almost as a colony. Frenchmen from the mainland sometimes denigrated Corsicans as half-African, and the island's coat of arms featured the head of a black man. The island had also been the site of a vigorous revolt for independence in the mid-eighteenth century, led by Pasquale Paoli, which Napoleon's own father had supported. Napoleon's Corsican background did not inspire him with any sympathy for Saint-Domingue's black population or its pretensions to autonomy, however. Napoleon often expressed his prejudices against black people, telling the former Convention deputy Antoine Thibaudeau, for instance, that "I am for the whites because I am white; I don't have any other reason, and that one is good enough. How could anyone have granted freedom to Africans, to men who didn't have any civilization, who didn't even know what a colony was, or what France was?"[2] Nevertheless, Napoleon was sufficiently pragmatic to consider the difficulties of restoring slavery in Saint-Domingue, and to consider the possible advantages he might gain if he could persuade the black population to identify with France. After his fall from power in 1815, Napoleon sometimes reflected on the opportunity he had missed. "With an army of twenty-five to thirty thousand blacks, what might I not [have undertaken] against Jamaica, the Antilles, Canada, the United States itself, or the Spanish colonies?" he told one of his companions in exile. In early 1802, he actually drafted a letter to Toussaint Louverture offering him a promotion and a chance to cooperate in a program of French military expansion in the Caribbean, although the letter was never sent.[3]

Napoleon's Fateful Decision

As he considered his various options, Napoleon was bombarded with advice from all sides about how to treat Toussaint Louverture and the blacks in Saint-Domingue. One person who apparently did not try to influence him was his wife, Josephine, even though she came from a slaveowning family in Martinique and owned a plantation in Saint-Domingue. Whereas Josephine did not try to sway Napoleon's policy, many other individuals in France did. As we have seen, Napoleon's minister of the navy, Alexandre Forfait, solicited opinions from a wide variety of people with interests in the colonies, and received letters and memoranda advocating everything from an alliance with Louverture to the immediate restoration of slavery in all its aspects. Some former colonists thought that they would have a better chance of reclaiming their plantations if the French government promised to maintain the policy of emancipation, whereas others demanded a complete return to the old regime. Republicans like Sonthonax and Louverture's black and mixed-race opponents joined with former plantation-owners in denouncing the misdeeds of the black general, "a man who owes his political existence ... and his important position to a government that he now refuses to recognize."[4] Even Louis Dufay, the representative from Saint-Domingue whose speech on 16 pluviôse Year II (4 February 1794) had persuaded the Convention to abolish slavery, now wrote, "for a long time, we have been too liberal and too tolerant with the blacks and the men of color."[5] Merchants in France's port cities, hard hit economically by the long-drawn-out war with Britain, looked forward eagerly to the end of hostilities and the resumption of the lucrative slave trade with the colonies. Principled opponents of slavery, such as Grégoire, continued to defend the freedom of the blacks, but they were aware that their arguments no longer carried the same weight as they had during the republican period.

As he listened to the conflicting voices in this debate, Napoleon also weighed the practical possibilities of intervention in the Caribbean and the situation in France's other colonies. Immediately after coming to power in 1799 he had planned to assemble a powerful naval force and send a significant number of troops to Saint-Domingue, but circumstances forced him to divert them to Egypt instead, where the army he had abandoned to return to France in 1799 was in dire straits. The ongoing war with Britain prevented him from planning any further overseas military operations for the time being. His armies' victories over Britain's continental ally Austria at Marengo and Hohenlinden in 1800 altered the situation, however. Austria prepared to end the war, and by March 1801 the British government, seeing no further chance of defeating the French, had begun putting out feelers about a peace settlement. Napoleon saw the opportunity not only to regain full control of the important Caribbean colonies, the only parts of pre-revolutionary France that had escaped from the country's control, but also to make France the dominant power in the Gulf of Mexico. The Louisiana territory, which Spain had ceded to France in 1800, would restore France's position on the North American continent, which it had lost after the Seven Years War in 1763. Napoleon calculated that Louisiana could provide food and supplies for Saint-Domingue and the other sugar islands, whose plantations would once again be an important part of the country's economy.

As Napoleon prepared to reclaim the colonies Britain had occupied, he had to decide whether to maintain slavery in Martinique, where the abolition decree of 1794 had never been applied because the island had been under British occupation. Napoleon had already decreed, shortly after coming to power, that slavery would be maintained in the Ile Bourbon (today's French department of Réunion in the Indian Ocean), and he soon made it clear that he would not grant freedom to the slaves in Martinique when France recovered it. Although it was theoretically possible to imagine a colonial empire in which slavery existed in some territories but not in others, Martinique's proximity to Guadeloupe and Saint-Domingue understandably raised concerns among the recently emancipated populations in France's other Caribbean colonies. As we have seen, Toussaint Louverture cited Napoleon's decision about Martinique as one of the reasons for his distrust of him. Napoleon, for his part, was also increasingly concerned about Louverture's actions. He learned of the black general's occupation of Spanish Santo Domingo just when the first British peace proposals were being floated, and the news undoubtedly made him more determined to assert his authority over Saint-Domingue. Louverture's colonial constitution reached Napoleon just as the treaty with Britain was being finalized, and provoked him to increase the size of his planned expedition.

Evaluating Napoleon's intentions with regard to Saint-Domingue is complicated by the fact that the French ruler, like Toussaint Louverture himself, knew the advantage of keeping his thoughts concealed. One of the numerous pro-slavery pamphlets published in France during the years prior to the Saint-Domingue expedition laid out a plan to restore French authority that certainly resembles what Napoleon actually did. Its author recommended the issuance of a secret decree reinstating slavery in the colony, to be made public only once French military control of Saint-Domingue had been established. If the blacks were willing to submit to their old masters, they would be spared any punishment, but if they tried to resist they would have to be "defeated and kept in complete subjection to forestall new misfortunes." Blacks who had held officer rank in the army would have to be removed from the colony altogether. "To avoid bloodshed, one could offer to send them back to their families" in Africa, the author suggested, leaving it to the reader to imagine how they would be dealt with if they balked at this idea.[6]

It is unlikely that this particular pamphlet actually guided Napoleon's decision-making, but the secret instructions issued to General Victoire-Emmanuel Leclerc, the expedition's commander, in 1801 followed a similar logic. Leclerc was told to proceed in three phases. He was to begin by issuing reassurances to the population and negotiating with Toussaint Louverture, promising him anything he wanted "in order to take possession of the strongholds and to get ourselves into the country." Once this was accomplished, however, Leclerc was to become "more demanding." He would order Louverture to give up his authority, and he would separate the black general from his supporters by confirming them in their military positions. Placed under Leclerc's control, the black army would then be used, alongside the white troops, to crush rebellious movements in the countryside. As soon as this was done, Leclerc was to proceed to the third and final phase of his mission. Not only Louverture but the other black generals, particularly Jean-Jacques Dessalines, were to be arrested; if they were captured carrying arms, they were to be "shot like rebels." All those of any color who had served as officers in Louverture's army or officials in his government were to be sent to France, and the black population was to be completely disarmed. White women who had violated European notions about racial hierarchy by having sexual relations with blacks were also to be deported.[7] Leclerc's instructions did not explicitly order the reintroduction of slavery in the colony. Leclerc was directed, however, to use deception and force to establish his control of Saint-Domingue, to impose a white military government purged of anyone who had participated in Toussaint Louverture's regime, and to render the black population completely defenseless.

The Leclerc Expedition

The expeditionary force that Leclerc was to command began assembling as soon as the preliminary peace agreement with Britain was signed in October 1801. It was one of the largest overseas military efforts any European power had ever undertaken. More than 20,000 soldiers, most of them experienced veterans of the wars France had been fighting since 1792, were dispatched to seven different Atlantic port cities, where an armada of ships prepared to take them and their supplies to the Caribbean. At the same time, a separate force of 3,600 men, commanded by General Antoine Richepance, headed for Guadeloupe, where Magloire Pélage, a man of mixed race, had led an uprising that overthrew the French military regime in 1801. Although they agreed to permit the French expedition, the British watched it warily: they feared that Napoleon might decide to use his troops to attack their valuable colony of Jamaica instead of sending them to Saint-Domingue. Nevertheless, British officials agreed that the experiment of emancipation in the French colony posed a danger to their own slave colonies in the Caribbean. In the United States, President Jefferson, a slaveholder himself, expressed no sympathy for Toussaint Louverture. On the other hand, however, Napoleon's ambitious plans worried him. If the French controlled New Orleans, they would be able to interfere with American commerce on the Mississippi River, and if they regained full control of Saint-Domingue, they could try to bar American traders from their lucrative trade with the colony. For the time being, American merchants could make good profits by supplying the French expedition, and Jefferson took comfort in the thought that "the conquest of St. Domingo will not be a short work. It will take consider-able time to wear down a great number of soldiers."[8]

The commander of the Saint-Domingue expedition, Leclerc, was a promising young general who had served with Napoleon in the campaign in Italy that had made Napoleon's own reputation. Leclerc was married to Napoleon's sister Pauline, a renowned beauty who accompanied him on the voyage that was supposed to consolidate his fame. Along with the troops, the ships carried a number of Toussaint Louverture's political op-ponents, such as André Rigaud and Alexandre Pétion, former leaders of the resistance to the black general in the South Province, and Jean-Bap-tiste Belley, the black deputy Sonthonax had sent to France to announce the emancipation decree of 1793. Napoleon also sent Louverture's two sons, who had been studying in France; they were to deliver to their father a letter from Napoleon calling on him to accept the authority of General Leclerc. Because of bad weather the fleet did not put to sea until 14 De-cember 1801, several crucial weeks later than originally planned; every-one understood the importance of getting the troops to Saint-Domingue in the winter, in hopes of concluding the campaign before the summer, which usually also brought an outbreak of tropical diseases among newly arrived Europeans. The plan was for the fleet to rendezvous at Samana Bay, off the coast of the Spanish section of Hispaniola, and then disperse to carry out simultaneous landings at the various ports of the island.

The opposition the French would have to face in Saint-Domingue was very different from the slave insurrection of 1791 to 1793. The long years of fighting against the British, the Spanish, and Rigaud's forces had given Toussaint Louverture a large body of trained troops, whose discipline impressed European observers; in all, they numbered around 20,000 at the time of Leclerc's landing, supplemented by another 10,000 local mili-tiamen. Louverture's corps of officers, headed by men like Dessalines and Henry Christophe, were also battle-hardened veterans. In the country-side, many of the black farm laborers were men who had participated in the fighting at some point during the revolution. Many of them had kept their muskets even when they returned home; Louverture had often em-phasized that their weapons were the ultimate defense of their freedom. In anticipation of an invasion, Louverture had hidden caches of weapons and supplies in various parts of the island's interior, where they could be distributed to the population in case of a war. At the same time, how-ever, Louverture's own policies had made some of the population regard him as a greater threat to their freedom than the French. His rigorous labor regulations, heavy-handedly enforced by the army, his protection of white landowners, and his efforts to control people's private lives alienated much of the black population. The *anciens libres*, the mixed-race population that regarded itself as naturally suited to govern the blacks because of its education and wealth, resented having to take orders from a black man whose ascent had blocked their ambitions to become the leaders of Saint-Domingue. Even some of Louverture's own generals thought his defiance of the French had been excessively confrontational.

Alerted to the impending arrival of the French by newspaper reports by the beginning of December 1801, Toussaint Louverture criss-crossed the territory inspecting his troops and fortifications. The violence of his reaction to Moïse's rebellion and his harshly worded proclamation to the population in November 1801 may well have reflected the anxiety he felt about the French threat even before he knew for sure that the fleet was on its way. Louverture is said to have actually observed the arrival of the French fleet in Samana Bay, and the sight of so many ships, all carrying well-armed troops, momentarily discouraged him. "We are going to die," he reportedly told his officers. "The whole of France has come to Saint-Domingue … She comes to avenge herself and force the blacks back into slavery."[9] Quickly recovering his nerve, however, he galloped back to the French part of the island to prepare to resist the occupation. Officially, the French insisted that since Louverture continued to acknowledge their sovereignty over Saint-Domingue, he should have no objection to French troops coming to the colony. Louverture responded that if the French recognized him as the colony's official governor, they should have requested his permission to come ashore. In reality, both sides were braced for combat. Any pretense to the contrary disappeared when General Rochambeau's units landed at Fort-Dauphin (then called Fort-Liberté) on the north coast, east of Cap Français, on 3 February 1802 and brutally massacred its outnumbered black defenders. This was the first of the many atrocities that would mark the fighting for the next two years and make the struggle for control of Saint-Domingue by far the bloodiest phase of the Haitian Revolution.

Resistance

Historians have differed sharply in their assessment of whether the confused and violent events of the first months following the French landings reflected a systematic plan of resistance directed by Toussaint

Louverture or whether they were the result of uncoordinated actions by his generals and the population at large. As was often the case during his career, Louverture kept out of sight at several crucial moments, and it is impossible to be sure whether his subordinates were always following his orders, or whether they were left to make decisions on their own. Once the fighting started, Louverture called on the entire population to rise up and set fire to the plantations and the island's cities, but it is not clear whether the peasants who took up arms were obeying him or acting spontaneously to defend their freedom. If there was an overall plan of resistance, some of Louverture's commanders quickly betrayed it. In the former Spanish territory of Santo Domingo, generals Augustin Clervaux and Paul Louverture, Toussaint's own brother, submitted to the French after only token resistance. In the South Province, where memories of the "war of the knives" of 1799–1800 were still strong, General Laplume, one of the mixed-race commanders Louverture had appointed to avoid the appearance of creating an exclusively black military elite, was persuaded to accept French authority without firing a shot.

The French encountered more resistance in their efforts to take over the island's two major cities, Cap Français and Port-au-Prince (still called, in 1802, by the new name – Port-Républicain – that it had received in 1793). When Leclerc himself tried to land at Cap Français, the black commander Henry Christophe insisted that he could not let the French troops ashore without permission from Toussaint Louverture himself. On behalf of the city's population, the mayor, a black man named César Télémaque, pleaded with Christophe not to carry out his threat to burn the city down if the French forced an entry, an indication of the willingness of some of the population to take their chances with the French rather than supporting Louverture, but Christophe remained inflexible. "You shall not enter the town of Le Cap until it is in ashes, and even then I will oppose you," he wrote to the French general. "You say that the French Government has sent to Saint-Domingue forces capable of vanquishing any rebels that may be found here; but it is you who have come to create them, among a people peaceful and obedient to France, by the hostile intentions that you express."[10] When the French warships managed to make their way past the fort guarding the harbor, Christophe set the example by setting fire to his own house before leading his troops out of the town to take up positions in the surrounding mountains.

In Port-au-Prince, Dessalines and his black soldiers also put up strong resistance to the French occupiers, although General Pierre Agé, the highest-ranking white officer in Louverture's army, and some of the mixed-raced commanders went over to their side. Driven out of the city, Dessalines retreated into the mountains dividing the West and North Provinces, rallying the population by spreading the rumor that the French had come to restore slavery. Along his route, Dessalines set fire to the towns and massacred hundreds of their white inhabitants. He and Toussaint Louverture, who had established his headquarters on his personal plantation at Ennery, urged the black *cultivateurs* in the countryside to take up arms and launch a guerrilla war against the French troops. "We are fighting an Arab-style war here," Leclerc wrote to Napoleon. "As soon as have we passed through, the blacks occupy the woods along the road and cut our communications."[11] As in earlier phases of the revolution, women contributed to the resistance along with the men. Some joined the armed guerrilla bands in the countryside; others took advantage of the fact that the French continued to let them cross the battle lines to bring food from the countryside into the cities to spy on French military movements.

Looking back on this early phase of the conflict later in the year, the black general Henry Christophe commented that it would have been better for the blacks not to try to confront the French army in regular battles. "If our system of resistance had been not to fight but to retreat and play on the fears of the field hands you would never have got at us. Old Toussaint never left off saying that, but nobody would listen to him," he told a French officer.[12] Establishing cooperation between the leaders of the guerrilla resistance movements – men like Petit Noël, Sylla, and Sans-Souci in the northern mountains and Lamour Dérance in the west – and Louverture's generals was not easy, however. Many of the guerrilla leaders had previously led revolts against Louverture's own government, sometimes fighting against the same generals who were now joining them against the French. The black generals, who had all acquired plantation properties under Louverture's rule, had a personal interest in enforcing the labor regulations that had fueled many of the rural population's revolts. Hoping to persuade Louverture to abandon his resistance, Leclerc sent his two sons and their tutor to deliver a letter from Napoleon, promising the black general that he would be generously treated if he accepted French authority and put himself under Leclerc's command. Although witnesses recorded that he was deeply moved to see his sons for the first time in six years, Louverture refused to be swayed by Leclerc's promises. "If General Leclerc really wants peace," he told the boys' tutor, "let him halt the march of his troops." His son Placide decided to join Toussaint's army, but his half-brother Isaac chose to remain with the French. Louverture's negative response to his letter gave Leclerc the pretext for a proclamation, dated 17 February 1802, declaring the black general an outlaw.

The fiercest fighting in the first months after the French landing took place in the mountains between the West and the North Provinces, where Leclerc had hoped to surround the troops loyal to Toussaint Louverture and Dessalines. In a fierce engagement at Ravine-à-Couleuvre, a steep-sided valley, Louverture's troops, supported by a large number of armed *cultivateurs*, showed that they could stand up to the best French soldiers in a pitched battle. The doctor Descourtilz, taken captive by Dessalines and spared because of his medical skills, was forced to treat the black soldiers, and thus became a witness to the most celebrated episode of this first stage of the military campaign, the siege of Crête-à-Pierrot, a small fort in the middle of the Cahos mountains where Dessalines made a stand. Heavily outnumbered by French units arriving from all directions, Dessalines's men dug trenches around the fort and inflicted heavy casualties on the overconfident white troops who tried to storm their position. When the French bombarded the fort, the black soldiers grimly hung on, with a courage that Descourtilz reluctantly acknowledged. "Deprived of water and food in this overwhelming heat, the troops had to chew on balls of lead in the hope of quenching their unbearable thirst," Descourtilz reported. "They suffered without complaint, out of a hope for vengeance."[13]

Descourtilz's memoirs give a sense of the forceful personality that would eventually enable Dessalines to replace Toussaint Louverture and defeat the French. In contrast to Louverture, Dessalines had been enslaved until the revolution, and his back was deeply scarred from the whippings he had suffered. His experiences had given him an abiding hatred of whites and the privileged members of the free colored caste. Prior to the French invasion, Descourtilz noted, Dessalines and Louverture had competed to recruit the island's best musicians for their private bands, but, whereas Louverture's group included white and mixed-race players, Dessalines's ensemble was entirely black. Even as he realized he would have to abandon his position at Crête-à-Pierrot, Dessalines still found ways to inspire his men. "Have courage, have courage, I tell you, the French can't hold out long in Saint-Domingue," he assured his officers, in his earthy Kreyol. "They will start off strongly, but soon they'll be slowed down by illness, and will die like flies. Hear what I say: if Dessalines surrenders to them a hundred times, he will betray them a hundred times … we'll harass them, we'll fight them, we'll burn their harvests, then we'll hide in our hills where they can't get us. They won't be able to hold the country, and they'll have to leave it. Then I'll make you independent. We don't need whites among us any more." As they besieged the fortress, the French troops were demoralized to hear the defenders singing their own republican war songs; General De La Croix commented that some of his men began to wonder if they were fighting against the ideals of freedom and equality they had sworn to defend. When the last black defenders made a breakout and escaped from the fortress, De La Croix admitted that they had "executed … a remarkable feat of arms."[14] Even today, the defense of Crête-à-Pierrot is one of the heroic episodes of the war celebrated in Haitian national memory.

The Illusion of a French Victory

Despite the courage and determination of their soldiers, Dessalines and Toussaint Louverture were unable to stop the advance of the heavily armed French troops. One by one, Louverture's generals accepted Leclerc's assurances that if they came over to the French side they would be allowed to retain their rank and continue to command their men. General Maurepas, who had initially fought hard to defend the northern coastal area around Port-de-Paix, abandoned the struggle at the end of February, after most of his own subordinates had already given in to the French. Maurepas's change of sides freed up the French units that had been opposing him to join the campaign against Louverture's main force, seriously weakening the resistance effort. By early April, after the end of the siege of Crête-à-Pierrot, Christophe, who had defied Leclerc and set fire to Cap Français in February, followed Maurepas's example, although he rejected Leclerc's effort to get him to betray Louverture. Dessalines, the last of Louverture's major field commanders to keep up the fight, finally did likewise. By the beginning of May, Louverture was isolated, with few troops left willing to oppose the French. Accompanied by an honor guard of several hundred heavily armed soldiers, Louverture arrived unexpectedly in Le Cap and announced that he was prepared to recognize Leclerc's authority. Leclerc, fearful of a confrontation with Louverture's escort, promised him that he could retire peacefully to his plantation, and that his soldiers and officers would be integrated into the French army. On 7 May 1802, Leclerc was able to write to Napoleon that "my present position is beautiful and brilliant ... all the rebel chiefs have submitted."

Despite the promises he had made to him, Leclerc always intended to eliminate Toussaint Louverture as quickly as possible, as his orders from Napoleon insisted. He was sure that Louverture was waiting for the moment when disease would weaken the French forces and he could resume the fight against them. In the meantime, Leclerc claimed, Louverture was secretly inciting the rural *cultivateurs* to continue their guerrilla resistance. On 7 June 1802, one of his officers, General Jean-Baptiste Brunet, set a trap for Louverture, luring him away from his plantation on the pretext of consulting him about the stationing of troops in the area. The normally suspicious Louverture was taken by surprise when French soldiers surrounded him, giving him no chance to resist. He was quickly disarmed and taken to the port of Gonaïves, where he was hustled on board a ship to be sent to France; his family was arrested the next day and deported with him.

As he boarded the ship that would carry him away from Saint-Domingue for good, Toussaint Louverture told its captain, "In overthrowing me, you have cut down only the trunk of the tree of the blacks' liberty in Saint-Domingue; it will grow back from its roots, because they are deep and numerous."[15] The harsh treatment inflicted on Louverture after his arrival in France showed how much Napoleon feared his influence. Separated from his family, who had been deported along with him, he was rushed across France to the Fort de Joux, a prison hundreds of miles away from the coast, and kept in solitary confinement. The cold, damp climate of his prison and the isolation in which he was kept soon undermined his health; he died on 7 April 1803, while the struggle for Saint-Domingue was still under way. As he had predicted, however, his exile and death brought the French no advantage: they would indeed learn that the black population could not be forced back into submission.

Although he had gotten Toussaint Louverture out of the way, General Leclerc recognized that his hold on the island remained precarious. Even before Louverture's capture and deportation, the tropical diseases that always took a heavy toll on newly arrived Europeans were beginning to eat away at his forces. On 8 May, just three months after his arrival, Leclerc reported to Paris that he had only 12,000 soldiers left out of the 20,000 he had arrived with, and that between 200 and 250 were falling sick every day. By June, a full-fledged epidemic of yellow fever was ravaging the army, killing the white troops while the blacks, largely immune to the mosquito-borne disease, remained healthy. Leclerc's letters became a continual litany of deaths and complaints about the lack of supplies and support from France. As he explained to his superiors, the dwindling number of French troops made it impossible for him to proceed with the plan to arrest the black military officers and disperse their units: increasingly, they were the only functional soldiers he had. In accordance with his instructions, Leclerc gave orders for the disarmament of the black population in the countryside, but he had no illusions about the obstacles to enforcing this unpopular policy: the white troops were in no condition to undertake difficult expeditions into the mountains, and the black troops could not be trusted.

For a few months, Dessalines, Christophe, and the other officers who had come over to the French side continued to follow Leclerc's orders; Dessalines was so vigorous in pursuing the guerrilla forces in the mountains that Leclerc himself called him "the butcher of the blacks." In August 1802, when another of Louverture's former generals, Charles Belair, inspired by his wife Sanite, tried to turn the black soldiers against the French, Dessalines arrested him and turned him over to the French, who had him and his wife shot. Sanite, who exhorted her husband to show courage as they were led to their execution, became one of the legendary heroines of the struggle against the French. Nevertheless, Leclerc realized the danger of having to rely so heavily on a largely black army with black commanders. The French had originally hoped that the officers and soldiers of mixed race would be more trustworthy, but they, too, were alienated by Leclerc's policies. A number of them had returned to Saint-Domingue with the expedition, but after Leclerc decided to send André Rigaud, Louverture's mixed-race rival, and some of his supporters back to France in May 1802, the others recognized that the French were determined to keep them, as well as the blacks, in a subordinate position.

Napoleon's Re-establishment of Slavery

Encouraged by the initial results of the Saint-Domingue expedition, Napoleon took new measures in France that were bound to inspire further resistance from the population in Saint-Domingue. On 20 floréal Year X (10 May 1802), he officially promulgated a law repealing the National Convention's abolition decree of 16 pluviôse Year II (4 February 1794) and authorizing the maintenance of slavery in those colonies, such as Martinique, where it had never been abolished. There was a certain amount of opposition to this measure – in the Tribunate, the most important house of the normally compliant Napoleonic legislature, the vote was 54 to 27, much less than the lopsided majority Napoleon's laws normally received – but not enough to seriously concern Napoleon. A press campaign, backed by former colonists and supporters of the regime, argued that the blacks, "by their ungratefulness to the government, by their insurrection against it, by their atrocities against the whites," had shown that they were nothing but "criminals who deserve to be punished," as Narcisse Baudry Deslozières, one of the contributors to this campaign, put it.[16] His book, dedicated to Napoleon's wife Josephine, formulated a new, biologically based racism that would pervade the western world for more than a century. Racist attitudes were also reflected in another decree, issued on 2 July 1802, prohibiting blacks and even people of mixed race from entering metropolitan France. Henri Grégoire, the most steadfast of revolutionary France's opponents of racism and slavery, answered these attacks in his *Of the Literature of the Negroes*, highlighting the intellectual accomplishments of black authors, but he was not able to publish his book until 1808.

News of the passage of the law of 20 floréal and of Napoleon's decision to maintain slavery in Martinique reached Saint-Domingue in August. A month later, in September, word of General Richepance's decision to restore slavery in all but name in Guadeloupe began to circulate. Convinced that the French meant to follow the same policy in Saint-Domingue, the leading black and mixed-race officers in Leclerc's army began to turn against the French. In mid-October, Alexandre Pétion, who had defended Jacmel against Dessalines's army during the "war of the knives" just two years earlier, went over to the insurgents, along with the black general Clervaux, and launched a surprise attack that almost overran Cap Français. Leclerc managed to beat back the enemy, but he knew his position was becoming hopeless. In reaction to the attack, the French army killed 1,200 black soldiers who had been part of the garrison in the city by drowning them in the harbor, an atrocity that increased the hatred against them. "Every day the party of the insurrection grows and mine diminishes, because of the losses among the whites and the desertions among the blacks," Leclerc wrote to Napoleon. Dessalines, who had been the most active in repressing the guerrilla bands during the summer, was clearly planning to betray the French. Leclerc had realized that the black general was no longer destroying the weapons he captured from the guerrillas, a sign that he was hiding them for later use, and that he "no longer mistreats the blacks, as he did before."[17]

By this point, as his black troops simply melted away into the mountains to join the uprising against him and the whites continued to die off, Leclerc had concluded that only a veritable genocide could maintain French authority in Saint-Domingue. "We must destroy all the Negroes in the mountains, men and women, sparing only children younger than twelve, destroy half those who live in the plains, and not leave in the colony a single man of color who has worn an officer's epaulette," he wrote in one of his last letters to Napoleon (Figure 5.1).[18] Fortunately, he had no forces left to carry out such a policy. Shortly after Pétion's and Clervaux's defections, Christophe and Dessalines, the two highest-ranking commanders from Louverture's army, also abandoned the French. At the end of the month, Leclerc came down with the deadly yellow fever that had decimated his army; within a few days he was dead. Command of the French forces passed to his second-in-command, General Rochambeau. Rochambeau was able to temporarily stabilize the military situation, thanks to the arrival of reinforcements from France and the slackening of the yellow fever epidemic that followed the end of the hot summer weather. Some whites began to think that the worst of the struggle was over. In February 1803, the merchant Jean-Joseph Borie in Cap Français ordered a shipment of goods including feather plumes for officers' helmets and fancy scarves for women, confidently telling his correspondents in Bordeaux that "they will bring me a pretty profit"; he dreamed of returning to France with a retinue of black servants.[19]

While the possibility of the reinstatement of slavery was a dream for Borie, it was a nightmare for the island's black population. The violence unleashed by the French expedition shattered the lives of members of all racial groups and overturned the new patterns of life that had begun to emerge after the abolition of slavery in 1793. In the northern coastal town of Port-de-Paix, for example, inhabitants lost their homes when the local black commander, Maurepas, burned the city before abandoning it in February 1802. In October 1802, an army of black *cultivateurs* seized the town and, according to some reports, massacred most of its white male population. Soon afterward, French troops commanded by General Brunet retook it and retaliated by killing as many black soldiers as they could. Traumatized survivors, many of them women, took refuge off the coast, on nearby Tortuga Island, where those who were lucky enough to

Figure 5.1 *The Mode of Exterminating the Black Army as Practised by the French*. From the start of their military invasion of Saint-Domingue in February 1802, the French used brutal tactics against the blacks, including the drowning of prisoners. Black forces retaliated by massacring white civilians and captured French soldiers. The two years of fighting in 1802–3 were the bloodiest phase of the Haitian Revolution. This illustration comes from the English army officer Marcus Rainsford's *An Historical Account of the Black Empire of Hayti*. Published in 1805, this was one of the first books in English about the struggle for Haitian independence.
Source: Courtesy of the John Carter Brown Library at Brown University.

have appropriate documents or testimonials from white acquaintances besieged the local notary, a refugee himself, to get certificates attesting that they had been legally free before Sonthonax's emancipation decree of August 1793, hoping that such papers would protect their freedom if the French won.[20]

Dessalines and the Growth of Resistance

The respite for the French during the winter of 1802–3 was only tempo-
rary. Although military action was limited, the insurrection was becoming better organized under the leadership of Dessalines (Figure 5.2), who
was officially proclaimed its overall leader at a meeting in the Arcahaye
plain in May 1803. As the twentieth-century Caribbean historian C. L.
R. James wrote in his classic *Black Jacobins*, Dessalines, in spite of his
frequent resort to brutality, was the leader the movement needed in the
all-out war that had now developed. "Dessalines was a one-sided genius,
but he was the man for this crisis, not Toussaint."[21] Louverture had never
been able to completely abandon his hope of achieving an understanding
with the French and a genuine cooperation between whites and blacks.
Dessalines lacked Louverture's subtlety, but he had a keen sense of the realities of power. He was single-mindedly devoted to defeating the French
and he saw no need for a continuing white presence in the country. Recognizing the importance of unity between the blacks and the mixed-race
population, however, Dessalines reconciled himself with the mixed-race
generals he had fought against during the "war of the knives" and left it
to two of them, Nicolas Geffrard and Pétion, to take control of the south,
the former stronghold of André Rigaud, where widespread revolts among
the local black *cultivateurs* had already undermined the French position.

For the first time since the start of the Haitian Revolution, the revolutionary movements representing the two non-white groups were finally united. Their goal was no longer to protect the rights the French
had granted them during the republican period, but instead to drive
the French out of Saint-Domingue entirely and make it an independent country. Writing to the governor of Jamaica in June 1803, Dessalines
told him, "all the ties that bound Saint-Domingue to France have been
broken."[22] As a sign of their determination the insurgents, now calling
themselves the "indigenous army," that is, the army of the native inhabitants of the island, abandoned the French tricolor flag, which they had
continued to use in 1802, and adopted a flag with just two stripes, one red
and one blue, symbolizing the union of the black and mixed-race populations and the exclusion of the whites.[23] Although the alliance among the
black and mixed-race leaders put an end to one of the most serious divisions among the population, conflicts between the generals directing the
organized opposition to the French and the leaders of the popular movements that had broken out in many parts of the countryside continued.

Figure 5.2   *Dessalines, the First Emperor of Haiti, in His Dress Uniform*. A contemporary portrait of Jean-Jacques Dessalines, the tough-minded leader who replaced Toussaint Louverture as leader of the black movement in 1802. Haitians remember him as the hero who defeated the French and proclaimed Haiti's independence. The elaborate costume he adopted symbolized the distance that he and the other formerly enslaved blacks had traveled in the course of the Haitian Revolution.
Source: Courtesy of the John Carter Brown Library at Brown University.

The rebel leader Sans-Souci, for example, who had fought against Christophe during the period when the black generals were supporting Leclerc, refused to subordinate himself to his former enemy. Christophe reacted by having Sans-Souci assassinated, and his followers retaliated by killing Paul Louverture, Toussaint Louverture's brother.

The divisions within the insurgent movement foreshadowed conflicts that would break out after the proclamation of Haitian independence, but they did not slow down the war against the French. The last French hopes of retaining the colony disappeared in the spring of 1803, with the renewal of the war with Britain. Neither government had fully trusted the other to live up to the terms of the peace treaty they had signed in March 1802, and by the beginning of the following year it was clear that hostilities would soon resume again. A year of peace had not been enough for France to rebuild its navy, and Napoleon knew that he would have to abandon his plans for a Caribbean empire centered on Saint-Domingue. His decision had momentous consequences for the United States. In early April 1803, having concluded that he had no chance of keeping the Louisiana territory, Napoleon directed his diplomats to offer to sell it to the young American republic, hoping to obtain some money for the coming war and to gain a grateful ally in his struggle against the British. The black uprising in Saint-Domingue, which had prevented Napoleon from consolidating French control of Louisiana, was thus crucial in opening the way for American expansion to the west. In Saint-Domingue itself, Rochambeau realized that he would not receive any more reinforcements. As soon as war was officially declared in May 1803, British ships began blockading the island's harbors, cutting off supplies, and British agents promised support to Dessalines's forces.

The last months of the French struggle in Saint-Domingue were grim ones for the population on both sides. As the number of his troops diminished, Rochambeau abandoned outlying settlements, concentrating on the defense of Port-au-Prince and Cap Français. Outside of Jérémie, in a region that white plantation-owners had successfully defended throughout the revolutionary period, furious whites almost lynched the French military commander when he announced that he had been ordered to withdraw his men. With no other hope of winning the war, Rochambeau resorted to a policy of terror, directed not only at his armed opponents but also at the civilians within his own lines. He had long detested the men of mixed race; according to a widely reported story, on one occasion he threw an elaborate party for a group of mixed-race women and then took them into a room where the bodies of their murdered husbands and brothers had been laid out. He accused the whites of not doing enough to help him, and had a Cap Français merchant who had objected to paying an emergency tax to help support the army shot. Black prisoners were executed en masse, provoking Dessalines to retaliate by hanging hundreds of captured French soldiers. An English officer who observed some of the last months of the war accused Rochambeau of unleashing savage dogs to tear helpless prisoners apart.[24] As the French hopes of victory collapsed,

Rochambeau continued to throw elaborate balls and entertainments for his officers and to pursue a very public courtship with a married woman, Leonora Sansay, whose novel about the last days of Cap Français, *Secret History, or The Horrors of Saint-Domingue*, vividly recreates the bizarre atmosphere of life in the besieged city.[25]

The French abandoned Port-au-Prince on 9 October 1803. On 18 November 1803, Dessalines's forces defeated the French at the battle of Vertières outside of Cap Français, leaving the city defenseless. Seeing that further resistance was hopeless, General Rochambeau and his troops gave themselves up to the British naval forces blockading the harbor, who took them back to England as prisoners. Napoleon's ill-advised effort to reimpose French authority in Saint-Domingue had cost the lives of some 50,000 French soldiers and sailors, and perhaps an equal or greater number of fighters on the side of the insurgents and civilians. The debacle was the worst defeat a French army had suffered since the early years of the Revolution, and it foreshadowed the disasters Napoleon would encounter in Spain after 1808 and in Russia in 1812. In his memoirs, dictated after his fall from power in 1815, Napoleon would look back on the decision to try to impose French authority in Saint-Domingue by force as one of his greatest mistakes. At the time, however, his tight control over the French press prevented the disaster from becoming a public issue. Within a few years, his stunning victories over rival European armies overshadowed the embarrassing failure in the Caribbean in French minds.

Creating Haiti

Having achieved their remarkable military victory, the black leaders were faced with the challenge of creating a new nation. Aided by educated secretaries who, ironically, produced documents that borrowed heavily from the bombastic rhetoric of the French they had just defeated, Dessalines and his colleagues drafted an initial proclamation, dated 29 November 1803, which was widely published in the newspapers in the United States and that suggested that they would continue many of Toussaint Louverture's policies. While announcing their independence and vowing never to tolerate the return of slavery, they still referred to the territory by its French name of Saint-Domingue. The three generals who signed the proclamation – Dessalines, Christophe, and Clervaux – apologized for the deaths of innocent whites during the fighting and promised to let white property-owners who had fled return to their plantations, provided that they "acknowledged the lawfulness of the cause for which we have been spilling our blood these twelve years."[26]

A subsequent document, dated 1 January 1804 and issued in the name of Dessalines alone, announced a more radical break with the past (Figure 5.3). According to legend, it was drafted by a young French-educated man of mixed race, Louis Boisrond-Tonnerre, who supposedly insisted that "in order to draw up our act of independence, we need the skin of a white to serve as a parchment, his skull as an inkwell, his blood for ink, and a bayonet for a pen."[27] Addressing the soldiers of his "indigenous army," Dessalines announced that the country would be called Haiti, an old Taino Indian name for the island of Hispaniola. By adopting this name, Dessalines and his colleagues identified their new nation with the island's original inhabitants and symbolically rejected not only Napoleonic France but the entire legacy of European colonization. Whereas the 29 November 1803 proclamation had struck a conciliatory tone, appealing to Frenchmen of good will, the new document lamented that "the French name still spreads gloom in our country" and denounced "the cruelties of this barbaric people." "There are still French people in our island, and you think yourselves free," Dessalines wrote, menacingly. Even as he warned the remaining French in the island of their coming fate, however, Dessalines was careful to reassure the world that Haiti would not lead an international crusade against slavery. "Let our neighbors breathe in peace," he said.[28] A "Haitian Hymn," written by one of Dessalines's supporters, exalted the victorious general and called on the population to give "Honor to his warrior's valor! Glory to his triumphant efforts!" because he had "assured your rights forever!"[29]

Dessalines had already shown that he meant to rid Haiti entirely of the French presence. Three days after Rochambeau's surrender, on 22 November 1803, he had 800 French prisoners of war who had been too ill to leave the island with the rest of the army put to death.[30] In February and March 1804, he personally supervised the massacre of the remaining white men in the colony, moving from city to city to see that his orders were carried out. As one white survivor of the killings in Jérémie noted, Dessalines compelled the free men of color to take part in them, "in order that they might not say afterwards they were innocent and thus lay all the murders perpetrated on the shoulders of the blacks alone."[31] Women and children were initially spared, but Dessalines eventually decided that they, too, needed to be eliminated. Many of his black soldiers balked at

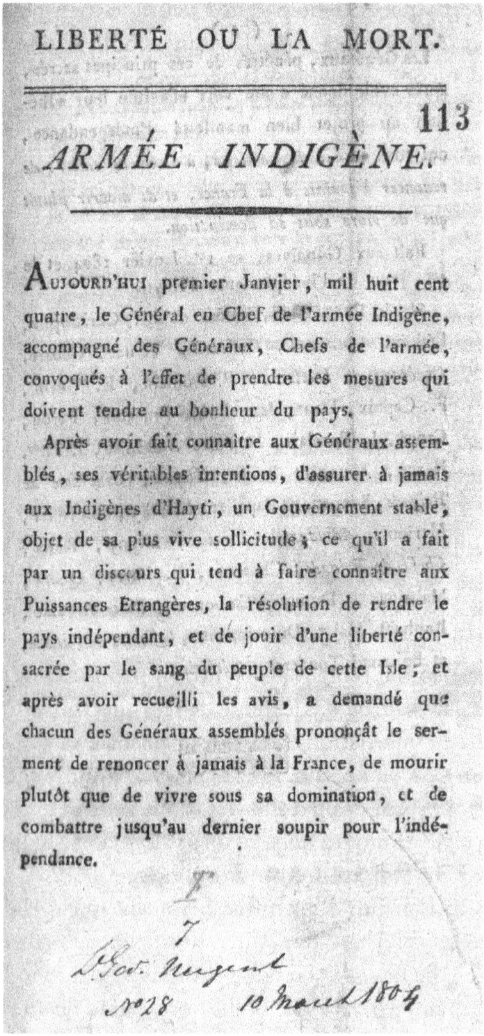

LIBERTÉ OU LA MORT.

113

ARMÉE INDIGÈNE.

Aujourd'hui premier Janvier, mil huit cent quatre, le Général en Chef de l'armée Indigène, accompagné des Généraux, Chefs de l'armée, convoqués à l'effet de prendre les mesures qui doivent tendre au bonheur du pays.

Après avoir fait connaitre aux Généraux assemblés, ses véritables intentions, d'assurer à jamais aux Indigènes d'Hayti, un Gouvernement stable, objet de sa plus vive sollicitude ; ce qu'il a fait par un discours qui tend à faire connaitre aux Puissances Etrangères, la résolution de rendre le pays indépendant, et de jouir d'une liberté consacrée par le sang du peuple de cette Isle ; et après avoir recueilli les avis, a demandé que chacun des Généraux assemblés prononçât le serment de renoncer à jamais à la France, de mourir plutôt que de vivre sous sa domination, et de combattre jusqu'au dernier soupir pour l'indépendance.

Figure 5.3 The Haitian Declaration of Independence, 1804. The discovery of an original printed copy of the Haitian Declaration of Independence in 2010, by the American scholar Julia Gaffield, caused great excitement. The Haitian declaration was only the second such act, following the American Declaration of Independence of 1776, and the first to assert the right of a non-white population to govern itself.

Source: The National Archives, UK, courtesy of Julia Gaffield.

this order, but by the end of April the white population had been virtually wiped out. Only a few doctors and other professionals were spared, along with a small number of Polish soldiers who had come to Saint-Domingue with Napoleon's expedition but deserted from the army, and a colony of German farmers who had been allowed to settle in the northwest of the island before the revolution. Far from trying to keep the massacres secret, Dessalines justified them in a public proclamation, announcing "We have given these true cannibals war for war, crimes for crimes, outrages for outrages. Yes, I have saved my country, I have avenged America."[32] In his mind, the killings were a brutal form of *Realpolitik*, necessary for Haiti's security: as long as there were French in the island, the former metropole might be able to use them to undermine the unity between blacks and people of color.

At the same time as he ruthlessly eliminated the remaining French population, Dessalines was eager to promote relations with other white countries, even those that permitted slavery. The British had supported the black forces against the French during the war, blockading Saint-Domingue's ports to prevent the arrival of supplies and reinforcements; they and the Americans were happy to continue trading with the new country, and the British even proposed signing a trade treaty with the new country, although Dessalines rejected their demand that Haiti limit its trade with other nations.[33] Determined to insist on Haiti's equality with France, Dessalines decided, when he learned that Napoleon was about the declare himself emperor, that the ruler of Haiti should have the same rank. In May 1805, he promulgated a written constitution, declaring himself emperor, and the country "sovereign and independent of all other powers in the universe." As Toussaint Louverture had done in 1801, Dessalines emphasized that "slavery is abolished forever" and that all citizens, regardless of skin color, were to have equal rights. Since any distinction of color "among children of a single family, whose father is the head of state, must necessarily cease, Haitians will be known from now on only under the generic name of 'blacks,'" the constitution announced. These were momentous initiatives; they made Haiti the first country in the world to make the abolition of slavery and of racial distinctions into constitutional principles. To forestall any future return of the whites, the constitution prohibited them from acquiring property in the country. This provision became one of the defining principles of Haitian independence; its cancellation during the occupation of the country by the United States in the early twentieth century still rankles with many Haitians.

Whereas the 1805 constitution took a strong stand against slavery and racial hierarchy, it offered the new nation's citizens few protections against arbitrary rule by their own government. Already, in his declaration of 1 January 1804, Dessalines had warned the population that "if ever you refused or grumbled while receiving those laws that the spirit guarding your fate dictates to me for your own good, you would deserve the fate of an ungrateful people."[34] Dessalines's constitution did not have the moralistic tone of Toussaint Louverture's document; Catholicism was no longer recognized as the state religion, although Dessalines was as hostile to the popular cult of *vodou* as Louverture had been, and divorce was explicitly permitted. On the other hand, however, Dessalines's plan went further than Louverture's in creating a militarized state. A citizen had to be a "good soldier," a provision that effectively excluded women from full citizenship, the territory was divided into six military divisions, and all generals were automatically members of the Council of State. Unlike the 1801 constitution, the 1805 document made no provision for any kind of legislative council to limit the power of the emperor, who was entitled to make laws, collect taxes, command the armed forces, and name his own successor. Whereas the 1801 constitution had mentioned a system of censorship as a limitation on press freedom and had guaranteed the right of petition, the 1805 constitution was completely silent about civil and political rights. In separate regulations, Dessalines continued the system of forced labor that Toussaint Louverture had created. The 1805 constitution thus maintained and even intensified the authoritarian tendencies of the "Louverturian state" that Dessalines's predecessor had erected.

A Historic Rupture

Although Dessalines's Haiti was hardly a model of democracy, it was nevertheless a revolutionary rupture in the history of the American world. Marcus Rainsford, a British officer who had visited the island in 1799, rushed into print in 1805 with his *Historical Account of the Black Empire of Hayti*, in order to underline the importance of what had happened. "It is on ancient record, that Negroes were capable of repelling their enemies, with vigour, in their own country; and a writer of modern date has assured us of the talents and virtues of these peoples; but it remained for the close of the eighteenth century to … exhibit, a horde of Negroes emancipating themselves from the vilest slavery, and at once filling the relations of society, enacting laws, and commanding armies, in the colonies of Europe," he wrote.[35] For white visitors, such as the American Condy Raguet, who was in Cap Français in 1804 and again in 1805, it was a shock to have to appear before a black official who treated visitors "with all the dignity and importance of a great man addressing his inferiors"; nowhere in the Atlantic world had whites ever found themselves in such a situation. Raguet's account emphasized the destruction caused by the long years of upheaval in the island, noting the ruinous condition of the former plantations and the poverty of the blacks who were now farming them, but he also commented on "the civility, which one meets with from the peasantry in travelling" and which ran counter to his assumptions about the blacks' backwardness. In the towns, he found men with "a degree of politeness and urbanity of manners scarcely conceivable," and he devoted a long chapter to the women of the country, pointing out that, in contrast to middle-class white women in the United States, "they are enabled to support themselves respectably, and to be highly useful to their country through their various employments."[36] In short, contrary to what most whites assumed would necessarily happen if blacks tried to form a country of their own, Raguet's letters showed that the new republic of Haiti was a functioning society, with a government, an economy, and a civilization of its own.

The long struggle that had begun with the twin uprisings of enslaved blacks and free men of color in August 1791 had finally culminated in the creation of an independent black-ruled state. In 1805, however, the future of Haiti remained uncertain. The dictatorial government Dessalines had created depended on the loyalty of the army and the unity of its commanders, many of whom had been enemies of the newly proclaimed emperor at earlier points in their careers. The conflict of interests between a rural black population eager to pursue their own interests and to manage their own lives, and a governing elite that still dreamed of restoring the profitable plantation system for its own benefit remained a critical problem. Napoleon's army had been defeated and, as long as France remained at war with Britain, there was little possibility of another invasion by the country's former rulers, but the European war would not last forever, and Haiti's rulers had to reckon with the prospect that France would some day try to recover the jewel of its overseas empire. For the moment, the other main powers in the Caribbean – Britain, the United States, and the Spanish empire – were willing to tolerate the new black nation, but all of them were slave powers that were bound to regard its principles as subversive. While the victory of 1804 had ended the military phase of the Haitian struggle for independence, the fate of the Haitian Revolution would remain unsettled for decades to come.

6

Consolidating Independence in a Hostile World

The Haitian declaration of independence issued on 1 January 1804 and Dessalines's constitution of 1805 are usually seen as the culmination of the series of events that has come to be called the Haitian Revolution. By defeating the French and eliminating almost all of the white population, the black and mixed-race inhabitants of Saint-Domingue had overthrown the island's old ruling class and opened the way for the creation of a new society from which slavery, the central institution of the old regime, had been completely abolished. The human cost of these achievements was a high one. A survey taken after the declaration of independence in 1804 estimated the population at only 380,000, a drop of almost a third from the figures in 1789. Whereas men had always outnumbered women among the enslaved population before the revolution, women made up the majority of the post-independence population, a sign of how many men had been killed in the fighting.[1] The vast majority of the deaths, certainly running to over 100,000 in the years from 1791 to 1803, had been among the black population. Despite the exaggerated accounts of massacres that circulated at the time, it is probable that the majority of the 30,000 whites in the colony in 1791 managed to escape to safety during the revolution, even though 10,000 may well have died, and the French military expeditions of 1792–3 and 1802–3 cost the lives of some 60,000 soldiers and sailors. The loss of life among the free population of

A Concise History of the Haitian Revolution, Second Edition. Jeremy D. Popkin.
© 2022 John Wiley & Sons Ltd. Published 2022 by John Wiley & Sons Ltd.

color – 28,000 people in 1791 – is harder to quantify, but the men in the group were heavily involved in the fighting at all stages of the revolution and presumably paid as heavy a toll as the members of other groups.

Post-Revolutionary Challenges

The long years of fighting from 1791 to 1803 had also caused considerable damage to property, although this affected the whites more than the victorious blacks, who had no reason to lament the destruction of the costly sugar-processing machinery on the plantations or of the masters' mansions. The island's cities, particularly Cap Français – now renamed Cap Haitien – and Port-au-Prince, had suffered heavily, although their port facilities were still functioning in 1804. The infrastructure built under the colonial regime, however, had been neglected since the start of the revolution. The irrigation systems vital for sugar-growing in drier regions had disintegrated, and many roads had deteriorated so badly that carriages could no longer use them, forcing travelers to go on horseback or by foot. The new nation of Haiti thus inherited little from its colonial past: its population would have to generate the resources to build its future. The survivors of the long years of warfare and disruption from 1791 to 1803 had undoubtedly been deeply changed by their experiences. The revolution had ended the import of new black captives, thus cutting off the constantly renewed connection with African cultures that they had provided. By 1803 there were no more newly arrived *bossales* unfamiliar with life in the Caribbean or the Kreyol language. In the course of the revolution, the distinctions between blacks from different ethnic groups and between *creoles* born in the colony and *bossales* must have become blurred as they all participated together in the fighting and suffered together at the hands of the French. Dessalines's insistence, in his 1805 constitution, that all Haitians, regardless of origin or skin color, now formed a single group reflected a certain reality: the revolution had forged a new national community, although not one as united as Dessalines hoped.

Despite the profound significance of the events of 1804 and 1805, not just for the people of the newly proclaimed nation of Haiti but for the entire western world, it would be a mistake to think that the story of the Haitian Revolution ended with the victory over the French and the establishment of a new "imagined community" of Haitian citizens.[2] Not until the middle of the nineteenth century was it clear what the lasting characteristics of Haitian society and politics would look like. Conflict over the country's future direction soon became so violent that Dessalines, the determined general who had defeated the French, was assassinated. For 14 years, from the beginning of 1807 to 1820, Haiti split apart, as the divisions between blacks and people of mixed race and between the northern and southern regions reasserted themselves in a simmering civil war. Instead of becoming one independent state, Haiti might well have developed into two rival countries.

Internal divisions were not the only threat to the future of the experiment launched in 1804. Despite the conclusiveness of the French defeat, few whites at the time believed that a society governed by people of African ancestry could endure; most assumed that it was just a matter of time before some outside power succeeded in reasserting control over the island. France, Haiti's former colonial overlord, refused to recognize the new country's independence, and former colonists and government officials there continued to discuss plans to reoccupy the territory for several decades after the independence declaration of 1804. In the meantime, the Spanish and Portuguese colonies in central and South America followed Haiti's lead in demanding their own independence, but, like the United States, they refused to recognize the black-ruled island as an equal partner in the new world of independent states that now made up the Americas. Disadvantaged by structural changes in the world economy that doomed any hope of recovering the prosperity of the colonial past, and marginalized by the rising tide of racial prejudice that characterized the nineteenth century, Haiti found itself condemned to a precarious existence from which, many would argue, it has never really been able to escape.

In the first years following independence, Haiti was protected from outside interference because of the ongoing Napoleonic wars. The British navy prevented France from trying to avenge its defeat, and the British government offered to make a trade treaty with Haiti, although Dessalines rejected the proposal on the grounds that it would make the country an economic dependency of the British empire. Even though their governments did not officially recognize Haiti's independence, British and, until Thomas Jefferson's embargo act of 1807 banning foreign trade, American merchants were happy to continue trading with the former French colony, as they had during Toussaint Louverture's years in power.

Despite these signs of the outside world's willingness to accept the existence of Haiti, the new country's rulers feared external threats. They immediately ordered construction of a massive mountaintop fortress, the

Citadelle La Ferrière, outside of Cap Haitien; it still stands today as a symbol of Haitian determination to defend its independence. The biggest threat to Haiti came from the eastern half of its own island. Toussaint Louverture had occupied this territory, the Spanish colony of Santo Domingo, in 1801, but when the other French forces surrendered to Dessalines at the end of 1803, the French general Jean-Louis Ferrand and his small army remained in control of it. The new Haitian government considered Ferrand's forces a serious threat. Their presence allowed France to claim that the fight for control of the island was still ongoing, and their possession of the ports in the eastern half of the island meant that if Napoleon sent a new expedition to attack Haiti, it would be able to land without opposition. Furthermore, in order to restore agricultural production in the Spanish territory, Ferrand maintained slavery there and even announced that prisoners taken in fighting with the Haitians would be considered as slaves.

In February 1805, Dessalines launched an invasion of Santo Domingo. Ferrand rallied the whites and people of color, warning them of their fate if "Dessalines, this rebellious slave, cruel enemy of all who are born free," succeeded. Even the 24,000 enslaved blacks in Santo Domingo were reluctant to welcome the Haitians; accustomed to a very different kind of life with a fair amount of independence on the cattle ranches in the area, they feared being subjected to the Haitian system of forced labor.[3] Nevertheless, Dessalines's forces advanced rapidly through the territory and laid siege to its capital. The appearance of a squadron of French warships, sent across the Altantic in an effort to draw British forces to the Caribbean so that Napoleon could launch an invasion of England, led Dessalines to make a hasty retreat: he feared that a new French invasion was about to begin. Determined to deprive his enemies of any possible resources for such a campaign, he ordered the devastation of the Santo Domingo countryside. Dessalines's failure to conquer Santo Domingo was an embarrassment for him, and the brutalities committed as the Haitian army retreated allowed the country's enemies to reinforce the notion that the new black nation was a dangerous menace to its neighbors. Ferrand's army remained in control of Santo Domingo until 1809, when the population there revolted in protest against Napoleon's invasion of Spain.

The Assassination of Dessalines

The appearance of French ships in 1805 was a false alarm; the main threat facing the new country came from internal conflicts that had been set aside during the struggle against the French. Once he was installed in power, "Dessalines's policies upset everyone," the modern Haitian historian Claude Moïse has written. As early as January 1804, Dessalines had issued decrees meant to limit the pretensions of wealthy landowners, a group that included many of the generals who had acquired plantations during the war, as well as members of the mixed-race population who had fought against him during the "war of the knives" in 1799–1800. Dessalines accused members of the latter group of acting as front men for whites who were still hoping to recover their properties. While he threatened the privileges of the wealthy, Dessalines also lost the support of the rural *cultivateurs* by continuing and intensifying the military discipline imposed on them. Meanwhile, his soldiers grumbled that they were not receiving their pay. In 1806, Alexandre Pétion and Étienne Gérin, two of the mixed-race generals Dessalines had relied on to drive the French out of the South Province, organized a conspiracy to overthrow him. They found support from some of the black generals, including Henry Christophe, the commander-in-chief of the army, who resented Dessalines's one-man rule. A manifesto drawn up by the plotters appealed to all the groups that had suffered under Dessalines's government: "Soldiers, you will be paid and clothed; cultivators, you will be protected; landowners, you will be guaranteed the possession of your properties."[4] On 17 October 1806, the conspirators ambushed and killed Dessalines as he was returning to Port-au-Prince from a trip to the North Province. Several of his closest supporters, including Capois-la-Mort ("Capois-Death"), the hero of the victory at Vertières three years earlier, were also killed.

At the time of his death Dessalines had become extremely unpopular: after his assassination, a crowd tore his body apart. According to legend, it was left to a local madwoman, Défilée-la-folle ("Crazy Défilée"), to gather the scattered remains and bury them. As time passed, however, attitudes toward the man who had rallied the population to defeat the French changed. Eventually, Dessalines became the only Haitian leader to be incorporated into the pantheon of *vodou* spirits or *lwa*, where he is recognized as one of the avatars of the warrior Ogou or Ogun.[5] In contrast to Toussaint Louverture, who had never entirely abandoned the hope of coexistence with the whites and who never took the ultimate step of declaring independence from France, Dessalines was transformed into a symbol of black liberation and national self-assertion. Haiti's national anthem, composed in 1904 to mark the hundredth anniversary of independence, is called "La Dessalinienne," and its words "United let us march! Let there be no traitors in our ranks! Let us be masters of our soil!" recall his ambition of bringing the different groups of the population together and eliminating white claims to property ownership. Whereas Toussaint Louverture remains better known in the world at large, in Haiti it is Jean-Jacques Dessalines, "this proud deity whose courage defied the murderous points of bayonets," as one twentieth-century Haitian historian called him,[6] who is seen as the embodiment of the revolutionary spirit and who is honored with statues and other monuments in the country's cities.

North versus South

The coalition of leaders who had organized the assassination of Dessalines was unable to maintain the unity he had imposed, and immediately fell apart over the question of how to govern the country. Henry Christophe, the black general whose power base was in the north of the country, assumed that he would now become the head of the government, but the southern generals, led by Alexandre Pétion, resisted his effort to assert control over their troops. The southern leaders packed the constitutional convention summoned to replace Dessalines's 1805 document and rammed through their own plan, which offered Christophe a position as a figurehead president while vesting real power in a Senate that his opponents would control. Had it succeeded, this plan would have substituted the rule of an oligarchy for the practice of one-man rule instituted by Toussaint Louverture and continued by Dessalines. While the country's small property-owning elite would have dominated the political system under the 1806 constitution, the tendency toward military dictatorship that had developed during the revolution might have been tempered. Instead, however, Christophe rejected the proposed constitution and established his own government, modeled after Dessalines's military regime, in the regions he controlled. His opponents then elected Pétion as the president of the southern part of the country. As open fighting developed between the two rival governments, the Senate transferred many of its powers to Pétion, thus establishing its own version of one-man rule. In 1816, a new constitution drawn up in the south gave Pétion the title of president for life, setting a pattern followed by most Haitian rulers in the first two-thirds of the nineteenth century.

The split between Christophe's government in the north and Pétion's in the south has often been described as a revival of the conflict between blacks and men from the mixed-race population, similar to the conflict between Toussaint Louverture and André Rigaud during the revolution. As in that period, the conflict did not entirely follow racial boundaries. The majority of the population in the south, including most of Pétion's soldiers, were black, whereas Christophe's inner circle of advisors included a number of educated men of mixed race. Nor did either side control a solid block of territory. A black leader named Goman seized control of the Grande Anse at the tip of the long southern peninsula and held it against Pétion's forces until 1819, and when the former mixed-race leader André Rigaud returned from France in 1810, he led much of the South Province in a breakaway movement that was only ended by his death in 1811. Meanwhile, for some years Christophe had to face a rebellion from supporters of Pétion in the island's northwestern region.

Neither Haitian state was able to gain a significant advantage over the other in the periodic rounds of fighting that broke out along their frontier in the West Province's Artibonite valley. Both tried to enlist support from the British, who controlled the seas around the island from their neighboring colony of Jamaica, but the British were happy to keep Haiti in a weakened condition by preventing either government from unifying the country under its control. Through pamphlets and newspapers, the two rival Haitian states also waged ideological war against each other. The southern government proclaimed itself a republic, identifying itself with the liberal principles of the western world, whereas Christophe converted the north into a kingdom in 1811, importing elaborate coronation robes from England and awarding noble titles to his main advisors. His propagandists claimed the heritage of Dessalines, insisting that Haiti needed a strong ruler to defend the country's independence.[7] After proclaiming himself king, Christophe built an elaborate palace at Milot, just below the fortress of La Citadelle. The ruins of this palace of Sans-Souci ("Without a care") still stand today, and together with the fortress, they are one of Haiti's main tourist attractions.

Both governments had to deal with the longstanding tension between the rural population's ambition to set up their own farms and the elite's desire to restore the profitable plantation system. Perhaps because he had a harder time maintaining the loyalty of his largely black army, Pétion proved more willing to break up plantations confiscated from white owners and distribute the land to the military, allowing even rank-and-file soldiers to establish small family farms. He continued to protect the large properties of the members of his own group, the *anciens libres*, however, and the result was a society divided between small farmers, mostly black, and large landowners, mostly of mixed race. Christophe was critical of Pétion's policy, which resulted in a drop in the production of export crops, and tried harder to prevent the breakup of the former plantations. Neither ruler was able to stop the process by which, as one recent historian has put it, the rural population went "maroon," escaping from the constraints of the market economy in order to make themselves subsistence farmers and ignoring government efforts to control them.[8]

Although he spent lavishly to glorify his rule, Christophe also made greater efforts than Pétion to improve education and medical care in his territories. Born in the British colony of Grenada and able to speak English, Christophe admired the British and even considered making English the official language of his kingdom. He cultivated contacts with the leaders of the British abolitionist movement and asked them to send teachers and doctors to the country. Whereas Christophe's goal, in theory, was to provide basic education for the entire population, Pétion's regime pursued an educational policy that concentrated on providing European-style schooling for the children of elite families. The decision that school instruction should be exclusively in French created a language barrier for most of the population, and set a pattern that has continued in Haiti down to the present day.

The Price of French Recognition

Although neither Christophe nor Pétion was willing to yield in the conflict dividing the island, both were united in resisting the prospect of a return of French rule. That possibility re-emerged following the defeat of Napoleon in 1814 and the restoration of the Bourbon monarchy under Louis XVI's brother, Louis XVIII. After the peace congress in Vienna, Britain, which had occupied Martinique and Guadeloupe again after the resumption of the war in 1803, returned them to the French, with their systems of slavery intact, and all the European powers recognized France's continuing claim to Saint-Domingue and its right to use force to recover it. Former plantation-owners were well represented in the French Restoration government; many of them were optimistic that Pétion and his mixed-race supporters would agree to put themselves under French authority in order to defeat Christophe.

When French agents tried to open negotiations with them, however, both rival Haitian governments rejected any proposals to renounce the freedom from slavery and the independence that had been won at such a high cost. In 1816 Christophe told one would-be French representative that "the Haitians will be unanimous on this point at least, to fight to extinction rather than submit again to the yoke of France and slavery."[9] Christophe's spokesman, the Baron de Vastey, published one of the first comprehensive condemnations of European colonialism written by a non-white author, indignantly denouncing it as nothing more than a conspiracy to oppress people of color throughout the world. Haiti's independence, he wrote, was only the first success for a movement in which "five hundred million men, black, yellow and brown, spread over the surface of the globe, are reclaiming the rights and privileges which they have received from the author of nature."[10] While Pétion was equally adamant in defending Haitian independence, he did suggest to the French that Haiti might be willing to compensate the former plantation-owners for their lost lands in order to obtain official recognition of its independence.

Eventually, a version of Pétion's proposal would become the basis for the acceptance of Haiti's independence, but for some years, under the pressure of the colonial lobby in the metropole, the French government rejected the idea. Meanwhile, the environment around Haiti was changing in important ways. When it proclaimed its independence in 1804, Haiti had been the only American territory outside of the United States that had freed itself from colonial rule. When Napoleon invaded Spain in 1808, however, revolts broke out in that country's American colonies. At the same time, the Portuguese royal family fled from the French and took refuge in its South American colony of Brazil. Initially, the "Americanos" who tried to seize power in the Spanish colonies proclaimed their loyalty to the deposed king of Spain, Fernando VII, but when the Spanish monarchy was restored in 1814 and attempted to reassert its control over its American territories, the local leaders who had emerged in the intervening years began to demand the right to govern themselves.

The most important of the Latin American revolutionaries, Simón Bolívar, took refuge in Pétion's Haitian republic in 1816, where he admired the authoritarian system of government; in exchange for helping him, Pétion made Bolívar promise that slavery would be abolished if he succeeded in establishing a free republic in South America. Addressing the congress drawing up a constitution for the new nation of Venezuela in 1819, Bolívar referred to the example of Haiti in urging them to abolish slavery, insisting that "one cannot be simultaneously free and enslaved except by violating at one and the same time the natural law, the political laws, and the civil laws."[11] Although the independence of the major Latin

American countries would not be fully established until the early 1820s, and slavery would not be ended in many of them until decades later, it was clear that the days of colonial rule in most of the region were numbered. In the face of this situation, French dreams of recovering Haiti looked increasingly unrealistic.

In these same years, important events were also taking place in Haiti itself. Pétion, named president for life of the southern republic in 1816, died in 1818, and was replaced by Jean-Pierre Boyer, another veteran mixed-race military officer who, like Pétion, had been involved in the insurrection launched by members of that group in 1791. Boyer succeeded in defeating the long-lasting Goman insurrection in 1819, thus bringing the whole of the south under his rule. He also seized the opportunity that presented itself in 1820, when Christophe, the ruler of the rival northern kingdom, suffered a stroke. In his weakened condition, Christophe was unable to prevent the outbreak of a mutiny in his own army and a general refusal to submit to his authoritarian rule. When Christophe committed suicide in his royal palace at Sans-Souci, Boyer quickly moved to occupy the north with his own forces, bringing the civil war that had begun in 1820 to an end (Figure 6.1). After eliminating Christophe's remaining loyalists, often by brutal methods, Boyer further expanded his territory in 1822 by occupying the eastern part of the island, the former Spanish colony of Santo Domingo. For the next 22 years Haiti was a much larger country than it is today, with a substantial Spanish-speaking population.

Boyer's success in bringing the whole island under his control made it clear to the French government that there was no realistic possibility of reconquering France's former colony by force. As the former Spanish colonies in South and Central America moved toward full independence, and as the United States announced a policy, the "Monroe Doctrine," of opposing any effort by European powers to impose their authority in the New World, French attention shifted to making sure that Haiti did not fall into the British or American spheres of economic influence. In spite of the French government's refusal to recognize its independence, trade between Haiti and its former imperial overlord had increased steadily after 1815; by the early 1820s, the island was furnishing France with half of its supply of coffee. For domestic reasons, however, the French government decided that it could not simply recognize Haitian independence without obtaining compensation for the former white colonists and their heirs, who constituted an influential lobby in French politics. In early 1825, the French government implemented a controversial plan to reimburse former French nobles for the property confiscated from them

Figure 6.1   Guillaume Guillon Lethière (1760–1832), *Le Serment des Ancêtres.*
Haitian memory highlights the agreement reached between the leaders of the black
and free colored movements, Jean-Jacques Dessalines and Alexandre Pétion, in 1802.
The union between the two groups paved the way for the final defeat of the French
in 1803 and the independence of Haiti. In 1806, however, Pétion helped organize the
assassination of Dessalines, which led to the division of the country into two rival
states. This painting, made after General Boyer reunified Haiti in 1820, served to
legitimize Boyer's claim that his regime, dominated by members of the light-skinned
minority, was the continuation of the struggle for freedom that had begun in 1791.
Source: Port-au-Prince, Musée national, © RMN/Gerard Blot.

during the French Revolution. Not wanting to leave the former Saint-
Domingue colonists as the only group that did not receive anything for
their losses, but unwilling to take on the additional expense of paying
them, the French put pressure on Haiti to compensate them. Boyer, for

his part, was eager to find a compromise that would end Haiti's diplomatic isolation.

Boyer was willing to consider paying some compensation to the former colonists for their lost lands, although not for their slaves, who, he pointed out, had been emancipated in 1793 by officials representing the French government, but he balked at the terms the French proposed. To break the deadlock, the French government finally dispatched a naval squadron, which arrived in Haiti in the spring of 1825. Its commander brought with him an ordinance drafted unilaterally by the French government that imposed very harsh terms on the Haitians. In exchange for French recognition of its independence, Haiti would have to pay an indemnity of 150 million French francs to the ex-colonists and allow importers of French goods to pay only half the tariffs charged on imports from other countries. If Haiti did not fulfill these commitments, the French reserved the right to withdraw their recognition of its independence. Boyer was warned that if he rejected the French ultimatum the French would bombard Port-au-Prince. These terms were so one-sided that Boyer kept them secret from the Haitian population. Nevertheless, he decided that he had no choice but to accept the French conditions, hoping to revise them later. The French government helped the Haitians negotiate a loan from French banks to cover the cost of the indemnity. Announcing the agreement, Boyer told Haitians that it "will legalize, in the eyes of the World, the rank that you have achieved, and to which Providence called you."[12]

The Consequences of the 1825 Arrangement

The financial terms of the 1825 arrangement proved impossible for Haiti to meet. Both the French officials who drafted it and Boyer himself still thought that, given peace and access to the French market, the island would quickly regain the prosperity it had known in the colonial era. In fact, however, sugar production in the island never recovered from the disruption of the revolution. Sugar cultivation had shifted to Cuba and Brazil, where growers used more efficient methods to process the cane; with a population unwilling to submit to disciplined labor in the fields and without resources to invest in the industry, Haiti could not compete with them. After 1825, the boom in coffee prices that had followed the end of the Napoleonic war came to an abrupt end as other countries began to produce the beans and flooded the market. By late 1826 Haiti was already in default on its loan payments. Boyer fended off French threats of direct intervention by arguing that if his government was overthrown Haitian payments would cease altogether. At several points in the 1830s, French military officials urged their government to take stronger action to force the Haitians to fulfill their promises, but the French government, more concerned about its new colonial venture in the North African territory of Algeria, which France had occupied in 1830, decided against the use of force. In 1838 Haiti and France agreed to a revised version of the 1825 arrangement. The amount of the indemnity was reduced and the time for repayment stretched out; in return, France finally renounced any threat of military intervention in Haiti. In legal terms, it was only with this agreement that Haiti finally achieved full recognition of its independence. Payments on the debt continued until 1883, and the French government finally certified that Haiti had paid off the indemnity in 1893. (Claims that the Haitians were still making payments to France until the mid-twentieth century confuse the payments required by the 1825 agreement with payments on a loan that Haiti was forced to take out during the American occupation of the country from 1915 to 1934. Those payments continued until 1947.)[13]

As Haitians today point out, their country was thus forced to purchase grudging recognition of the independence its people had won on the battlefield by going heavily into debt. The terms imposed on Haiti in 1825 were an early example of "neocolonialism," a strategy under which more developed countries continue to exploit poorer parts of the world even after conceding formal independence to their former colonies. The spectacle of an impoverished, largely black country having to struggle to pay off the descendants of former white slaveowners is certainly an ugly one. As the date of the bicentennial of Haitian independence approached in 2003, the Haitian president at the time, the radical populist Jean-Bertrand Aristide, launched a campaign to demand that France reimburse Haiti for the cost of the indemnity imposed in 1825, plus accumulated interest that Aristide calculated brought the reparations due to his country to some 21 billion dollars. "We're not looking for pity, no, but for you to acknowledge that we have the right to recuperate a part of what has been stolen from us," Aristide said.[14] The French government rejected Aristide's demand, and French irritation with him for raising the issue has been cited as one reason why that country joined the United States in forcing him to leave office in February 2004. How much the 1825 indemnity, as opposed to other factors such as the fall of the price of coffee and internal instability, contributed to the present-day impoverishment of Haiti is difficult to calculate. Haiti's economic condition was actually better during the mid-nineteenth century, when it was still making indemnity payments, than in the years following 1890, when the loan had been paid off but when foreign financial interests gained increased influence in the country.[15] Nevertheless, the memory of the one-sided arrangement imposed by France, which likes to call itself "the country of the Rights of Man," on the Haitian people, who had had to struggle so hard against the French to gain those rights, remains a bitter one.

In Boyer's mind, the main reason for accepting the onerous terms of the 1825 arrangement was that it enabled Haiti to break out of the international isolation in which the country had been confined since 1804. Until France abandoned its claims to its former colony, Haitians traveling outside the country had no legal protection and foreign investors were reluctant to do business there. Even the newly independent Spanish-speaking republics, not wanting to antagonize France, had refused to acknowledge Haiti's independence, excluding the country from a Pan-American Congress held in Panama in 1826. Other European and Latin American countries followed France's lead in recognizing Haiti's sovereignty, although the United States, under the influence of politicians from the southern slave states, refused to do so until 1862, in the midst of the American Civil War. Haiti's small but influential light-skinned elite, of which Boyer himself was a member, also welcomed the restoration of cultural ties with the former metropole. As in the colonial period, they were now able to send their children to be educated in France. In spite of bitter memories of the war for independence, French culture still served as the model that educated Haitians wanted to emulate. "The highest compliment which it is possible to offer to a Haytien black is ... that he resembles a Frenchman in his personal manners," an American visitor in the 1830s noted.[16] Members of this educated elite considered themselves naturally suited to govern the country and to serve as "guides" for the majority of the black population, who remained illiterate and spoke only Kreyol. Although all Haitians recognized their African ancestry, there were few contacts between the black republic in the Americas and the continent from which those ancestors had come. Educated Haitians, eager to establish their status as part of the "civilized" western world, adopted European prejudices toward the black populations of Africa.

Haiti under President Boyer

The quarter-century of Boyer's rule, from 1818 until his overthrow in 1843, was one of the longest periods of political stability in Haiti's history. To the recently emancipated black population in the nearby island of Jamaica, "a society waiting for evidence of what the Negro race can do and become," Haiti under his rule was an inspiration.[17] Boyer followed in the tradition of one-man rule begun by Toussaint Louverture and continued by Dessalines, Christophe, and Pétion, and his government certainly favored the interests of the wealthy, light-skinned descendants of the pre-revolutionary "men of color." The army also continued to play a central role in national life. Even after 1825, Boyer argued that a large military was necessary to ward off a possible French invasion. His control over the army allowed Boyer to tolerate the existence of a largely powerless parliament and other civil institutions; he knew that he could count on the troops to back him in any conflict. In this respect, Haiti resembled the newly independent nations of Latin America, which also tended to be controlled by lighter-skinned property-owners and by strongmen depending on military support.

The Rural Code Boyer issued in 1826, even longer and more elaborate than the series of ordinances regulating farm labor begun by Sonthonax and Polverel in 1793 and carried on by Toussaint Louverture and Dessalines, officially classified the rural population as a distinct group with limited rights and subject to special regulations. Boyer also oversaw the introduction of comprehensive codes of civil and criminal law, heavily influenced by the French law codes enacted under Napoleon. Among other things, Haiti copied the French laws that prevented women from owning property in their own name and subjected them to the authority of their fathers or husbands. Despite the undemocratic features of its various law codes, Haiti thus took its place among the "civilized" nations of the period; on paper, at least, the powers of government and the rights of citizens were regulated by written laws, even if those laws were not always respected. As an African American journalist wrote in 1827, "the people have a regular and enlightened government of the republican form – more liberal, perhaps, in its operation than any now existing in Europe … The public offices are filled by native citizens of talents and character – they have their judges and courts, and other establishments like ourselves."[18] At a time when even such major European powers as Austria, Prussia, and Russia still lacked any form of written constitution or parliamentary institutions, post-revolutionary Haiti was certainly not a "backward" country.

The Rural Code was connected to the 1825 arrangement with France, since Boyer argued that a restoration of the plantation system would be necessary to raise income-producing crops to pay off the debt the country had contracted. In fact, however, like his predecessors, Boyer was unable to enforce his regulations. In spite of Boyer's laws, rural Haiti continued to evolve, as it had since the beginning of the revolution, in the direction of a peasant society, with individual families occupying land without legal title, cultivating crops to feed themselves and producing coffee as a source of cash income. Successful farmers consolidated their holdings and built *lakous*, multi-generational rural households living together under the control of a family patriarch. Although Boyer's regime continued to recognize Catholicism as the state religion, the *lakou* provided a framework for the practice of the *vodou* rituals to which most of the population remained devoted. Despite the harsh inequalities in Haitian society, the standard of living of the rural population was better than that in the other Caribbean islands, where slavery still prevailed.

By the early 1820s, Haiti had also developed a small commercial middle class. At the beginning of the decade, this group's spokesmen campaigned, like business interests in the United States, for tariff protection that would keep them from being undersold by foreign competitors. The Boyer government, however, succumbed to pressure from the British and French to keep tariffs low in exchange for purchasing Haitian export crops. In 1822 Boyer had one particularly outspoken critic, Félix Darfour, arrested and shot for accusing the government of favoring foreigners over its own citizens. The agreement imposed by France in 1825 aggravated Haiti's dependence on foreign commerce by granting favorable terms to imports from France. Haiti's urban elites profited from these arrangements, but they showed no interest in investing in institutions, such as public schools, that would have benefited the poorer classes of the population.

Although both countries were the product of revolutionary uprisings against colonial rule, Haiti cannot fairly be compared to the United States, the most successful of the new American republics born during the western hemisphere's "age of revolutions." Before the revolution, the French colony of Saint-Domingue had been an extreme example of a slave society, in which everything had been done to prevent the majority of the population from acquiring property, literacy, and the experience of self-government. In the United States, despite the importance of slavery, the majority of the population at the time of the revolution consisted of free people who had already constructed a thriving civil society. The United States possessed incomparably greater natural resources and a diversified economy that was not dependent on a small range of export crops. Because of the European origin of most of the population, the United States was quickly accepted as a full participant in the white-dominated world order of the day. Haiti's success in emerging from its revolutionary crisis is more appropriately measured against that of the other countries of Central and South America and the islands of the Caribbean. By those standards, Haiti appeared, as of the early 1840s, to have achieved a modest but respectable level of development.

Despite some successes, the Boyer regime did not fully succeed in putting the country on the path to stability and democracy. Its weaknesses, and the underlying tensions in Haitian society, became evident in 1843, when a group of liberal reformers, frustrated by Boyer's authoritarianism, overthrew his government. The reformers drafted a constitution that called for the end of military rule and a government with a careful balance of powers between the legislature and the president, but they were never able to put it into effect. The population in the Spanish half of the island seized the opportunity to revolt against the Haitian occupation begun in 1822, an ambitious general set up his own government in the north, and a major peasant revolt in the south demanded a fairer distribution of property. In the face of these threats, many of the reformers, themselves members of the country's wealthy elite, abandoned their progressive ideas and called for a government headed by a military strongman to restore order. The Spanish-speaking territory of Santo Domingo was lost for good, reducing Haiti to its present-day dimensions. The Piquet movement, as the peasant revolt in the south was called, showed that democratic ideas had taken root among the population, but the response of Haiti's post-revolutionary elites demonstrated that they were unwilling to take any steps in that direction.[19] By 1847 Haiti had come under the rule of a black general, Faustin Soulouque, who crowned himself emperor in 1848 and instituted a dictatorship that recalled Dessalines's short-lived regime.

Claude Moïse, author of a fundamental study of the history of Haiti's political system, has written that, down to the present, Haiti has continued to alternate between regimes that look back to the authoritarian traditions that first developed during the struggles of the revolutionary period and that were embodied in Pétion's constitution of 1816, which Boyer continued to follow, and the more liberal ideals incorporated in the unsuccessful constitution of 1843.[20] Nevertheless, in the first half of the nineteenth century Haiti's political history was in some ways not that different from that of its former colonial ruler, France, which also saw the repeated failure of movements for greater democracy. In 1851 Napoleon III, nephew of the French leader who had tried and failed to force the blacks of Saint-Domingue back into slavery, copied Faustin Soulouque by overthrowing the democratic Second Republic established three years earlier and proclaiming himself emperor. If Haiti today has fallen behind other countries in terms of its ability to provide a good life for its people, we cannot conclude that this is solely a result of the legacy inherited from its revolution. Instead, the reasons for Haiti's current problems must be sought primarily in more recent historical developments. These include both internal issues – above all, the failure to integrate the poorer classes of the population into society – and external ones, notably the role of foreign economic interests and the intervention of foreign governments, particularly the United States, which occupied Haiti militarily from 1915 to 1934 and has intervened directly in the country on several subsequent occasions.

The Impact of the Haitian Revolution

While the impact of the Haitian Revolution was felt especially in the island itself, the historic events that had taken place there starting in 1791 also affected many other parts of the world. Slavery was such a central institution throughout the Americas that the revolt of 1791 and the declarations of emancipation in 1793 were bound to send shock waves throughout the hemisphere. The Haitians' victory over the French in 1803 and Haiti's declaration of independence in 1804 challenged the notion that white people, because of their supposedly higher level of civilization, were naturally destined to rule the whole world. Haiti's success in defending its independence in the years after 1804, despite the many internal and external problems confronting it, made this challenge a continuing issue. It is no accident that the most thorough and convincing refutation of racist claims about black inferiority to be published in the nineteenth century was the Haitian author Anténor Firmin's *Equality of the Human Races* (1885).

The Haitian Revolution inspired great hopes among enslaved populations elsewhere and among abolitionists in Britain and the United States. It generated corresponding fear among slaveholders and advocates of white superiority. Nevertheless, it is easy to exaggerate the direct impact of the Haitian Revolution. The Haitian Revolution had a limited effect on slavery in other parts of the Americas, and it certainly did not stem the tide of racialist pseudo-science that pervaded the western world throughout the nineteenth century and well into the twentieth. People of African descent in other parts of the Americas did look to Haiti as an inspiration, but no other enslaved black population was able to imitate the Haitian example and free itself. For a long time, the economic interests behind slavery and the cultural investment in racial hierarchy proved more powerful than the liberating inspiration of the Haitian Revolution. Only with the abolition of the last bastions of American slavery in the second half of the nineteenth century and the sweeping movement of decolonization in the mid-twentieth century did it become possible to see the Haitian Revolution as the precursor of a new world.

Even before the achievement of Haitian independence, contact with blacks from the island who had reached the other parts of the Americas may have helped stimulate slave conspiracies such as the Coro uprising in Venezuela and the slave revolt in Curaçao in 1795 and Gabriel's rebellion in Virginia in 1800. After the declaration of Haitian independence in 1804, British abolitionists cited that event to show the necessity of banning the slave trade: if slaveowners knew that they could not import new human chattels, the abolitionists claimed, they would recognize that they needed to improve the treatment of the blacks they held in slavery, and would eventually act on their own to do away with the institution without driving their enslaved workers to the point of violent rebellion. In 1807, 18 years after it had first considered the issue, the British Parliament finally accepted this argument and abolished the slave trade. The legislation committed the British government to put pressure on other countries to follow its lead, so that British colonies would not be disadvantaged compared to their rivals; in 1815, the British insisted that other European countries prohibit their citizens from slave trading as part of the conditions imposed in the Vienna peace treaty. The United States, in accordance with a provision in its own constitution that had been passed in 1788, before the start of the Haitian uprising, cut off the import of new captives from Africa beginning in 1808, as did many of the newly independent countries that broke away from the Spanish empire after 1810. Even if the events in Haiti helped stimulate the passage of the British law, however, it took many decades before the slave trade was actually ended. Other European countries, most notably Portugal, continued to defy pressure to stop slave imports. The all-time record for the number of captives shipped to the Americas in a single year was set in the 1820s, with Brazil as their major destination, and the trade continued to operate without much interference through the 1840s. Not until the second half of the nineteenth century was the Atlantic slave trade finally halted.

If Haitian independence had little immediate effect on the slave trade, it had even less impact on the institution of slavery itself. Despite the Haitian example, the slave societies of the New World expanded more rapidly in the decades after 1804 than ever before. With the help of exiled Saint-Domingue plantation-owners, who found themselves dispersed throughout the Americas, new sugar-producing centers arose in Brazil, Cuba, and Louisiana. Nowhere was the influence from Saint-Domingue greater than in New Orleans, where more than 9,000 refugees – a group that had gone to Cuba in 1803, almost equally divided among whites, free people of color, and enslaved blacks – arrived together in 1809. Expelled from Cuba as part of the Spanish empire's revolt against Napoleon, they joined earlier arrivals from Saint-Domingue and descendants of the French settlers expelled from Acadia (Nova Scotia) in the 1750s to give the region its distinctive French-flavored culture. As the western world's appetite for the product continued to grow, more blacks than ever were put to forced labor raising and processing sugar cane. At the same time, Eli Whitney's invention of the cotton gin in 1794, which facilitated the processing of cotton bolls into fiber ready for spinning, opened the way for an enormous expansion in the growth of another product dependent on slave labor. The United States, which had been the destination for only 4% of the total number of Africans shipped to the Americas, rose to become the country with the largest number of enslaved blacks until the Civil War of 1861–5 resulted in their emancipation. Cuba and Brazil, the two Latin American countries whose slaveholders benefited the most from the opportunities created by the independence of Haiti, were also the last places where slavery was finally abolished, in 1886 and 1889 respectively. For eight decades after 1804, an independent, black-governed Haiti coexisted with flourishing slave societies, some of them, like the Spanish colonies of Cuba and Puerto Rico, where slavery was ended in 1873, only a few miles from its shores.

Just as its success did not lead to the immediate abolition of either the slave trade or slavery itself in other parts of the world, the achievement of Haitian independence in 1804 also did not halt the spread of European colonial empires, but it did help reshape the nature of colonialism. The

Haitian Revolution and the growth of abolitionist sentiment in Britain, France, and the Americas discouraged any idea of creating new overseas slave colonies. Instead, Europeans began to think of ways of obtaining the tropical commodities they wanted by encouraging their production in Africa itself. As Henri Grégoire, a leading defender of abolition during the French Revolution and a staunch supporter of Haitian independence, wrote in 1815, "Certainly France … could and should have brought civilization to the shores of Senegal, where, without regrets and without dangers, she could have created prosperous colonies with rich soil, and closer to the mother country than the Antilles, a part of which has already escaped from her."[21] Under the pretext of bringing prosperity and progress to what they called "the dark continent," Europeans steadily encroached on African autonomy, until by the end of the nineteenth century almost all of Africa had been carved up into European colonies. One of the pretexts Europeans put forward for these intrusions was the need to suppress the slave trade. In its place, however, they introduced various forms of forced labor to compel African populations to produce the products Europeans wanted.

The example of Haiti undoubtedly had some influence on patterns of black resistance to slavery in the Americas in the nineteenth century, although its effects in this regard, too, were somewhat mixed. Enslaved blacks who succeeded in reaching Haiti could claim freedom and become citizens, and some black sailors on ships from the United States did so, although they had to learn a new language and new customs to accommodate themselves to Haitian life. White officials throughout the Americas were convinced that the Haitian example inspired slave conspiracies. The leader of the Aponte conspiracy in Cuba in 1812 had acquired a book with portraits of the leaders of the Haitian uprising, including Toussaint Louverture and Henry Christophe, and used it to inspire his followers.[22] According to one of his supporters, Denmark Vesey, the organizer of a slave plot in South Carolina in 1822, "was in the habit of reading to me all the passages in the newspapers that related to St. Domingo." Another member of the group testified that Vesey had told them "that we were fully able to conquer the whites, if we were only unanimous and courageous, as the St. Domingo people were."[23] Nevertheless, some rebellious blacks saw the Haitian Revolution less as an inspiration than as a model to be avoided. The insurgents whose uprisings in the British colonies of Demerara in 1826 and Jamaica in 1831–2 helped propel the British Parliament to abolish slavery in its colonies in 1833 were careful to prevent their followers from killing whites or destroying their plantations; they made it clear from the start that they sought to negotiate an improvement in their conditions, not to take over or destroy the colonies.[24]

Haiti in the Eyes of the World

Whether or not it inspired them with thoughts of launching their own insurrections, the example of the Haitian Revolution certainly gave blacks in the rest of the Americas a new sense of pride. In his *Appeal to the Coloured Citizens of the World*, published in 1829, David Walker, often considered the founder of black nationalism, hailed Haiti as "the glory of the blacks and terror of tyrants ... They are men who would be cut off to a man, before they would yield to the combined forces of the whole world."[25] Despite his admiration for Haiti, Walker opposed the idea that blacks from the United States should migrate to the black republic, but earlier in the 1820s a movement had been organized to promote that idea. "Go to that *highly favored*, and as yet *only land*, where the sons of Africa appear as a civilized, well-ordered and flourishing nation," one preacher urged.[26] Haitian President Boyer eagerly encouraged the plan, promising to provide land and support for the emigrants, and as many as 6,000 blacks, most of them freedmen from the northern and border states, may have made the trip to the island. For most of the emigrants, unfortunately, Haiti proved a disappointment. Working and living conditions in the tropical heat were arduous, and they had difficulty adjusting to an unfamiliar language and culture. The American blacks, often devout Protestants, reacted strongly against the mixture of Catholicism and *vodou* beliefs that constituted the majority religion in Haiti. Talk of promoting American black settlement in Haiti was revived in the late 1850s, until the outbreak of the Civil War and the abolition of slavery in the United States raised blacks' hopes for a better future in their native country.

While the Haitian Revolution and the existence of an independent black nation were sources of inspiration for black populations in the Americas, they generated fear and concern among whites in the United States and Europe. Through 1804, the events of the Haitian Revolution were regularly covered in the press on both sides of the Atlantic; modern scholars have speculated that the German philosopher G. W. F. Hegel's famous analysis of the "master–slave relationship" and its consequences for the consciousness of both masters and slaves may have been inspired by news reports about the French defeat in 1803, although Hegel never explicitly mentioned Haiti and his comments about black people were generally negative.[27] Interest in the unexpected victory of Dessalines and his troops over the supposedly invincible French army resulted in a flurry of publications in the years immediately after 1804, most of them, like Louis Dubroca's *Life of J. J. Dessalines*, "this monster covered with blood and crimes," very unfavorable to the Haitians. Originally published in Paris, Dubroca's work was translated into many languages, including a Spanish edition put out in Mexico in 1806. Within a few years, however, interest in the subject fell off sharply; what the modern Haitian American scholar Michel-Rolph Trouillot has called the "silencing" of the Haitian Revolution had begun.[28]

The little the white world's collective memory did retain about the events between 1791 and 1804 was almost entirely negative. Passing references to them almost invariably stressed the violence of the black assault on the white population. A French newspaper, reviewing the memoir of a survivor of Dessalines's massacres in 1812, wrote that the former colony of Saint-Domingue had "exceeded all other places in the horrible disasters and the shocking crimes of which it was the theater." The French army, the journalist added, had only been defeated because it had had to fight "a horrible army of Negroes, ten times more numerous than it was ..."[29] Post-revolutionary Haiti was depicted as a poverty-stricken country subject to military dictators. When the agreement of 1825 allowed them to resume direct communication with the country, French opponents of slavery, such as Grégoire, were disappointed to discover that it was not the prosperous democratic society they had imagined. The American author Jonathan Brown, who visited the country in 1833–4, concluded that "as a nation the blacks of St. Domingo are in a retrograde movement as regards intellectual improvement, and no obstacle seems to exist to prevent this descent into barbarism."[30]

On both sides of the Atlantic, interest in Haiti and in the events of the Haitian Revolution was tied to the ongoing debate about the institution of slavery and to the development of theories about racial hierarchy. Even those opposed to slavery, like the great French author Victor Hugo, whose first novel, *Bug-Jargal*, is the story of a noble black man who sacrifices his own life to save a white man and the white woman they both love during the Haitian Revolution, felt obliged to condemn the violence of the Haitian Revolution. The black hero of Hugo's novel, which appeared in 1826 as the French government was finally moving to make its ban on slave trading effective, reproaches the leader of the insurrection, asking "is it necessary … that the only sign of our passage should always be a spot of blood or a blaze of fire?"[31] In 1840 the former Saint-Domingue plantation-owner Peter Chazotte published his memoir of his escape from Dessalines's massacres to refute what he called "the nefarious lies propagated by American fanatics" who wanted to see slavery abolished in the United States.[32] Arthur Gobineau, whose *Moral and Intellectual Diversity of the Races*, published in 1855, was the most influential statement of the theory of white racial superiority for nearly a century, announced that "the history of independent Haiti is nothing but a long series of massacres … the savage instincts of the population reign supreme."[33] A negative view of Haiti and of the revolution that had created it thus became deeply anchored in the white-dominated cultures of the United States and Europe. The abolition of slavery in the remaining French colonies in 1848 and the end of the institution in the United States after the Civil War diminished the outside world's interest in Haiti and its revolutionary past, but did nothing to alter this prejudicial view of the Haitian Revolution.

Although the white world remembered the Haitian Revolution as a time of horrors, it made an exception for the movement's main leader, Toussaint Louverture. As early as 1803, the great British Romantic poet William Wordsworth had hailed the black leader, then languishing in Napoleon's prison, as a martyr for liberty. "Wear … in thy bonds a cheerful brow," Wordsworth urged Louverture. "There's not a breathing of the common wind/That will forget thee: thou hast great allies:/Thy friends are exultations, agonies,/And love, and man's unconquerable mind."[34] White abolitionists in the United States compared Louverture to George Washington, although the black abolitionist William Wells Brown pointed out that "Toussaint liberated his countrymen; Washington enslaved a portion of his." The pioneering British feminist Harriet Martineau's 1839 novel about Louverture, *The Hour and the Man*, was widely read. Even white southerners saluted Louverture, primarily because of his attempts to protect the whites in Saint-Domingue and his willingness to impose a system of forced labor on the black population; one of them called him "the only truly great man yet known of the Negro race."[35]

Writing the History of the Haitian Revolution

At the same time as the white world was making the Haitian Revolution a byword for horror and violence, two Haitian authors were writing the first scholarly histories of the events that had led from the slave uprisings to the country's independence. Thomas Madiou's *Histoire d'Haïti*, published in 1847, and Alexis Beaubrun Ardouin's *Études sur l'histoire d'Haïti*, which appeared in 1853, were both written by members of the country's educated mixed-race elite who had, ironically, been driven into exile in France by the political upheavals of the early 1840s in Haiti. The two authors hated each other – Ardouin claimed that he had written his book to correct the errors in Madiou's work – and both are often criticized today as apologists for the "mulatto" minority to which they themselves belonged; Ardouin in particular repeatedly insisted that his group had a natural mission to protect and civilize the blacks. Nevertheless, both were determined to produce serious works of history that would meet the standards of the leading European scholars of the time, and their works are still indispensable for research on the subject. Madiou and Ardouin both relied largely on French documents, as all historians of the subject have to do, but they used those documents to show that the black and mixed-race insurgents were far different from the bloodthirsty savages depicted in most publications about the country. The history of the Haitian uprising, according to Madiou, was the story of the "African … confronting his master, to whom he owed nothing, with the moral force of a being unjustly treated, and who takes back the rights that he had never consented to yield."[36]

Outside of Haiti, serious scholarship on the Haitian Revolution remained limited until well into the twentieth century. Particularly after the major European powers agreed among themselves, at the Congress of Berlin in 1885, to carve up the African continent into white-ruled colonies, the existence of the black-ruled republic of Haiti appeared to be a historical anomaly. As the United States increased its involvement in the Caribbean region Haiti's very independence was threatened: in 1915 American Marines landed in the island, beginning a military occupation that lasted until 1934. For the descendants of Toussaint Louverture and Jean-Jacques Dessalines, the experience of seeing their country taken over by white foreigners from a country in which blacks were treated as second-class citizens was a brutal one. For the first time, Haiti's intellectual class ceased to insist on their European culture and began to take pride in their African ancestry. "We gradually forced ourselves to believe we were 'colored' Frenchmen," the Haitian anthropologist and diplomat Jean Price-Mars wrote in his classic essay on Haitian folklore, *So Spoke the Uncle* (*Ainsi parla l'oncle*). "For mercy's sake, my friends, let us no longer scorn our ancestral heritage."[37]

A turning point in the historiography of the Haitian Revolution occurred in 1938, with the publication of the British Caribbean author C. L. R. James's history of the event, *The Black Jacobins*. In a vividly written narrative, James underlined the vital contribution that the black population of Saint-Domingue had made to the movement for freedom during the revolutionary era. His title linked the movement in Saint-Domingue to the Jacobins in revolutionary France, indicating his conviction that the two revolutions had been intimately connected and that the struggle for freedom in France itself would not have succeeded without the impetus provided by the blacks in the colony. In the decades after World War II, James's account of the making of Haitian independence took on added resonance as the populations of European colonies in Africa and Asia demanded their freedom. In France, the Martiniquan author Aimé Césaire, one of the leading voices of anti-colonialism, reinforced James's message in his essay, *Toussaint Louverture: The French Revolution and the Colonial Question*, first published in 1960.[38] Instead of being seen as an obscure event outside the mainstream of world history, the Haitian Revolution now began to appear as the precursor of modern movements for liberation throughout the non-western world.

In 1991 the United Nations Educational, Scientific and Cultural Organization (UNESCO) declared the anniversary of the outbreak of the slave insurrection of 22–23 August 1791 a world holiday of freedom. Not since the time of the events themselves has there been so much attention paid to the dramatic upheavals of the years from 1791 to 1804. It is now widely recognized that the Haitian Revolution is central to the understanding of the process in which our modern definitions of liberty and equality emerged in the decades around 1800. Through their actions, the participants in the Haitian Revolution made it clear that liberty was incompatible with slavery and that equality had to extend to people of all races. The independence of Haiti is an integral part of the story of movements for independence in the Americas, and it stands at the origin of the anticolonial movement that has now shaped the history of the entire world. Similarly to the French Revolution, however, the story of the Haitian Revolution also highlights the challenges of establishing a democratic society in the wake of a violent upheaval. Like all the great events of world history, the Haitian Revolution forces us to confront fundamental questions, not just about the past, but about the world in which we live.

Afterword: The Earthquake Crisis of 2010 and the Haitian Revolution

It is a sad irony that, just as the story of the Haitian Revolution was achieving a new visibility in modern consciousness, the world's attention was suddenly riveted on the country by an enormous catastrophe. On 12 January 2010, a massive earthquake struck Haiti's capital city of Port-au-Prince, killing more than 200,000 people and doing enormous damage to buildings, roads, and other installations. The aftermath of this disaster cast a cruel light on the weaknesses of Haiti's political institutions, as the government seemed unable to shape an effective response. Aid from around the world flowed into the stricken country, but even this influx of support from abroad raised questions about how Haiti could maintain the independence it won in 1804 while relying so heavily on foreign assistance. An epidemic of cholera, introduced into the country by United Nations troops who had been sent to Haiti to help stabilize political conditions, dramatized the consequences of the country's inability to determine its own destiny. As the poorest victims of the "goudougoudou," a Kreyol word invented to capture the low, rumbling sound of the earthquake, struggled to put shattered lives back together, the gap between the country's ruling elites and the mass of the population, a legacy rooted in its historical past, yawned wider than ever. In 2010, some Haitians dared to hope that the shock of the January 2010 disaster would generate a new spirit of purpose and unity in their country, enabling it to truly realize the hopes for a better life that had inspired their ancestors during the revolutionary period, and that the outside world would finally recognize the need to change the unequal arrangements that have so often

A Concise History of the Haitian Revolution, Second Edition. Jeremy D. Popkin.
© 2022 John Wiley & Sons Ltd. Published 2022 by John Wiley & Sons Ltd.

drained the country's resources. Others feared, however, that their country was doomed to slide even further into poverty and to see even more of its talented and educated people leave to pursue better opportunities abroad. In July 2021, Haiti was plunged into a new crisis by the assassination of its president Jovenel Moïse, which raised the specter that the country might fall into civil conflict and the possibility of foreign intervention.

Haiti's needs in the present remain so urgent that studying what happened there 200 years ago may seem like a diversion from the country's real problems. Few students there even have the opportunity that those in other countries do to spend time learning about the events of the Haitian Revolution. Certainly, however, the history of the Haitian Revolution is not irrelevant to Haiti's efforts to deal with its current issues. People of all countries draw inspiration from past moments when their ancestors came together to meet daunting challenges. The problems facing Haitians today are worrisome, but they are not more terrifying than those that faced the insurgents in August 1791, when they launched their uprisings against the solidly entrenched system of colonial slavery and racism. Haitians sometimes despair of finding effective leadership for their country, but no one, in 1791, could have predicted the talents that the humble former enslaved black man Toussaint of Bréda would prove to possess. Political disunity is a discouraging aspect of Haiti today, but the issues of the present are not more divisive than those that separated the rival groups that finally came together to win the country's independence. To deal with the problems currently facing their country, Haitians will need to use all of their resources. The memory of their country's struggle for independence is one of those sources of strength on which they can draw.

For those of us in the outside world, it remains equally important to understand the Haitian Revolution and its significance. This account of the Haitian uprising has tried to avoid the pitfalls of a purely celebratory narrative. Nevertheless, readers of it should recognize the tremendous achievement of the Haitian revolutionaries. As Laurent Dubois, one of the most important recent contributors to the study of the Haitian Revolution, has written, the Haitian movement "was a central part of the destruction of slavery in the Americas, and therefore a crucial moment in the history of democracy, one that laid the foundation for the continuing struggles for human rights everywhere."[1] When we remember that the Haitian uprising was the only successful slave revolt in recorded history, we can appreciate the difficulties that Boukman, Toussaint Louverture,

Dessalines, and the thousands of other men and women who participated in the revolution had to overcome. At the same time, the story of the Haitian Revolution is a sobering reminder to those who would like to see western European civilization as the source of modern ideas about liberty and equality. The same revolutionary leaders in the United States and France who formulated those ideas in such eloquent language were prepared to fight to the death to maintain the enslavement of blacks throughout the Atlantic world. It was Toussaint Louverture's Haitian constitution of 1801, and not the constitutions of the United States or revolutionary France, that first declared "There can be no slaves in this territory; servitude is abolished within it forever." If the recognition of the equal worth of all human beings is to be the basis of a truly universal set of values for the world, we need to acknowledge that this principle was first articulated as a result of the struggles of people of African descent in the French colony of Saint-Domingue.

While scholars outside of Haiti have accorded increasing importance to the Haitian Revolution in their studies of the origins of modernity, historians from Haiti itself have sometimes sounded a more cautionary note. They recognize that the legacy of the revolution included the destruction of slavery, but they know that it also saw the erection of the "Louverturian state," an authoritarian model of government whose influence still affects Haiti today. Writing in 2009, the Haitian scholars Michel Hector and Laënnec Hurbon regretted that when present-day Haitian politicians look back at their country's revolution, they "take from this glorious past a cult of violence and a despotic mode of government marked by shows of force and summary executions of enemies."[2] Hector's and Hurbon's views are not universally shared among Haitians, as many of the contributions to the lavishly illustrated volume *Revolutionary Freedoms: A History of Survival, Strength and Imagination in Haiti*, published in 2006, demonstrate.[3] Nevertheless, their words are a reminder that the meaning of the Haitian movement, like that of other revolutions, cannot be reduced to a simple slogan. Like the heirs of the American and French revolutions, Haitians today, and those who sympathize with their struggles, have a complicated legacy to ponder.

Recent Scholarship on the Haitian Revolution

Students and other readers eager to learn more about the Haitian Revolution are fortunate in being able to take advantage of the enormous increase in scholarship about the subject in the past few decades, as well as of the unprecedented access to primary sources on the topic made possible by the internet. The major contributions to the historical understanding of the events of the years from 1791 to 1804 that have appeared since the mid-1980s have been published mainly in English and French. Since this book is intended primarily for English-speaking readers, the discussion that follows emphasizes publications in that language, but students should be aware of the importance of the many contributions of Haitian and French historians that are still accessible only in French, the most important of which are referenced here. The overwhelming majority of the primary sources on the subject are also available only in French. Jeremy D. Popkin, "The Haitian Revolution Comes of Age," *Slavery and Abolition* v. 42, no. 2 (June 2021) 382–401 surveys scholarship on the Haitian Revolution from 2010 to 2020.

Two invaluable collections of translated primary source documents on the Haitian Revolution are Laurent Dubois and John D. Garrigus, *Slave Revolution in the Caribbean 1789–1804* (2nd edn, 2017) and David Geggus, *The Haitian Revolution: A Documentary History* (2014). Jeremy D. Popkin, *Facing Racial Revolution: Eyewitness Accounts of the Haitian Uprising* (2007), includes excerpts from authors who experienced these events. In 2010, the John Carter Brown Library in Providence, Rhode Island, a world-famous research library devoted to the early history of the Americas, put all of its extremely rich materials about the Haitian Revolution online (www.brown.edu/Facilities/John_Carter_Brown_Library). Although the majority of these texts are in French, there are a number of items in English as well. Some Haitian Revolution materials are also available online through the Gallica collection on the website of the Bibliothèque nationale de France (www.bnf.fr) The events of the Haitian Revolution were covered extensively in the American press at the time; most of these newspapers can now be found online.

In retrospect, a number of publications of the 1980s or early 1990s signaled the beginning of a new era in the study of the Haitian Revolution, even though most of the major works issued in those years attracted little attention when they first appeared. Among those publications that are still essential reading on the subject are Robert Louis Stein's biography, *Léger-Félicité Sonthonax: The Lost Sentinel of the Republic* (1985), French scholar Yves Bénot's *La Révolution française et la fin des colonies* (1987), and Carolyn Fick's *The Making of Haiti: The Saint-Domingue Revolution from Below* (1991), as well as the numerous publications of David Geggus. Stein rescued Sonthonax from nearly two centuries of oblivion and demonstrated his central role in the process of emancipation.[1] Bénot underlined the importance of the issue of slavery in the politics of the French Revolution, while Fick broke away from the long tradition of accounts focused on the role of leaders, particularly Toussaint Louverture, in order to highlight the role of the mass of the population in fighting for its freedom. Geggus showed the range of unexploited archival sources available for the study of the subject. He also peeled away myths that had accumulated around such key moments of the revolution as the Bois Caïman ceremony of 1791 and Toussaint Louverture's decision to ally himself with the French in 1794.[2]

Interest in the topic of the Haitian Revolution grew rapidly during the 1990s and the first decade of the twenty-first century, as a new struggle for democracy began in Haiti itself after the end of the era of the dictatorships of François Duvalier and his son Jean-Claude Duvalier in 1986, and as the bicentennial of the French Revolution brought new attention to that movement's debates about slavery. Building on the insights of Yves Bénot's work, other scholars, such as Jean-Daniel Piquet, in his *L'Émancipation des Noirs dans la Révolution française (1789–1795)* (2002), delved into the contradictions of the French revolutionaries' actions on slavery, including their hesitation about voting to abolish slavery, as well as Napoleon's attempt to regain control over the colony, and the connections between events in Saint-Domingue and those in France. Bénot and a number of other French scholars contributed to an important volume on the occasion of the bicentennial of the emancipation decrees of 1793 in Saint-Domingue and 1794 in France, which was translated into English as *The Abolitions of Slavery from Léger-Félicité Sonthonax to Victor Schoelcher, 1793, 1794, 1848*.[3] Marcel Dorigny has edited or co-edited a number of other collaborative volumes on aspects of the French abolition movement that are available only in French.[4] Scholars from all over the world contributed to the collective volume edited by David Geggus and Norman Fiering, *The World of the Haitian Revolution* (2009).

Laurent Dubois's *Avengers of the New World: The Story of the Haitian Revolution* (2004) was the first comprehensive overview of the subject in any language in many years, and has been a great stimulus to interest in the field. Dubois's book has largely replaced the earlier one-volume English-language histories of the revolution, such as Thomas Ott, *The Haitian Revolution 1789–1804* (1973), the first academic monograph to use the phrase "The Haitian Revolution" in its title, although C. L. R. James, *The Black Jacobins: Toussaint Louverture and the San Domingo Revolution* (originally published in 1938), remains a classic for its assertion of the world-historical importance of the Haitian movement. Michel-Rolph Trouillot, *Silencing the Past: Power and the Production of History* (1995), is an impassioned denunciation of historians' refusal to give proper recognition to the significance of the Haitian Revolution, an accusation that no longer accurately reflects the state of scholarship in the field.

The history of colonial Saint-Domingue, a topic long neglected after the breakup of France's overseas empire, has attracted new attention in recent years. Alan Forrest, *The Death of the French Atlantic: Trade, War, and Slavery in the Age of Revolution* (2020), puts the Haitian Revolution in the context of the fate of France's Atlantic empire from the mid-eighteenth century to the end of the Napoleonic wars. The early years of the colony's development are covered in the general works of Philip K. Boucher, *France and the American Tropics to 1700: Tropics of Discontent?* (2008), and James Pritchard, *In Search of Empire: The French in the Americas, 1670–1730* (2004). Trevor Burnard and John Garrigus, *The Plantation Machine: Atlantic Capitalism in French Saint-Domingue and British Jamaica* (2016) compares the two most important eighteenth-century sugar colonies; Paul Cheney, *Cul de Sac: Patrimony, Capitalism, and Slavery in French Saint-Domingue* (2017) is an illuminating case study of one Saint-Domingue plantation at the end of the Old Regime. Robert Louis Stein's *The French Slave Trade in the Eighteenth Century: An Old Regime Business* (1979) and *The French Sugar Business in the Eighteenth Century* (1988) explain two fundamental features of the colonial economy. Doris Garraway, *The Libertine Colony: Creolization in the Early French Caribbean* (2005), and Madeleine Dobie, *Trading Places: Colonization and Slavery in Eighteenth-Century French Culture* (2010), analyze writing about culture and race in pre-revolutionary French literature. Sue Peabody, *"There Are No Slaves in France": The Political Culture of Race and Slavery in the Ancien Régime* (1996), outlines official French policy toward blacks in the metropole, and Jennifer L. Palmer. *Intimate Bonds: Family and Slavery in the French Atlantic* (2016) examines the impact of colonial families on French society. James E. McClellan, *Colonialism and Science: Saint-Domingue in the Old Regime* (1992), deals with the development of white intellectual life in the colony. The French historian Charles Frostin's *Les Révoltes blanches à Saint-Domingue aux XVIIe et XVIIIe siècles* (1975, reissued 2008) is an essential study of the white colonists' political attitudes. Malick Ghachem, *The Old Regime and the Haitian Revolution* (2011) makes a provocative and persuasive argument that black ideas about freedom grew out of the colonial legal system more than the thought of the European Enlightenment.

Neither the fundamental study of the slavery system in the French Caribbean, Gabriel Debien, *Les Esclaves aux Antilles françaises (XVIIe–XVIIIe siècles)* (1974), nor the more recent survey of the subject by Frédéric Régent, *La France et ses esclaves* (2007), have been translated into English. Jean Fouchard, *The Haitian Maroons: Liberty or Death* (1981), makes a case for the extent of slave resistance, and Julius S. Scott, *The Common Wind: Afro-American Currents: Communication in the Age of the Haitian Revolution*, (2018 (orig. 1986)) explores how news circulated among enslaved populations in the Caribbean.[5] Bernard Moitt, *Women and Slavery in the French Antilles, 1635–1848* (2001), and Arlette Gautier, *Les Soeurs de Solitude* (1985), are studies of the condition of enslaved women in the French colonies. Publications highlighting the role of the free people of color in pre-revolutionary Saint-Domingue include John Garrigus, *Before Haiti: Race and Citizenship in French Saint-Domingue* (2006), Stewart King, *Blue Coat or Powdered Wig: Free People of Color in Pre-Revolutionary Saint Domingue* (2001), and the dissertation of French scholar Dominique Rogers, "Les Libres de couleur dans les capitales de Saint-Domingue: Fortune, mentalités et intégration à la fin de l'ancien régime" (1999).

Crucial aspects of the Haitian Revolution's early years are illuminated in David Geggus's numerous articles, a selection of which are collected in his *Haitian Revolutionary Studies* (2002), and in Jeremy D. Popkin, "Sailors and Revolution: naval mutineers in Saint-Domingue, 1790–1793,"

French History 26 (Dec. 2012), 460–81; "The French Revolution's Royal Governor: General Blanchelande and Saint Domingue, 1790–92," *William and Mary Quarterly*. 3ʳᵈ ser., 71 no. 2 (April 2014), 203–28; "A Colonial Media Revolution: The Press in Saint-Domingue, 1789–1793," *The Americas* 75 (2018), 3–25; and "Port-au-Prince and the Collapse of French Imperial Authority, 1789–1793," *French Historical Studies* 44, no. 1 (2021), 59–84. Jeremy D. Popkin, *You Are All Free: The Haitian Revolution and the Abolition of Slavery* (2010), provides a detailed account of the mission of Sonthonax and Polverel, the issuance of the emancipation proclamations of 1793, and the way in which events in Saint-Domingue precipitated the French National Convention's abolition decree of 4 February 1794. Elizabeth Colwill, "Gendering the June Days: Race, Masculinity, and Slave Emancipation in Saint Domingue," *Journal of Haitian Studies* 15 (2009), 103–24, and "'Enfans de l'Amérique': Configuring Creole Citizenship in the Press, 1793," *Journal of Haitian Studies* 15 (2009), 168–79, look at crucial aspects of the emancipation process. Judith Kafka, "Action, Reaction, and Interaction: Slave Women in Resistance in the South of Saint-Domingue, 1793–94," *Slavery and Abolition* 18 (1997), 48–72, documents the role of women in the transition to freedom.

The upsurge of interest in the Haitian Revolution as a collective movement that began in the 1980s shifted attention away from Toussaint Louverture, but recent years have seen the publication of no less than three new English-language biographies of the movement's main leader, all drawing on new documentary discoveries about his early life. Philippe Girard, *Toussaint Louverture: A Revolutionary Life* (2016) sees him as motivated primarily by personal ambition; Sudhir Hazareesingh, *Black Spartacus: The Epic Life of Toussaint Louverture* (2020) gives more credit to his dedication to freedom for the black population, and Charles Forsdick and Christian Hogsberg, *Toussaint Louverture: A Black Jacobin in the Age of Revolutions* (2017) follows C. L. R. James in interpreting Louverture as a revolutionary who ultimately lost the trust of the Haitian masses. It is a reflection of the difficulties besetting Haiti that there is no scholarly edition of Toussaint Louverture's letters and papers, many of which continue to be cited on the basis of inaccurate published versions from the nineteenth century. Louverture's memoirs, which cover only his career as a French official in the colony, have been translated by Philippe Girard: *The Memoir of Toussaint Louverture* (2014). A selection of documents by and about Toussaint Louverture in English is George Tyson, Jr., ed., *Toussaint Louverture* (1973). Translations of some of his letters and proclamations can be found online at www.marxists.org/reference/archive/toussaint-louverture/index.htm. His correspondence with General Laveaux has been published by Gérard Laurent, *Toussaint Louverture à travers sa correspondance (1794–1798)* (1953). Other key actors in the Haitian Revolution have received much less attention than Louverture. Robert Louis Stein's *Sonthonax* (1985) is a portrait of the French official who played a central role in the achievement of emancipation, and Gérard Laurent's four-volume work on *Le Commissaire Sonthonax à Saint-Domingue* (1965–74) contains much valuable information on his activities. Several scholars are currently preparing biographies of Jean-Jacques Dessalines, whose life has not yet benefited from any English-language study.

David Geggus, *Slavery, War, and Revolution: The British Occupation of Saint-Domingue, 1793–1798* (1982), explains the consequences of the British invasion. The involvement of the Spanish colonies of Cuba and Santo Domingo in the Haitian Revolution is explored in Graham Nessler, *An Islandwide Struggle for Freedom: Revolution, Emancipation, and Reenslavement in Hispaniola, 1789–1809* (2016) and Ada Ferrer, *Freedom's Mirror: Cuba and Haiti in the Age of Revolution* (2014). Ashli White, *Encountering Revolution: Haiti and the Making of the Early Republic* (2010), and James Alexander Dun, *Dangerous Neighbors: Making the Haitian Revolution in Early America* (2016) cover the impact of refugees and news from Saint-Domingue in the United States during the 1790s, and Nathalie Dessens, *From Saint-Domingue to New Orleans: Migration and Influences* (2007), explains the refugees' impact in Louisiana. The involvement of the United States in the Haitian Revolution is the subject of Gordon S. Brown, *Toussaint's Clause: The Founding Fathers and the Haitian Revolution* (2005), and Tim Matthewson, *A Proslavery Foreign Policy: Haitian–American Relations During the Early Republic* (2003). David Geggus and Barry Gaspar, eds., *A Turbulent Time: The French Revolution and the Greater Caribbean* (1997), and David Geggus, ed., *Impact of the Haitian Revolution in the Atlantic World* (2001), look at the impact of the Haitian Revolution in various parts of the Americas. William S. Cormack, *Patriots, Royalists, and Terrorists in the West Indies* (2019) is a detailed account of the revolutionary era in France's two other major Caribbean colonies, Martinique and Guadeloupe.

The Leclerc expedition and the violence accompanying the struggle for independence have been studied more closely than the republican period of 1794 to 1801. Paul Roussier, ed., *Lettres du Général Leclerc* (1937), is an essential documentary source. The background to Napoleon's policy is outlined in Yves Bénot, *La Démence coloniale sous Napoléon* (1991). The bloody war of independence is recounted in Philippe Girard, *The Slaves Who Defeated Napoleon: Toussaint Louverture and the Haitian War of Independence* (2011). Several of Girard's articles extend his research on the subject: "Napoleon Bonaparte and the Emancipation Issue in Saint-Domingue, 1799–1803," *French Historical Studies* 32 (2009), 587–618, "Caribbean Genocide: Racial War in Haiti, 1802–4," *Patterns of Prejudice* 39 (2005), 138–61, "*Rebelles* with a Cause: Women in the Haitian War of Independence, 1802–04," *Gender and History* 21 (2009), 60–85, "Birth of a Nation: The Creation of the Haitian Flag and Haiti's French Revolutionary Heritage," *Journal of Haitian Studies* 15 (2009), 135–50, "Jean-Jacques Dessalines and the Atlantic System: A Reappraisal," *William and Mary Quarterly* 69, no. 3 (July 2012), 549–82, "French Atrocities during the War of Independence," *Journal of Genocide Research* 15, no. 2 (2013), 133–49. Girard's critical view of the Haitian movement has been challenged in Sudhir Hazareesingh's recent biography of Toussaint Louverture and in Jean-Pierre Le Glaunec, *The Cry of Vertières: Liberation, Memory, and the Beginning of Haiti* (2014), which also details the development of historical memory in Haiti after the Revolution.

Julia Gaffield, *The Haitian Declaration of Independence: Creation, Context, and* Legacy (2016) situates the 1804 declaration in its historical context; Deborah Jenson, "Dessalines's American Proclamations of Haitian Independence," *Journal of Haitian Studies* 15 (2009), 72–102, shows how the document was circulated in the United States. Julia Gaffield, *Haitian Connections in the Atlantic World: Recognition after Revolution* (2015) challenges the standard narrative of the outside world's hostility to the new Haitian state after 1804.

Haitian history after 1804, long a neglected subject in English-language scholarship, has attracted new attention in recent years. Alyssa Sepinwall, *Haitian History: New Perspectives* (2013) includes selections by a number of leading scholars covering Haitian history from the revolutionary period to the moment of the 2010 earthquake. David Nicholls, *From Dessalines to Duvalier: Race, Colour and National Independence in Haiti* (new edn., 1996), was for many years the standard account of post-revolutionary Haitian history in English; it has now been challenged by Laurent Dubois, *Haiti: The Aftershocks of History* (2012). Hubert Cole, *Christophe King of Haiti* (1967), is a biography of one of the post-revolutionary period's key figures. Johnhenry Gonzalez, *Maroon Nation: A History of Revolutionary*

Haiti (2019) offers a positive reassessment of the outcome of the Haitian Revolution for the country's peasantry. Deborah Jenson, *Beyond the Slave Narrative: Politics, Sex and Manuscripts in the Haitian Revolution* (2011), initiated a new interest in Haitian political writing from this period. Marlene L. Daut's two publications, *Tropics of Haiti: Race and the Literary History of the Haitian Revolution in the Atlantic World, 1789–1865* (2016) and *Baron de Vastey and the Origins of Black Atlantic Humanism* (2017), persuasively demonstrate the importance of Haiti and of Haitian authors in the Atlantic culture of the nineteenth century, and Chelsea Stieber, *Haiti's Paper War: Post-Independence Writing, Civil War, and the Making of the Republic, 1804–1954* explores rival Haitian traditions of political thought. Mimi Sheller, *Democracy after Slavery: Black Publics and Peasant Radicalism in Haiti and Jamaica* (2000), and Matthew J. Smith, *Liberty, Fraternity, Exile: Haiti and Jamaica after Emancipation* (2014) provide comparisons between the two Caribbean islands in the wake of the abolition of slavery. Robert Fatton, Jr., *The Roots of Haitian Despotism* (2007), explains the impact of the revolutionary era on Haiti's modern political institutions. In French, key publications include Claude Moïse, *Constitutions et luttes de pouvoir en Haïti (1804–1987)* (1988), Jean-Pierre Brière, *Haïti et la France, 1804–1848: La Rêve brisée* (2008), and Michel Hector and Laënnec Hurbon, eds., *Genèse de l'État haïtien (1804–1859)* (2009).

Studies of nineteenth-century reactions to Haiti in the United States include Alfred N. Hunt, *Haiti's Influence on Antebellum America: Slumbering Volcano in the Caribbean* (1988), Leon D. Pamphile, *Haitians and African Americans: A Heritage of Tragedy and Hope* (2001), and Brandon Byrd, *The Black Republic: African Americans and the Fate of Haiti* (2020). Sibylle Fischer, *Modernity Disavowed: Haiti and the Cultures of Slavery in the Age of Revolution* (2004), analyzes reactions to the Haitian Revolution in the Caribbean. Susan Buck-Morss, *Hegel, Haiti, and Universal History* (2009), makes an admittedly speculative case for the influence of the Haitian Revolution on the German philosopher Hegel's thought. Doris L. Garraway, ed., *Tree of Liberty: Cultural Legacies of the Haitian Revolution in the Atlantic World* (2008), is an important collection of articles on literary legacy of the Haitian Revolution, both in Haiti itself and in the wider world.

In addition to historians, novelists have helped to increase interest in the Haitian Revolution. Leonora Sansay's *Secret History, or, The Horrors of Saint-Domingue*, one of the first fictional treatments of the subject, has been republished in an edition edited by Michael J. Drexler (2007). Émeric

Bergeaud, *Stella: A Novel of the Haitian Revolution*, translated and edited by Lesley S. Curtis and Christen Mucher (2015), makes a classic nineteenth-century Haitian novel about the Revolution accessible to Anglophone readers. The African American novelist Arna Bontemps, a major figure in the "Harlem Renaissance" of the 1920s and 1930s, dramatized the opening moments of the slave uprising in *Drums at Dusk* (1939). Cuban novelist Alejo Carpentier's *The Kingdom of This World*, first published in Spanish in 1949, is a classic that was one of the founding works of the Latin American tradition of "magic realism" in literature. More recently, Madison Smartt Bell's epic trilogy, *All Souls' Rising* (1995), *Master of the Crossroads* (2000), and *The Stone that the Builder Refused* (2004), and Isabelle Allende's *Island Beneath the Sea* (2010), have brought the story of the Haitian Revolution to life for English-speaking readers. Alyssa Sepinwall, *Slave Revolt on Screen: The Haitian Revolution in Film and Video* (2021) examines contemporary representations of the Revolution in non-print media, and Rachel Douglas, *Making the Black Jacobins: C. L. R. James and the Drama of History* (2019) shows how James not only wrote a history of the Haitian Revolution but also produced powerful stage plays about it.

Notes

Abbreviations

AN   Archives nationales (Paris).
CAOM   Centre d'Archives d'Outre-Mer (Aix-en-Provence).

Introduction

1 *Discours fait à l'assemblée nationale, le 3 novembre 1791*, 2.
2 [Gabriel] Gros, *Historick Recital, of the Different Occurrences in the Camps of Grande-Reviere [sic], Dondon, Sainte-Suzanne, and others, from the 26 of October, 1791, to the 24ᵗʰ of December, of the same year* (Baltimore: Samuel and John Adams, 1793), in Jeremy D. Popkin, *Facing Racial Revolution: Eyewitness Accounts of the Haitian Insurrection* (Chicago: University of Chicago Press, 2007), 138.
3 Michel-Rolph Trouillot, *Silencing the Past: Power and the Production of History* (Boston, MA: Beacon Press, 1995).

Chapter 1: A Colonial Society in a Revolutionary Era

1 James Pritchard, *In Search of Empire: The French in the Americas, 1670–1730* (Cambridge: Cambridge University Press, 2004), 424; Paul Butel, *Histoire des Antilles françaises* (Paris: Perrin, 2007), 184.
2 Justin Girod de Chantrans, *Voyage d'un Suisse dans les Colonies d'Amérique*, ed. Pierre Pluchon (1785; Paris: Taillandier, 1980), 128.
3 John Thornton, "African Soldiers in the Haitian Revolution," *Journal of Caribbean History* 25 (1991), 58–80.
4 Malick Ghachem, *The Old Regime and the Haitian Revolution* (2011).

A Concise History of the Haitian Revolution, Second Edition. Jeremy D. Popkin.
© 2022 John Wiley & Sons Ltd. Published 2022 by John Wiley & Sons Ltd.

5 Recent discoveries about Toussaint Louverture's early life are incorporated in the biographies by Sudhir Hazareesingh, *Black Spartacus: The Epic Life of Toussaint Louverture* (New York: Farrar, Straus and Giroux, 2020) and Philippe Girard, *Toussaint Louverture: A Revolutionary Life* (New York: Basic Books, 2016).

6 Anon., "Manuscrit d'un voyage de France à Saint-Domingue," John Carter Brown Library, cited in Jeremy D. Popkin, *Facing Racial Revolution: Eyewitness Accounts of the Haitian Uprising* (Chicago, IL: University of Chicago Press, 2007), 38–40. The French text of this manuscript has been edited by David Geggus: *Voyage de France à Saint-Domingue. Transcription d'un manuscript inédit* (Paris: L'Harmattan, 2021).

7 AN, 5 mi 1434, deposition of Mirande, n.d.

8 "Esclaves bienfaisance," in ANOM, Moreau de Saint-Méry papers, F 3 198.

9 Cited in Laurent Dubois and John Garrigus, *Slave Revolution in the Caribbean 1789–1804* (New York: Bedford/St. Martin's, 2006), 56.

10 Sue Peabody, *"There Are No Slaves in France": The Political Culture of Race and Slavery in the Ancien Régime* (New York: Oxford University Press, 1996), 106–20.

11 Letter of Pierre Céloron de Blainville, 8 May 1785, cited in Gabriel Debien, *Les Esclaves aux Antilles Françaises (XVIIe–XVIIIe siècles)* (Basse-Terre and Fort-de-France: Sociétés d'histoire de la Guadeloupe et de la Martinique, 1974), 486.

12 On the debates about slavery and colonial rights during the first stages of the French Revolution, see Jeremy D. Popkin, "Saint-Domingue, Slavery, and the Origins of the French Revolution," in Thomas Kaiser and Dale Van Kley, eds., *From Deficit to Deluge* (Stanford, CA: Stanford University Press, 2011).

13 *Courrier de Provence*, no. 30 (20–21 Aug. 1789).

14 François Raimond letterbook, 1 Oct. 1789, in *Correspondance de Julien Raimond, avec ses frères, de Saint-Domingue, et les pièces qui lui ont été adressés par eux* (Paris: Cercle social, Year II [1793]), 4.

15 John Garrigus, *Before Haiti: Race and Citizenship in French Saint-Domingue* (New York: Palgrave Macmillan, 2006), 248–9.

16 Baron de Beauvois, *Idées sommaires sur quelques règlements à faire par l'Assemblée coloniale; par M. le baron de Beauvois, conseiller au Conseil-supérieur du Cap, correspondant de l'Académie royale des Sciences, ci-devant associé de la Société royale des sciences & arts de Saint-Domingue* (Cap-Français: Batilliot, 1790), 36–40.

Chapter 2: The Uprisings, 1791–1793

1 For the Creole text, see Carolyn Fick, *The Making of Haiti: The Saint-Domingue Revolution from Below* (Knoxville, TN: University of Tennessee Press, 1991), 93. The historical evidence about the Bois Caïman ceremony is carefully presented in David Geggus, "The Bois Caïman Ceremony," in his *Haitian Revolutionary Studies* (Bloomington, IN: Indiana University Press, 2002), 81–92.

2 Anon., "La Révolution de Saint-Domingue," cited in Popkin, *Facing Racial Revolution: Eyewitness Accounts of the Haitian Uprising* (Chicago, IL: Chicago University Press, 2007), 50, 53.

3 Gros, "Historick Recital," cited in Popkin, *Facing Racial Revolution*, 124; Anon., "La Révolution de Saint-Domingue," AN, Col. F 3 141; testimony of Marie Jeanne Jouette, in Popkin, *Facing Racial Revolution*, 158.

4 *Concordat passé entre les citoyens du Port-au-Prince & les citoyens de couleur de la même partie de Saint-Domingue* (1791).

5 "Evaluation de la quantité des nègres révoltés dans les dix paroisses en insurrection," AN, D XXV 113, d. 897.

6 Letter of First Civil Commission to Minister of the Navy, 23 Dec. 1791, AN, D XXV 1, d. 2.

7 "La Révolution de Saint-Domingue," cited in Popkin, *Facing Racial Revolution*, 57.

8 AN, D XXV 1, d. 4.

9 Ibid.

10 Bryan Edwards, *An Historical Survey of the Island of Saint Domingo* (London: John Stockdale, 1801), 11.

11 Gelston and Saltonstall letterbook, 28 Sept. 1791, in New York Historical Society.

12 Jean-Philippe- Guy le Gentil Paroy, *Mémoires du Comte de Paroy*, ed. Etienne Charavay (Paris: Plon, 1895), 292.

13 The most accessible version of this letter is Nathalie Piquionne, "Lettre de Jean-François, Biassou et Belair, juillet 1792," *Chemins critiques* 3 (1997), 206–10. Roume mentioned his letter to the black leaders and the royalist Colonel Cambefort's interception of their response in his justification of his conduct after he returned to France (AN, D XXV 3, d. 31). This explains how Cambefort came to be the first person to publish the letter, as part of his own defense of his record in Saint-Domingue after he returned to France in January 1793. The letter was then reprinted in the anti-slavery journalist Milscent's *Créole patriote*.

14 Joseph Paul Augustin Cambefort, *Mémoire justificatif* (1793), pt. 3, p. 9.

15 Cited in Antonio del Monte y Tejada, *Historia de Santo Domingo*, 3 vols. (Trujillo, 1952–3), 3:xii.

16 Biassou to abbé de la Haye, AN, D XXV 5, d. 48.

17 *Compte rendu à l'assemblée nationale, par M. Saint-Léger, commissaire civil pour l'isle de Saint-Domingue, le 2 juin 1792, l'an 4e de la liberté* (Paris: Imprimerie nationale, 1792), 27. On "Romaine la prophetesse," see Terry Rey, *The Priest and the Prophetess: Abbé Ouvière, Romaine Rivière, and the Revolutionary Atlantic World* (NY: Oxford University Press, 2016).

18 Toussaint Louverture, letter of 8–27 Aug. 1793, AN, AA 55, d. 1511.

19 Sonthonax and Polverel, report to Convention, 18 June 1793, AN, D XXV 5, d. 51.

20 On the involvement of the Spanish colonies in the Haitian Revolution, see Graham T. Nessler, *An Islandwide Struggle for Freedom: Revolution, Emancipation and Reenslavement in Hispaniola, 1789–1809* (Chapel Hill NC: University of

North Carolina Press, 2016), and Ada Ferrer, *Freedom's Mirror: Cuba and Haiti in the Age of Revolution* (NY: Cambridge University Press, 2014).

21 Account A, ANOM, Col. F 3 198.

22 Copy of letter from Toussaint and Moïse, 25 June 1793, AN, D XXV 20, d. 200.

23 Samuel G. Perkins, "Sketches of St. Domingo from January, 1785, to December, 1794," *Proceedings of the Massuchusetts Historical Society*, 2nd ser. 2 (1886), 363, 358–9.

24 Toussaint Louverture, letter of 29 Aug. 1793, AN, AA 53, d. 1490.

25 Fick, *The Making of Haiti*, 168–82.

26 Cited in Judith Kafka, "Action, Reaction, and Interaction: Slave Women in Resistance in the South of Saint-Domingue, 1793–94," *Slavery and Abolition* 18 (1997), 54.

Chapter 3: Republican Emancipation in Saint-Domingue, 1793–1798

1 Laurent Dubois and John D. Garrigus, *Slave Revolution in the Caribbean 1789–1804* (New York: Bedford/St. Martin's, 2006), 132.

2 Toussaint Louverture, letter of 18 May 1794, in Gérard Laurent, *Toussaint Louverture à travers sa correspondance (1794–1798)* (Madrid: Industrias Graficas España, 1953), 103.

3 Sonthonax and Polverel to Toussaint Louverture, June 1794, AN, D XXV 23, d. 232.

4 Sonthonax to Laveaux, 8 June 1794, AN, CC 9 A 8.

5 Toussaint Louverture to Laveaux, 13 June 1795, 14 Sept. 1795, and 30 pluviôse Year IV, in Laurent, *Toussaint Louverture à travers sa correspondance*, 182, 229–30, 317.

6 Toussaint Louverture, proclamation of 25 Apr. 1796, ibid., 381.

7 Toussaint Louverture to Laveaux, 19 July 1794 and 31 Aug. 1796, ibid., 123, 428.

8 *Nouvelles politiques* (Paris), 12 June 1795.

9 Laurent, *Toussaint Louverture à travers sa correspondance*, 278.

10 "My Odyssey," cited in Popkin, *Facing Racial Revolution: Eyewitness Accounts of the Haitian Uprising* (Chicago, IL: Chicago University Press, 2007), 266.

11 Boissy d'Anglas, speech to National Convention, 4 August 1795, in *Réimpression de l'Ancien Moniteur*, v. 26, issue of 23 thermidor Year II (10 Aug. 1795).

12 Cited in Robert Louis Stein, *Léger-Félicité Sonthonax: The Lost Sentinel of the Republic* (Rutherford, NJ: Fairleigh Dickinson Press, 1985), 137.

13 Cited in ibid., 168.

14 Toussaint Louverture, open letter to the Directory, cited in Dubois and Garrigus, *Slave Revolution*, 148–53.

15 Cited in ibid., 154–5.

16 *Discours prononcé par Sonthonax, sur la situation actuelle de Saint-Domingue, 16 pluviôse Year VI* (Paris: Imprimerie nationale, 1798), 14.

17 Jean Fouchard, *Les Marrons du Syllabaire* (Port-au-Prince: Henri Deschamps, 1953), 121.

18 Michel-Etienne Descourtilz, *Voyages d'un naturaliste* (1809), cited in Popkin, *Facing Racial Revolution*, 274–5.

19 Article from Charlestown newspaper, in *Nouvelles politiques* (Paris), 29 June 1795.

20 Laurent, *Toussaint Louverture à travers sa correspondance*, letter of 24 Sept. 1798, 452–4.

21 Cited in Gérard Laurent, *Le Commissaire Sonthonax à Saint-Domingue*, vol. 2: *L'Organisateur* (Port-au-Prince: La Phalange, 1965), 117.

22 Printed letter, signed Poncignon, 29 ventôse Year V, from Philadelphia, in Bibliothèque nationale, MS n.a.f. 6846 (Sonthonax papers); *Nouvelles politiques* (Paris), 29 June 1795.

23 Kenneth R. Maxwell, "The Generation of the 1790s and the Idea of Luso-Brazilian Empire," in Dauril Alden, ed., *Colonial Roots of Modern Brazil* (Berkeley, CA: University of California Press, 1973), 120.

Chapter 4: Toussaint Louverture in Power, 1798–1801

1 Sabine Manigat, "Les Fondements sociaux de l'état Louverturienne," in Michel Hector, ed., *La Révolution française et Haïti: Filiations, ruptures, nouvelles dimensions*, 2 vols. (Port-au-Prince: Société Haïtienne d'histoire et de géographie et Éditions Henri Deschamps, 1995), 1:130–42.

2 Cited in Beaubrun Ardouin, *Études sur l'histoire d'Haïti*, 11 vols. (1853–60; Port-au-Prince: Dr. François Dalencour, 1958), 3:86.

3 Cited in Christian Schneider, "Le Colonel Vincent, officier du génie à Saint-Domingue," *Annales historiques de la Révolution française*, no. 329 (2002), 101–22.

4 Cited in Gordon S. Brown, *Toussaint's Clause: The Founding Fathers and the Haitian Revolution* (Jackson, MS: University Press of Mississippi, 2005), 136.

5 Cited in Ardouin, *Études*, 4:14.

6 Stevens, letter of 24 June 1799, in George Tyson, Jr., ed., *Toussaint L'Ouverture* (Englewood Cliffs, NJ: Prentice Hall, 1973), 97.

7 Michel-Etienne Descourtilz, *Voyages d'un naturaliste* (1809), 3:261, cited in Popkin, *Facing Racial Revolution: Eyewitness Accounts of the Haitian Uprising* (Chicago, IL: Chicago University Press, 2007).

8 Toussaint Louverture, forced labor decree of 12 Oct. 1800, in Tyson, ed., *Toussaint Louverture*, 52–6.

9 Decree of 25 Nov. 1801, cited in Tyson, ed., *Toussaint L'Ouverture*, 59–64; Constitution of 1801, cited in Laurent Dubois and John D. Garrigus, *Slave Revolution in the Caribbean 1789–1804* (New York: Bedford/St. Martin's, 2006), 168–70.

10 Cited in Tyson, ed., *Toussaint L'Ouverture*, 84.
11 Cited ibid., 74.
12 Cited in Victor Schoelcher, *Vie de Toussaint Louverture* (Paris, 1889), 309–10.
13 Descourtilz, *Voyages*, cited in Popkin, *Facing Racial Revolution*, 277.
14 Cited in Tyson, ed., *Toussaint L'Ouverture*, 83.
15 Descourtilz, *Voyages*, cited in Popkin, *Facing Racial Revolution*, 278–9.
16 Pamphile De La Croix, *La Révolution d'Haïti* (original title *Mémoires pour servir à la Révolution de Saint-Domingue*), ed. Pierre Pluchon (1819; Paris: Karthala, 1995) 244-5; Descourtilz, *Voyages*, 3:342, cited in Popkin, *Facing Racial Revolution*.
17 Cited in Tyson, ed., *Toussaint L'Ouverture*, 86, 84.
18 Descourtilz, "Caractère des nègres créoles à Saint-Domingue," *Voyages*, 3:188–234, cited in Popkin, *Facing Racial Revolution*.
19 Cited in Schneider, "Le Colonel Vincent".
20 Documents in AN, CC 9 A 27.
21 Emilio Cordero Michel, "Toussaint en Saint-Domingue Espagnol," in Alain Yacou, ed., *Saint-Domingue espagnol et la révolution nègre d'Haïti* (Paris: Karthala, 2007), 251–7.
22 Decree of 29 Oct. 1801, cited in Schoelcher, *Vie de Toussaint L'Ouverture*, 287.
23 Cited ibid., 300.
24 Cited ibid., 304.
25 Pierre Pluchon, *Toussaint Louverture: Un révolutionnaire noir d'Ancien Régime* (1979; 2nd edn., Paris: Fayard, 1989), 406.
26 De La Croix, *La Révolution d'Haïti* 277.
27 Cited in Schoelcher, *Vie de Toussaint L'Ouverture*, 299.
28 Julius S. Scott, *The Common Wind: Afro-American Currents in the Age of Haitian Revolution* (London: Verso, 2018), 207.
29 Pluchon, *Toussaint Louverture*, 253, 435; Laurent Dubois, *Avengers of the New World: The Story of the Haitian Revolution* (Cambridge, MA: Belknap, 2004), 247.

Chapter 5: The Struggle for Independence, 1802–1806

1 The course of the fighting is covered in Philippe Girard, *The Slaves Who Defeated Napoleon: Toussaint Louverture and the Haitian War of Independence 1801–1804* (Tuscaloosa AL: University of Alabama Press, 2011).
2 Cited in Yves Bénot, *La Démence coloniale sous Napoléon* (Paris: La Découverte, 1991), 89.
3 Philippe R. Girard, "Napoleon Bonaparte and the Emancipation Issue in Saint-Domingue, 1799–1803," *French Historical Studies* 32 (2009), 601–2.
4 Paul Alliot, memorandum of 19 prairial Year VIII, AN, CC 9 A 27.
5 Cited in Thierry Lentz et al., *Napoléon, l'esclavage et les colonies* (Paris: Fayard, 2006), 108.
6 *De l'affranchissement des noirs, ou Observations sur la loi du 16 pluviôse, an deuxième, et sur les moyens à prendre pour le rétablissement des Colonies, du*

Commerce et de la Marine, 29. This anonymous pamphlet is catalogued under the date of 1797 in the Bibliothèque nationale de France, but it may have been published in the early years of the Consulate. In any event, the strategy of deception it proposes strongly resembles what Napoleon actually did.

7 "Notes pour servir aux instructions à donner au capitaine général Leclerc," in *Lettres du Général Leclerc,* ed. Paul Roussier (Paris: Société de l'histoire des colonies françaises, 1937), 263–74.

8 Cited in Gordon S. Brown, *Toussaint's Clause: The Founding Fathers and the Haitian Revolution* (Jackson, MS: University Press of Mississippi, 2005), 211.

9 Pamphile De La Croix, *La Révolution d'Haïti,* 283.

10 Cited in Hubert Cole, *Christophe King of Haiti* (1967; New York: Viking, 1970), 84.

11 Leclerc to Napoleon, 19 Feb. 1802, in *Lettres du Général Leclerc,* ed. Roussier, 102.

12 Cited in Cole, *Christophe King of Haiti,* 120.

13 Michel-Etienne Descourtilz, *Voyages d'un naturaliste* (1809), cited in Popkin, *Facing Racial Revolution,* 308.

14 Descourtilz, *Voyages,* cited ibid., 306; De La Croix, *Mémoires,* 335.

15 Cited in Victor Schoelcher, *Vie de Toussaint Louverture* (Paris, 1889), 349.

16 Cited in Claude Wanquet, "Un réquisitoire contre l'abolition de l'esclavage: *Les égarements du nigrophilisme* ["The Errors of Negrophilia"] de Louis Narcisse Baudry Deslozières (mars 1802)," in Yves Bénot and Marcel Dorigny, eds., *Rétablissement de l'esclavage dans les colonies françaises: Aux origines d'Haïti 1802* (Paris: Maisonneuve et Larose, 2004), 43.

17 Leclerc to Napoleon, 26 Sept. 1802, in *Lettres du Général Leclerc,* ed. Roussier, 245–6.

18 Leclerc to Napoleon, 7 Oct. 1802, ibid., 256.

19 Borie papers, Historical Society of Pennsylvania, MS 1602.

20 Elizabeth Colwill, "Bearing Witness to Freedom: Memory Traces, Counter-Histories, and the Collective Trauma of Slavery," paper for conference on "*Stories of Saint-Domingue, Stories of Haiti: Representations of the Haitian Revolution, 1804–2009*" UCLA, 2009, cited with permission.

21 C. L. R. James, *The Black Jacobins: Toussaint Louverture and the San Domingo Revolution* (1938; New York: Vintage, 1963), 361.

22 Letter of 23 June 1803, cited in Julia Gaffield, "'The good understanding which ought always to subsist between the two islands': Haiti and Jamaica in the Atlantic World, 1803–1804," *William and Mary Quarterly* 69, no. 3 (July 2012), 583.

23 Popular accounts of the Haitian Revolution often repeat the story that Dessalines created the design for the national flag at the Arcahaye conference, by tearing the white strip out of a French tricolor flag, and even name a certain Catherine Flon, "the Haitian Betsy Ross," as the seamstress who sewed the first new flag together. A recent article by Philippe R. Girard, "Birth of a Nation: The Creation of the Haitian Flag and Haiti's French Revolutionary Heritage," *Journal of Haitian Studies* 15 (2009), 135–50, claims that the bicolor flag was already in use before the Arcahaye conference.

24 The story that Rochambeau trained dogs to kill black prisoners has been questioned in a recent study, Georges H. Lutz, "Un avatar de la domestication canine: Les Chiens à esclaves: "Buscadores' de Cuba et de Saint-Domingue," in Marcel Dorigny, ed., *Haïti: Première République noir* (Paris: Société française d'histoire d'outre-mer, 2004), 61–81. Lutz argues that the dogs were used, as they had been for years throughout the Caribbean, to track blacks in the mountains, not to kill them.

25 Leonora Sansay ["Mary Hassal"] (1808), *Secret History, or, The Horrors of Saint-Domingue*, ed. Michael J. Drexler (Peterborough, ON: Broadview Editions, 2007).

26 Proclamation, dated Fort Dauphin, 29 Nov. 1803, in *Poulson's Daily Advertiser* (Philadelphia), 5 Jan. 1804. Deborah Jenson drew attention to the importance of this document in her article, "Dessalines's American Proclamations of the Haitian Independence," *Journal of Haitian Studies* 15 (2009), 72–102.

27 Cited in Laurent Dubois, *Avengers of the New World: The Story of the Haitian Revolution* (Cambridge, MA: Belknap, 2004), 298.

28 In 2010 Julia Gaffield discovered the first known printed copy of this declaration in the British National Archives.

29 "Hymne Haitien", printed copy in British National Archives, carton 137/111.

30 Lentz et al., *Napoléon, l'esclavage et les colonies*, 108, 163.

31 Peter S. Chazotte, *Historical Sketches of the Revolution and the Foreign and Civil Wars in the Island of St. Domingo* (New York: Wm. Applegate, 1840), cited in Popkin, Facing Racial Revolution, 355.

32 Cited in Beaubrun Ardouin, *Études sur l'histoire d'Haïti*, 11 vols. (1853–60; Port-au-Prince: Dr. François Dalencour, 1958), 6:16.

33 Gaffield, "'The good understanding'".

34 Cited in Laurent Dubois and John D. Garrigus, *Slave Revolution in the Caribbean 1789–1804* (New York: Bedford/St. Martin's, 2006), 191.

35 Marcus Rainsford, *An Historical Account of the Black Empire of Hayti: Comprehending a view of the Principal Transactions in the Revolution of Saint Domingo; with Its Antient and Modern State* (London: James Cundee, 1805), x–xi. Rainsford's account has been republished with a useful introduction: Paul Youngquist and Grégory Pierrot, eds., *An Historical Account of the Black Empire of Hayti* (Durham, NC: Duke University Press, 2013).

36 Condy Raguet, "Memoirs of Hayti," cited in *Secret History*, ed. Drexler, 293–312.

Chapter 6: Consolidating Independence in a Hostile World

1 Jonathan Brown, *The History and Present Condition of St. Domingo*, 2 vols. (Philadelphia, PA: William Marshall, 1837), 2:149–50.

2 The suggestive notion that nations should be understood as "imagined communities" held together by their citizens' conviction that they share an identity with each other comes from the anthropologist Benedict Anderson's, *Imagined Communities* (London: Verso, 1991).

3 Alain Yacou, "L'Ère de la France en Saint-Domingue espagnol: Le Gouvernement du général Ferrand," 482, and Emilio Cordero Michel, "Dessalines en Saint-Domingue espagnol," 432, both in Alain Yacou, ed., *Saint-Domingue espagnol et la révolution nègre d'Haïti* (Paris: Karthala, 2007).

4 Claude Moïse, *Constitutions et luttes de pouvoir en Haïti (1804–1987)*, 2 vols. (Montreal: Éditions du CIDHICA, 1988), 1:34–5.

5 Joan Dayan, *Haiti, History, and the Gods* (Berkeley, CA: University of California Press, 1995), 17–19.

6 Gerard M. Laurent, *Six Études sur J. J. Dessalines* (Port-au-Prince: Les Presses libres, n.d.), 142.

7 The ideological differences between the two Haitian states are probed in Chelsea Stieber, *Haiti's Paper War: Post-Independence Writing, Civil War, and the Making of the Republic, 1804–1954* (NY: NYU Press, 2020).

8 See Johnhenry Gonzalez, *Maroon Nation: A History of Revolution Haiti* (New Haven CT: Yale University Press, 2019).

9 Cited in Hubert Cole, *Christophe King of Haiti* (1967; New York: Viking, 1970), 235.

10 Cited in David Nicholls, *From Dessalines to Duvalier: Race, Colour and National Independence in Haiti*, rev. edn. (New Brunswick, NJ: Rutgers University Press, 1996), 45. On Vastey, see Marlene Daut, *Baron de Vastey and the Origins of Black Atlantic Humanism* (NY: Palgrave Macmillan, 2017).

11 Cited in Jeremy Adelman, *Sovereignty and Revolt in the Iberian Revolution* (Princeton, NJ: Princeton University Press, 2006), 363.

12 Cited in Julia Gaffield, "The Racialization of International Law after the Haitian Revolution: The Holy See and National Sovereignty", *American Historical Review* 125, no.3 (June, 2020), 848.

13 On the 1825 arrangement and its subsequent alterations, see Jean-François Brière, *Haiti et la France, 1804–1848: Le Rêve brisé* (Paris: Karthala, 2008). On the loan to American banks, see Hans Schmidt, *The United States Occupation of Haiti, 1915–1934* (New Brunswick, NJ: Rutgers University Press, 1995), 161–5.

14 Cited in Peter Hallward, *Damming the Flood: Haiti, Aristide and the Politics of Containment* (London: Verso, 2007), 226.

15 Michel Hector, "Jalons pour une périodisation," in Michel Hector and Laennec Hurbon, eds., *Genèse de l'État haïtien (1804–1859)* (Paris: Éditions de la Maison des sciences de l'homme, 2009), 37–8.

16 Brown, *History and Present Condition*, 2:276.

17 *Jamaica Standard and Royal Gazette*, December 1838. Cited in Matthew J. Smith, *Liberty, Fraternity Exile: Haiti and Jamaica after Emancipation* (Chapel North Carolina Press, 2014), 31.

18 *Genius of Universal Emancipation*, cited in Leon D. Pamphile, *Haitians and African Americans: A Heritage of Tragedy and Hope* (Gainesville, FL: University Press of Florida, 2001), 28.

19 On the Piquet rebellion, see Mimi Sheller, *Democracy after Slavery: Black Publics and Peasant Radicalism in Haiti and Jamaica* (Gainesville, FL: University Press of Florida, 2000).

20 Moïse, *Constitutions et luttes de pouvoir*, 1:112.

21 Cited in Christopher Miller, *The French Atlantic Triangle: Literature and Culture of the Slave Trade* (Durham, NC: Duke University Press, 2008), 485–6.

22 Ada Ferrer, "Speaking of Haiti: Slavery, Revolution, and Freedom in Cuban Slave Testimony," in David Geggus and Norman Fiering, eds., *The World of the Haitian Revolution* (Bloomington, IN: Indiana University Press, 2009), 237.

23 *An Account of the Late Intended Insurrection among a Portion of the Blacks of this City* (Charleston: Corporation of Charleston, 1822), 42, 39.

24 Seymour Drescher, *Abolition: A History of Slavery and Antislavery* (New York: Cambridge University Press, 2009), 255–63.

25 David Walker, *Appeal to the Coloured Citizens of the World*, ed. Peter P. Hinks (1829; University Park, PA: Penn State University Press, 2000), 23.

26 Cited in Floyd J. Miller, *The Search for a Black Nationality: Black Emigration and Colonization 1787–1862* (Urbana, IL: University of Illinois Press, 1975), 79.

27 See Susan Buck-Morss, *Hegel, Haiti, and Universal History* (Pittsburgh, PA: University of Pittsburgh Press, 2009).

28 Trouillot, *Silencing the Past*.

29 *Journal de l'Empire*, 20 May 1812.

30 Brown, *History and Present Condition*, 2:288–9.

31 Victor Hugo, *Bug-Jargal* (Boston, MA: D. C. Heath, 1889), 127.

32 Peter S. Chazotte, *Historical Sketches of the Revolution and the Foreign and Civil Wars in the Island of St. Domingo* (New York: Wm. Applegate, 1840), cited in Popkin, *Facing Racial Revolution*, 339.

33 Arthur Gobineau, *The Moral and Intellectual Diversity of Races*, trans. H. Hotz (Philadelphia, PA: J. B. Lippincott, 1856), 195.

34 William Wordsworth, "To Toussaint L'Ouverture" (1803), cited in George Tyson, Jr., ed., *Toussaint Louverture* (Englewood Cliffs, NJ: Prentice Hall, 1973), 114.

35 Citations in Alfred N. Hunt, *Haiti's Influence on Antebellum America: Slumbering Volcano in the Caribbean* (Baton Rouge, LA: Louisiana State University Press, 1988), 93, 89–90.

36 Thomas Madiou, *Histoire d'Haïti*, 3 vols. (1847; Port-au-Prince: Henri Deschamps, 1989), 1:x.

37 Jean Price-Mars, *So Spoke the Uncle (Ainsi parla l'oncle)*, trans. Magdaline W. Shannon (Washington, DC: Three Continents Press, 1983), 8, 218.

38 Aimé Césaire, *Toussaint Louverture: La Révolution française et la question coloniale*, 2nd edn. (Paris, 1962).

Afterword: The Earthquake Crisis of 2010 and the Haitian Revolution

1 Dubois, *Avengers of the New World*, 7.
2 Michel Hector and Laënnec Hurbon, "Introduction: Les Fondations," in Michel Hector and Laënnec Hurbon, eds., *Genèse de l'État haïtien (1804–1859)* (Paris: Éditions de la Maison des sciences de l'homme, 2009), 22. For other Haitian writing on the history of the revolutionary era, see the contributions to Michel Hector, ed., *La Révolution française et Haïti: Filiations, Ruptures, Nouvelles Dimensions*, 2 vols. (Port-au-Prince: Société Haïtienne d'histoire et de géographie et Éditions Henri Deschamps, 1995), and Laënnec Hurbon, ed., *L'Insurrection des esclaves de Saint-Domingue (22–23 août 1791). Actes de la table ronde internationale de Port-au-Prince (8 au 10 décembre 1997)* (Paris: Karthala, 2000).
3 Cécile Accilien, Jessica Adams, and Elmide Méléance, eds., *Revolutionary Freedoms: A History of Survival, Strength and Imagination in Haiti* (Coconut Beach, Fla.: Caribbean Studies Press, 2006).

Recent Scholarship on the Haitian Revolution

1 Another important publication on Sonthonax is Marcel Dorigny, ed., *Léger-Félicité Sonthonax: La Première Abolition de l'esclavage. La Révolution française et la Révolution de Saint-Domingue* (1987; 2nd edn., Paris: Société française d'histoire d'outre-mer, 2005).
2 A number of Geggus"s articles have been collected in David Geggus, *Haitian Revolutionary Studies* (Bloomington, IN: Indiana University Press, 2002).
3 Marcel Dorigny, ed., *The Abolitions of Slavery from Léger-Félicité Sonthonax to Victor Schoelcher, 1793, 1794, 1848* (1995; New York: Berghahn, 2003).
4 Marcel Dorigny and Bernard Gainot, eds., *La Société des Amis des Noirs 1788–1799: Contribution à l'histoire de l'abolition de l'esclavage* (Paris: Éditions UNESCO, 1998); Yves Bénot and Marcel Dorigny, *Grégoire et la cause des Noirs* (Paris: Société d'histoire d'outre-mer, 2000); Yves Bénot and Marcel Dorigny, eds., *Rétablissement de l'esclavage dans les colonies françaises: Aux origines d'Haïti 1802* (Paris: Maisonneuve et Larose, 2004); Marcel Dorigny, *Haïti première république noir* (Paris: Société française d'histoire d'outre-mer, 2004).
5 Fouchard, a Haitian scholar, was replying to a long article by a French author, Yvan Debbasch, who argued that the extent of *marronnage* had been exaggerated. See Yvan Debbasch, "Le Marronnage: Essai sur la désertion de l'esclave antillais," *Année sociologique* 3rd ser. (1961), 1–112, (1962), 117–95.

Index

A Concise History of the Haitian Revolution, Second Edition. Jeremy D. Popkin.
© 2022 John Wiley & Sons Ltd. Published 2022 by John Wiley & Sons Ltd.